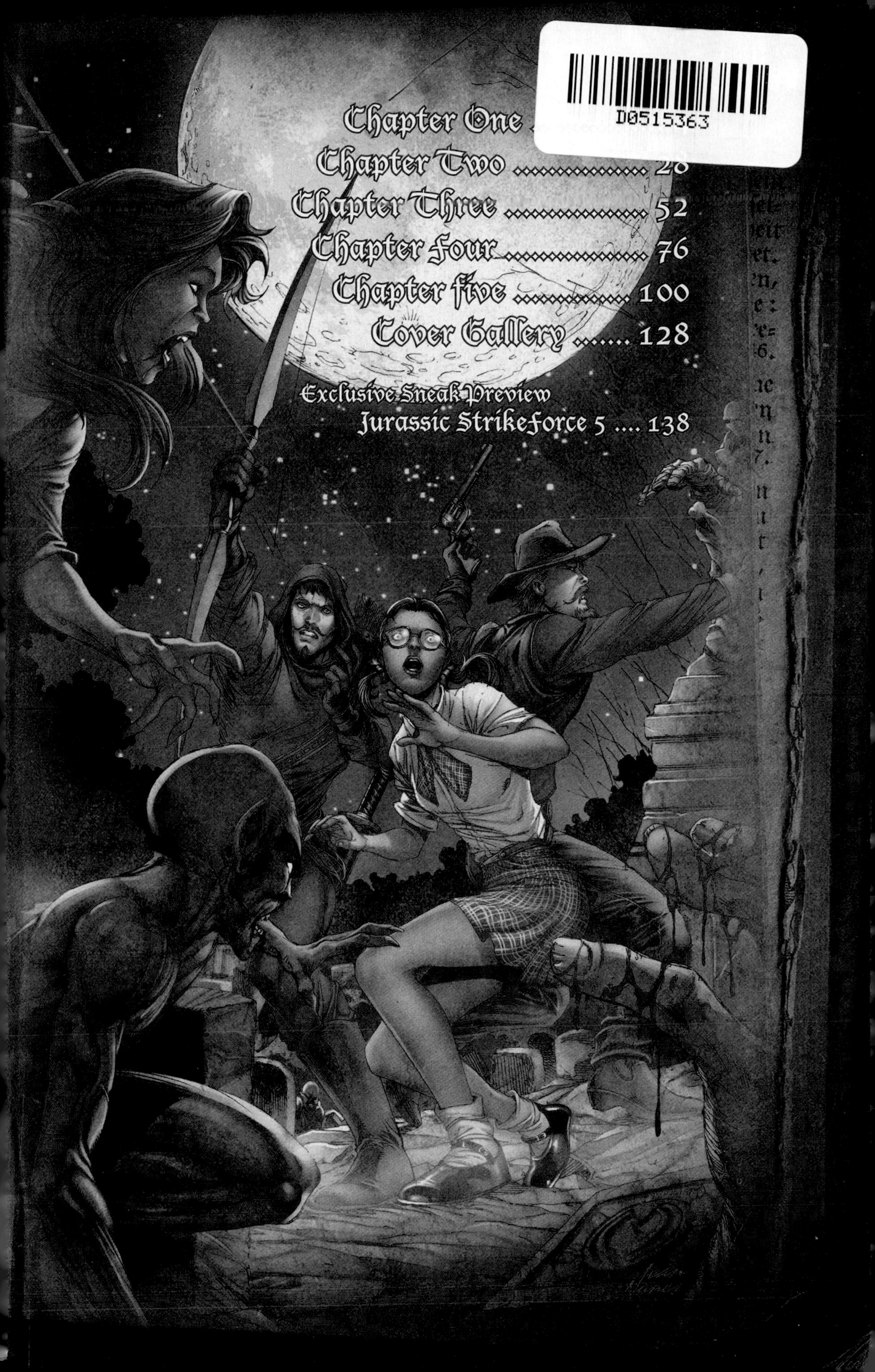

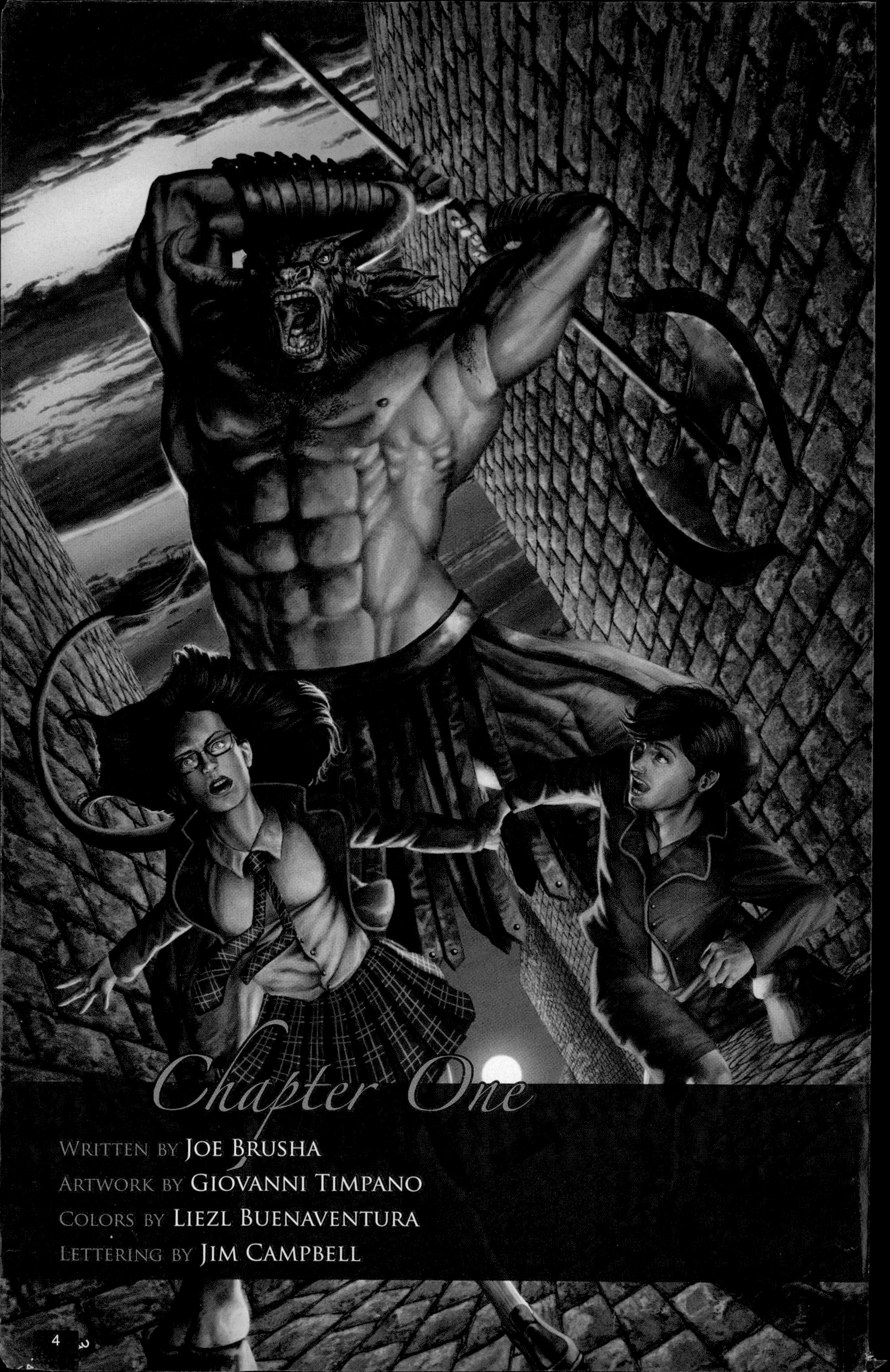

Chapter One

Written by Joe Brusha
Artwork by Giovanni Timpano
Colors by Liezl Buenaventura
Lettering by Jim Campbell

Grimm Fairy Tales *Presents*
the Library

zenescope

Grimm Fairy Tales presents
the Library

WRITTEN BY
JOE BRUSHA

ARTWORK BY
GIOVANNI TIMPANO

TRADE DESIGN BY
CHRISTOPHER COTE

ART DIRECTION BY
ANTHONY SPAY

EDITED BY
RALPH TEDESCO

THIS VOLUME REPRINTS THE
COMIC SERIES GRIMM FAIRY TALES
THE LIBRARY ISSUES #1-5 PUBLISHED
BY ZENESCOPE ENTERTAINMENT

WWW.ZENESCOPE.COM

FIRST EDITION, MAY 2012
ISBN: 978-1-937068-97-4

ZENESCOPE ENTERTAINMENT, INC.
Joe Brusha • President & Chief Creative Officer
Ralph Tedesco • Editor-in-Chief
Jennifer Bermel • Director of Licensing & Business Development
Raven Gregory • Executive Editor
Anthony Spay •Art Director
Christopher Cote • Production Manager
Dave Franchini • Direct Market Sales & Customer Service
Stephen Haberman • Marketing Manager

WWW.ZENESCOPE.COM
FACEBOOK.COM/ZENESCOPE

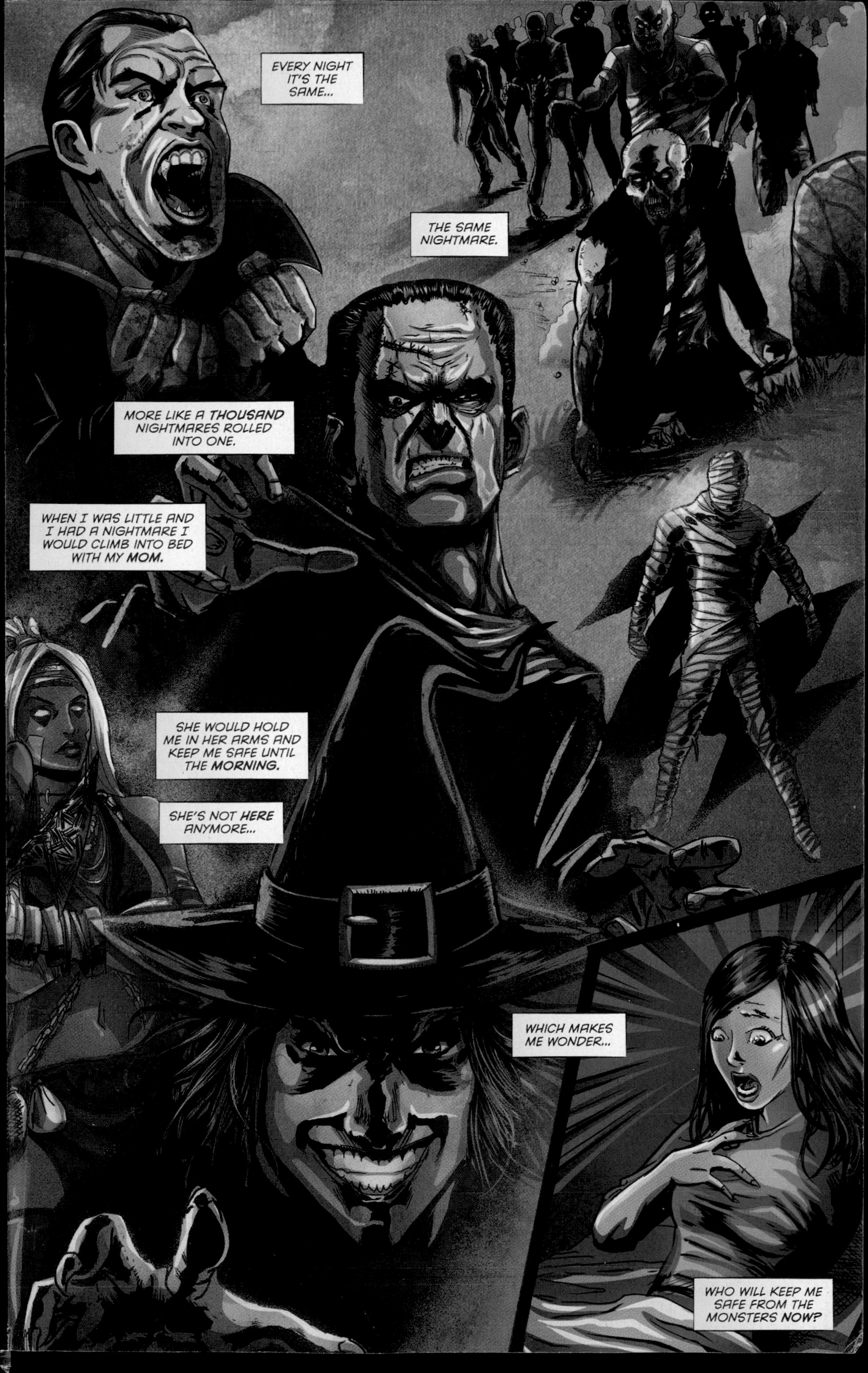
EVERY NIGHT IT'S THE SAME...
THE SAME NIGHTMARE.
MORE LIKE A THOUSAND NIGHTMARES ROLLED INTO ONE.
WHEN I WAS LITTLE AND I HAD A NIGHTMARE I WOULD CLIMB INTO BED WITH MY MOM.
SHE WOULD HOLD ME IN HER ARMS AND KEEP ME SAFE UNTIL THE MORNING.
SHE'S NOT HERE ANYMORE...
WHICH MAKES ME WONDER...
WHO WILL KEEP ME SAFE FROM THE MONSTERS NOW?

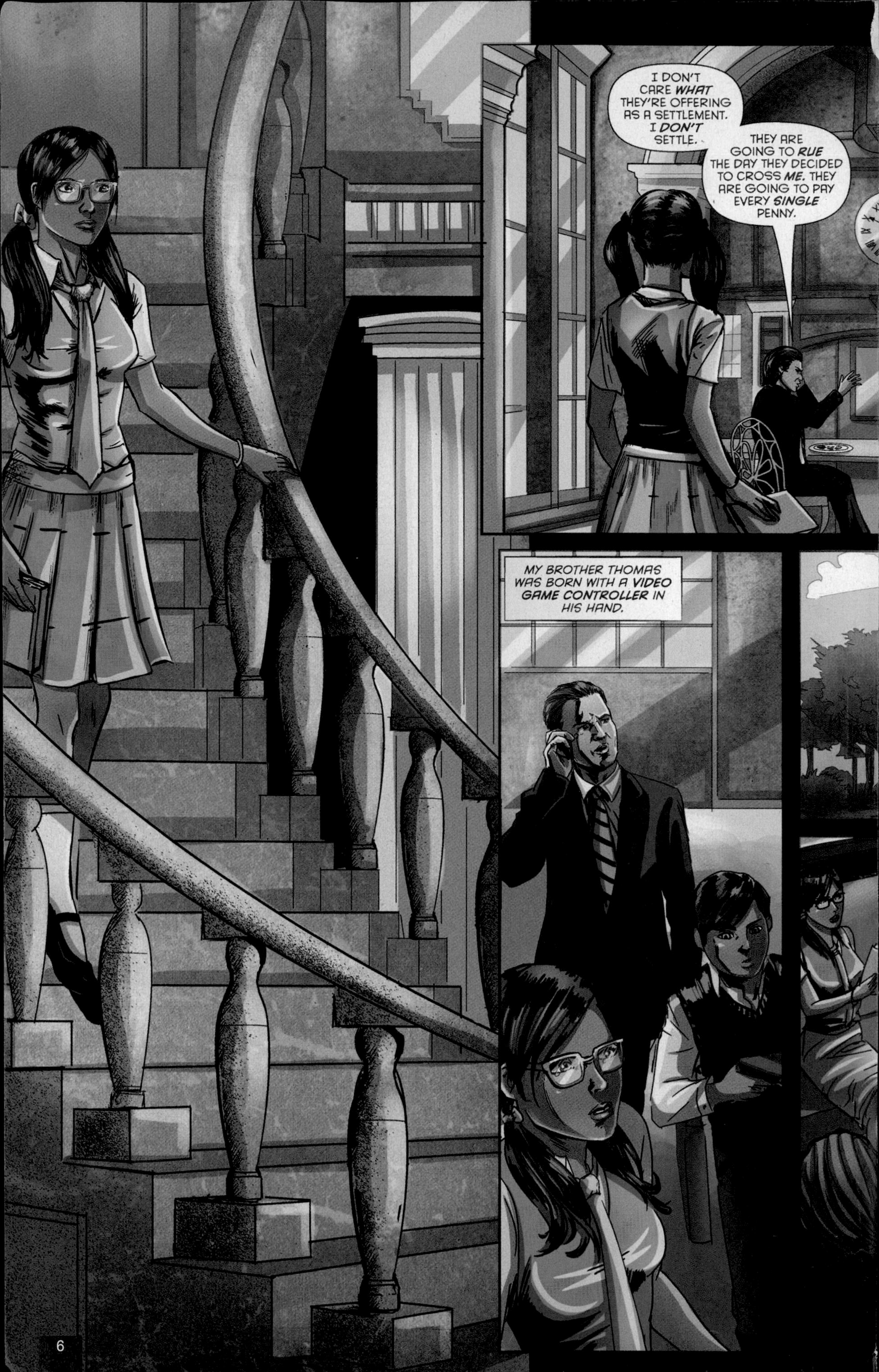
I DON'T CARE *WHAT* THEY'RE OFFERING AS A SETTLEMENT. *I DON'T* SETTLE.
THEY ARE GOING TO *RUE* THE DAY THEY DECIDED TO CROSS *ME.* THEY ARE GOING TO PAY EVERY *SINGLE* PENNY.
MY BROTHER THOMAS WAS BORN WITH A *VIDEO GAME CONTROLLER* IN HIS HAND.

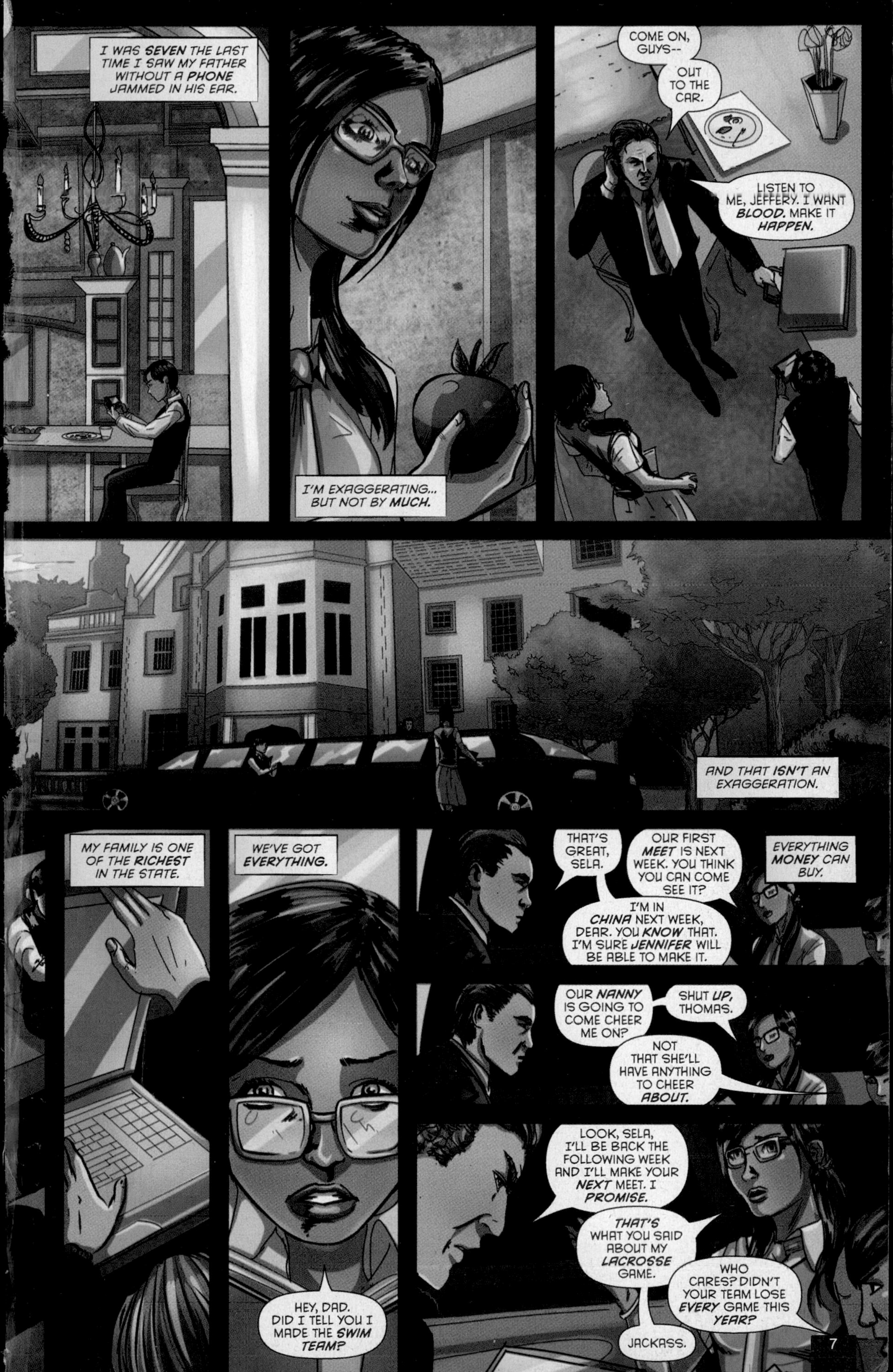
I WAS SEVEN THE LAST TIME I SAW MY FATHER WITHOUT A PHONE JAMMED IN HIS EAR.
I'M EXAGGERATING... BUT NOT BY MUCH.
COME ON, GUYS--
OUT TO THE CAR.
LISTEN TO ME, JEFFERY. I WANT BLOOD. MAKE IT HAPPEN.
AND THAT ISN'T AN EXAGGERATION.
MY FAMILY IS ONE OF THE RICHEST IN THE STATE.
WE'VE GOT EVERYTHING.
HEY, DAD. DID I TELL YOU I MADE THE SWIM TEAM?
THAT'S GREAT, SELA.
OUR FIRST MEET IS NEXT WEEK. YOU THINK YOU CAN COME SEE IT?
EVERYTHING MONEY CAN BUY.
I'M IN CHINA NEXT WEEK, DEAR. YOU KNOW THAT. I'M SURE JENNIFER WILL BE ABLE TO MAKE IT.
OUR NANNY IS GOING TO COME CHEER ME ON?
SHUT UP, THOMAS.
NOT THAT SHE'LL HAVE ANYTHING TO CHEER ABOUT.
LOOK, SELA, I'LL BE BACK THE FOLLOWING WEEK AND I'LL MAKE YOUR NEXT MEET. I PROMISE.
THAT'S WHAT YOU SAID ABOUT MY LACROSSE GAME.
JACKASS.
WHO CARES? DIDN'T YOUR TEAM LOSE EVERY GAME THIS YEAR?

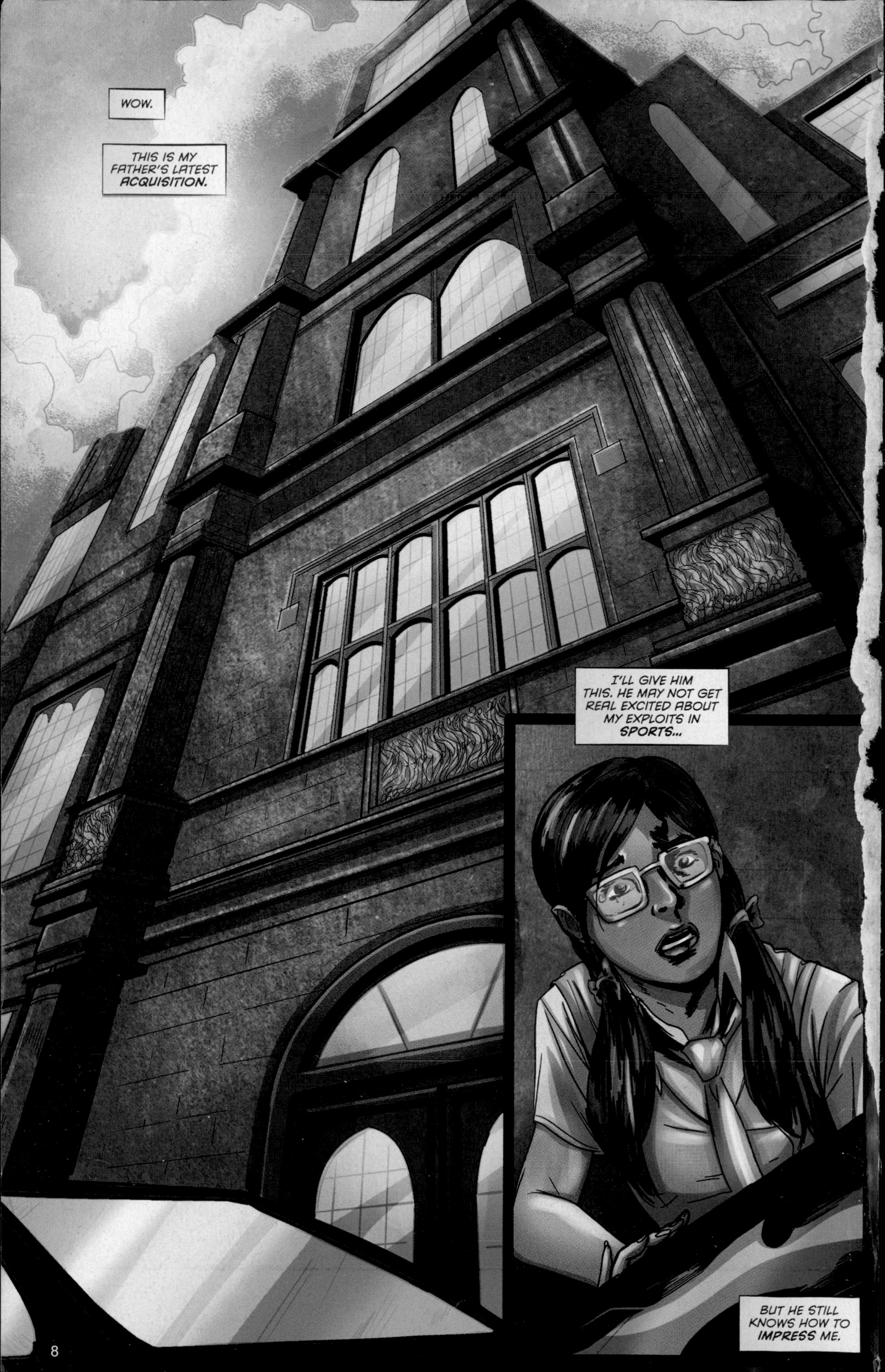
WOW.
THIS IS MY FATHER'S LATEST ACQUISITION.
I'LL GIVE HIM THIS. HE MAY NOT GET REAL EXCITED ABOUT MY EXPLOITS IN SPORTS...
BUT HE STILL KNOWS HOW TO IMPRESS ME.

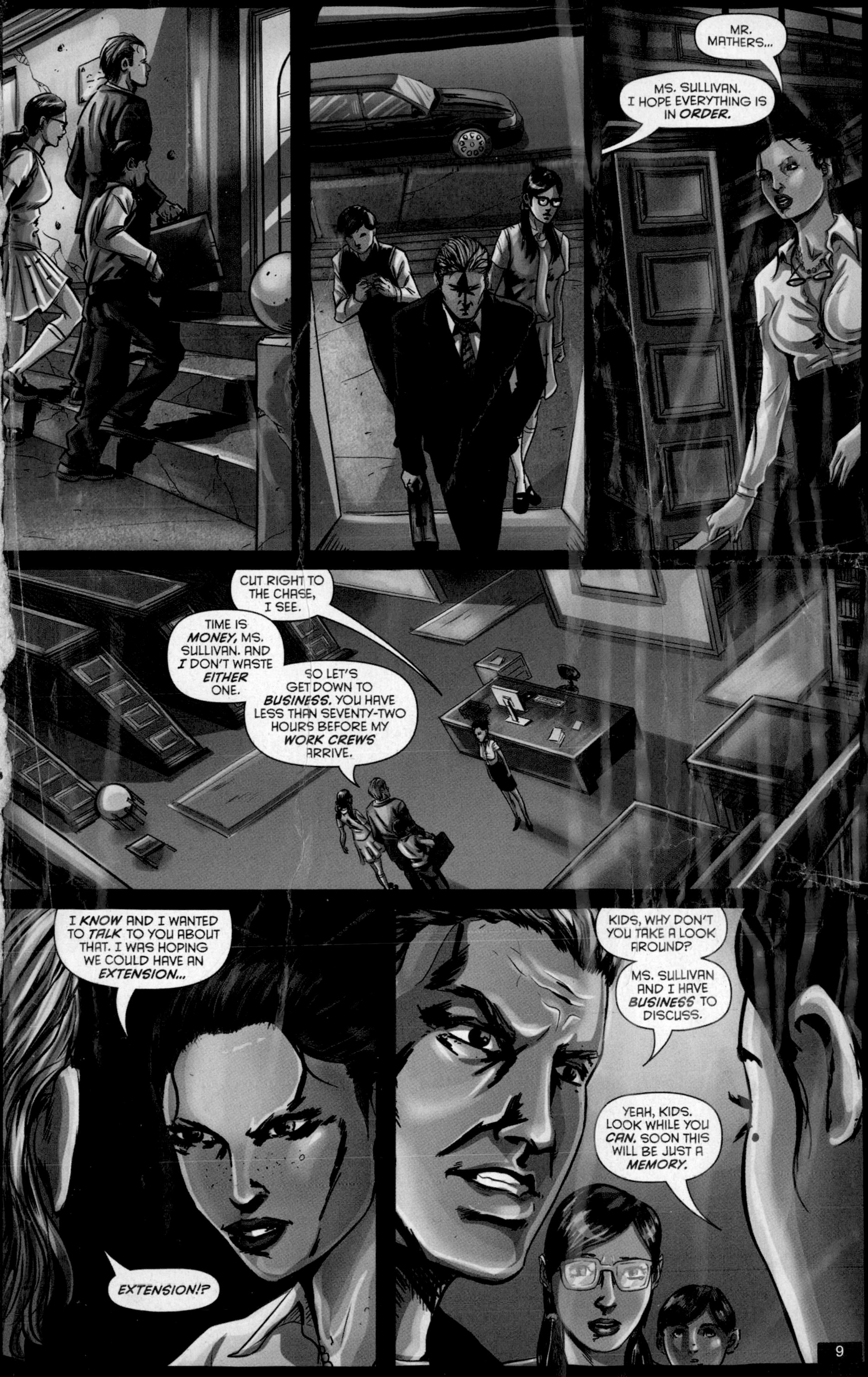
MR. MATHERS...
MS. SULLIVAN. I HOPE EVERYTHING IS IN ORDER.
CUT RIGHT TO THE CHASE, I SEE.
TIME IS MONEY, MS. SULLIVAN. AND I DON'T WASTE EITHER ONE.
SO LET'S GET DOWN TO BUSINESS. YOU HAVE LESS THAN SEVENTY-TWO HOURS BEFORE MY WORK CREWS ARRIVE.
I KNOW AND I WANTED TO TALK TO YOU ABOUT THAT. I WAS HOPING WE COULD HAVE AN EXTENSION...
EXTENSION!?
KIDS, WHY DON'T YOU TAKE A LOOK AROUND?
MS. SULLIVAN AND I HAVE BUSINESS TO DISCUSS.
YEAH, KIDS. LOOK WHILE YOU CAN. SOON THIS WILL BE JUST A MEMORY.

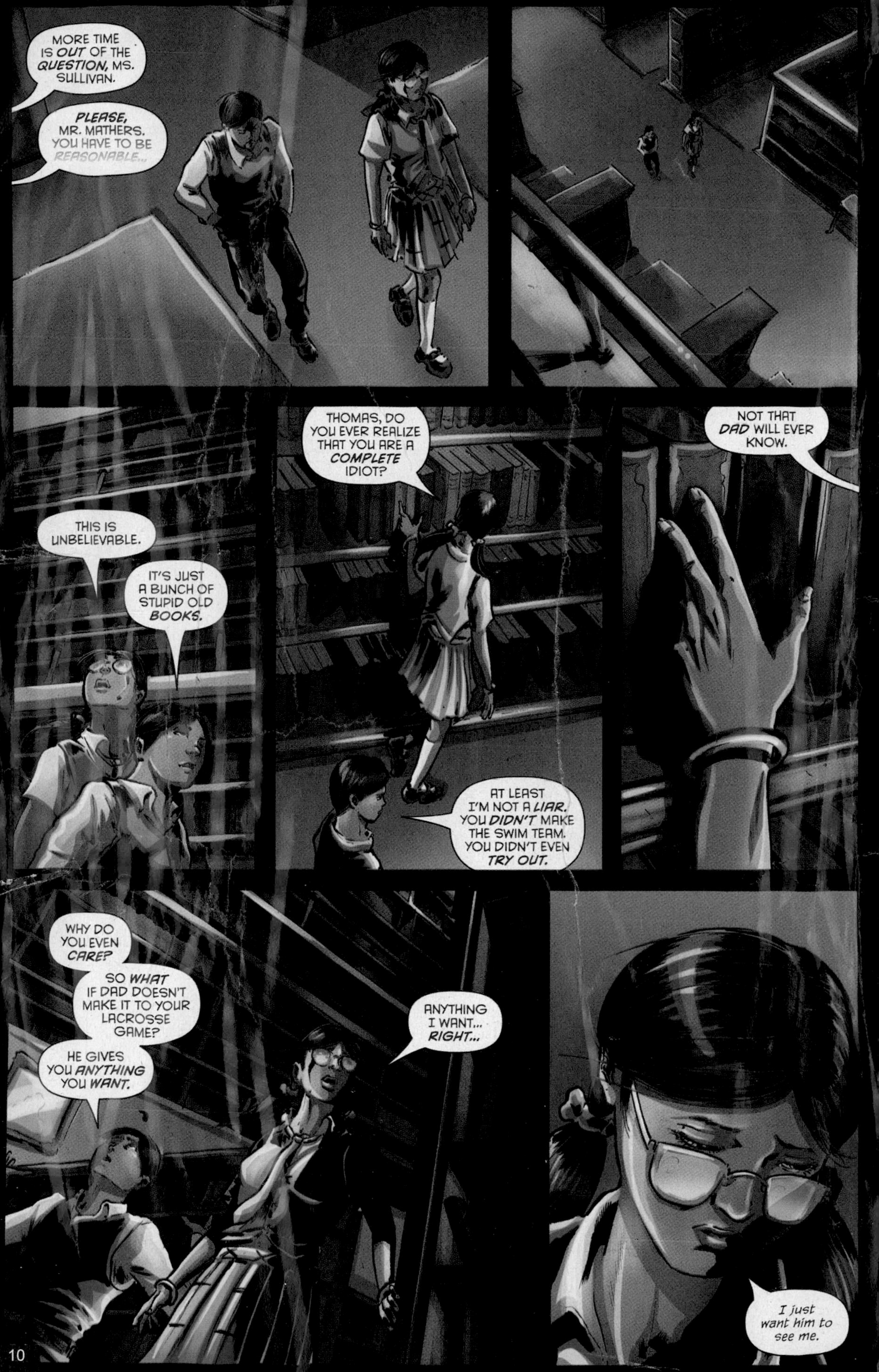
MORE TIME IS OUT OF THE QUESTION, MS. SULLIVAN.
PLEASE, MR. MATHERS. YOU HAVE TO BE REASONABLE...
THIS IS UNBELIEVABLE.
IT'S JUST A BUNCH OF STUPID OLD BOOKS.
THOMAS, DO YOU EVER REALIZE THAT YOU ARE A COMPLETE IDIOT?
AT LEAST I'M NOT A LIAR. YOU DIDN'T MAKE THE SWIM TEAM. YOU DIDN'T EVEN TRY OUT.
NOT THAT DAD WILL EVER KNOW.
WHY DO YOU EVEN CARE?
SO WHAT IF DAD DOESN'T MAKE IT TO YOUR LACROSSE GAME?
HE GIVES YOU ANYTHING YOU WANT.
ANYTHING I WANT... RIGHT...
I just want him to see me.

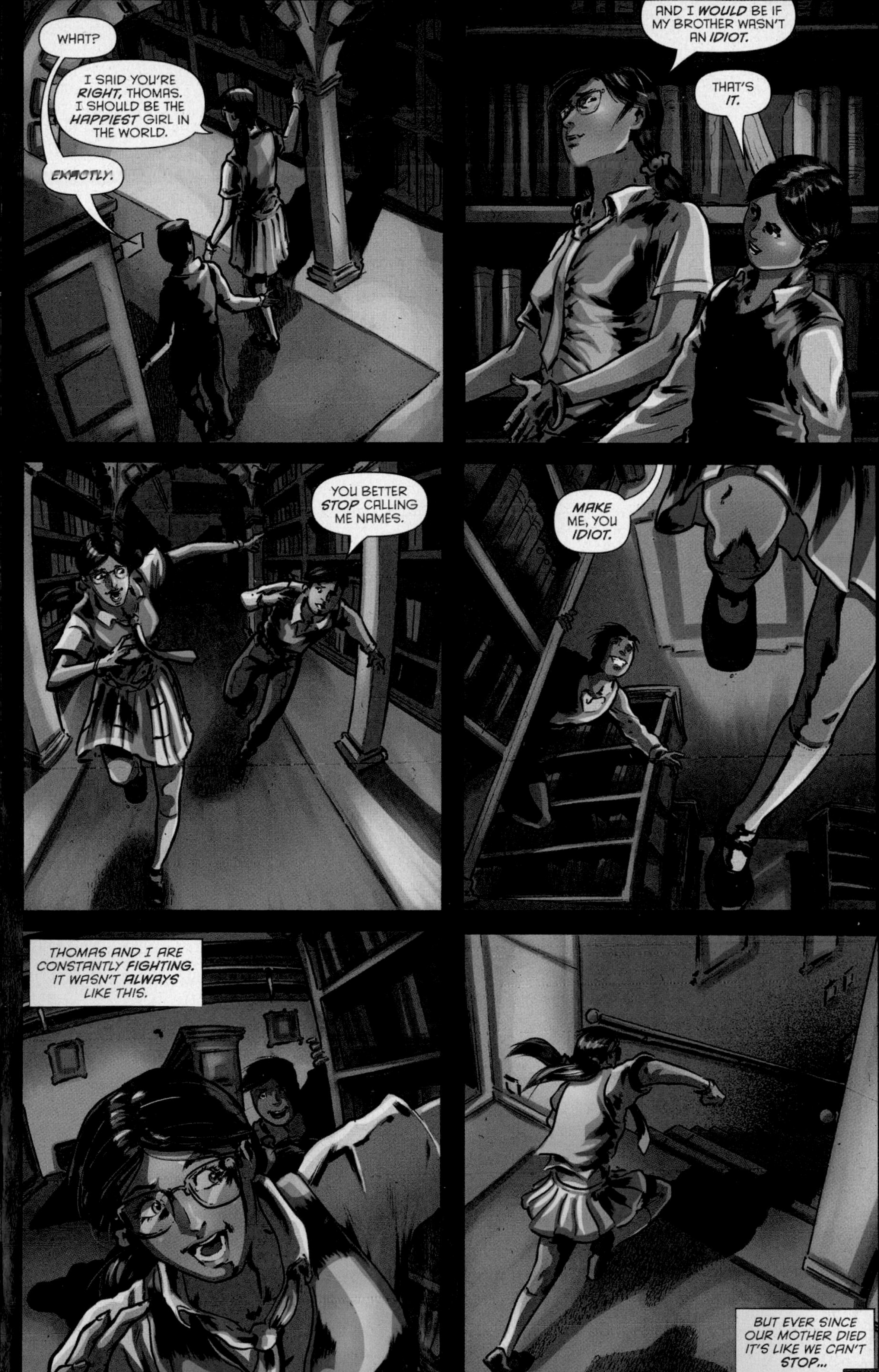
WHAT?
I SAID YOU'RE RIGHT, THOMAS. I SHOULD BE THE HAPPIEST GIRL IN THE WORLD.
EXACTLY.
AND I WOULD BE IF MY BROTHER WASN'T AN IDIOT.
THAT'S IT.
YOU BETTER STOP CALLING ME NAMES.
MAKE ME, YOU IDIOT.
THOMAS AND I ARE CONSTANTLY FIGHTING. IT WASN'T ALWAYS LIKE THIS.
BUT EVER SINCE OUR MOTHER DIED IT'S LIKE WE CAN'T STOP...

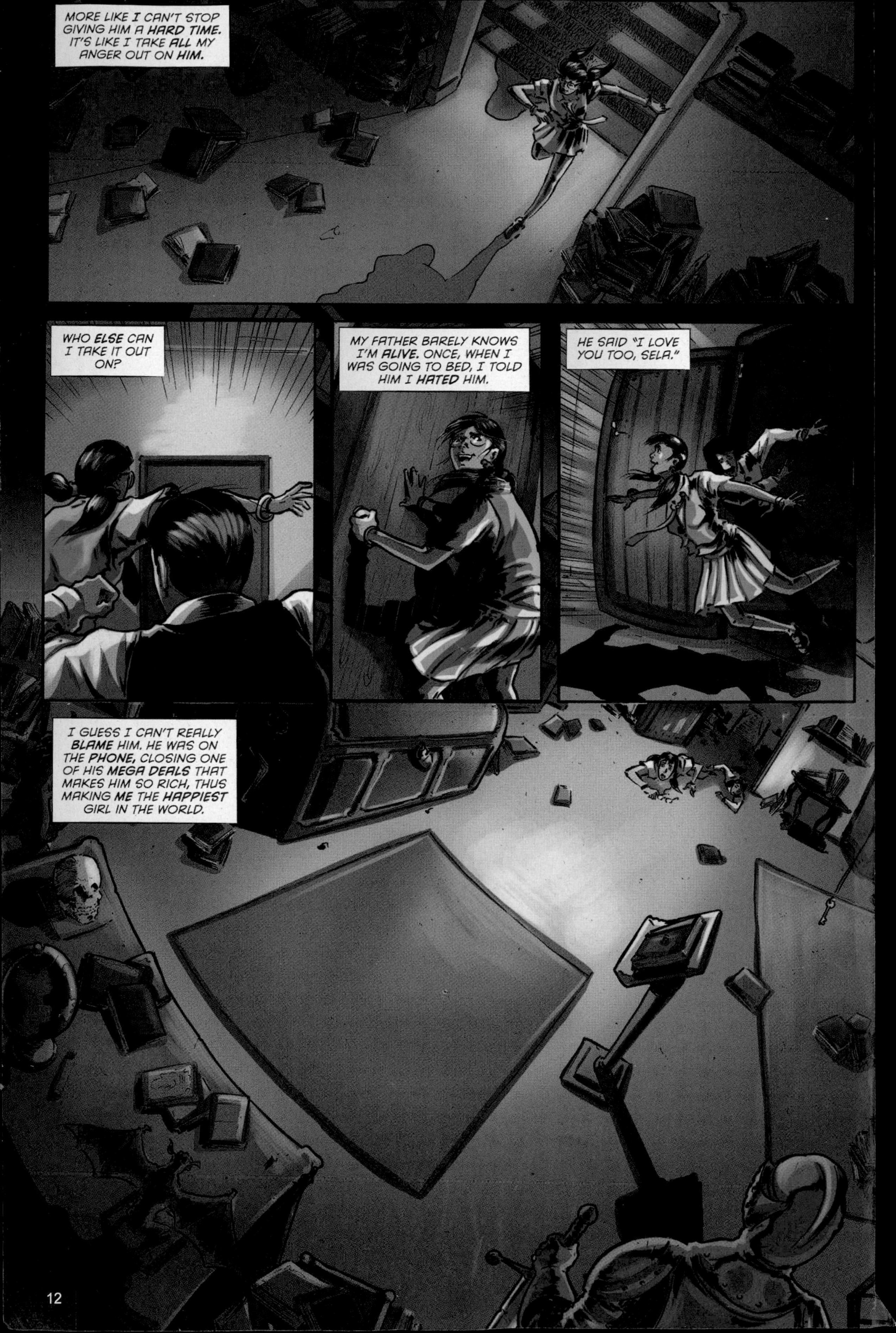

MORE LIKE I CAN'T STOP GIVING HIM A HARD TIME. IT'S LIKE I TAKE ALL MY ANGER OUT ON HIM.
WHO ELSE CAN I TAKE IT OUT ON?
MY FATHER BARELY KNOWS I'M ALIVE. ONCE, WHEN I WAS GOING TO BED, I TOLD HIM I HATED HIM.
HE SAID "I LOVE YOU TOO, SELA."
I GUESS I CAN'T REALLY BLAME HIM. HE WAS ON THE PHONE, CLOSING ONE OF HIS MEGA DEALS THAT MAKES HIM SO RICH, THUS MAKING ME THE HAPPIEST GIRL IN THE WORLD.

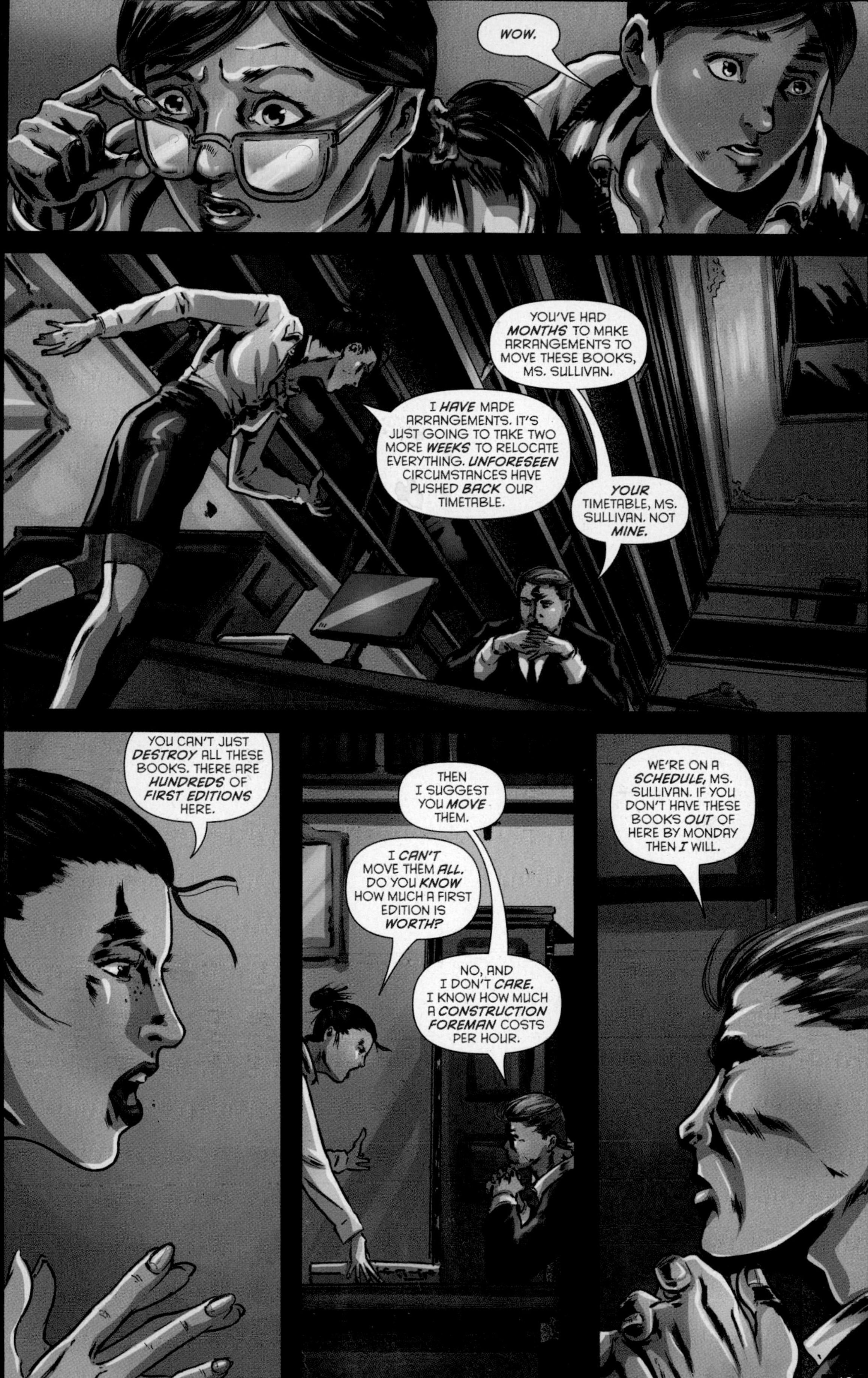
WOW.
YOU'VE HAD MONTHS TO MAKE ARRANGEMENTS TO MOVE THESE BOOKS, MS. SULLIVAN.
I HAVE MADE ARRANGEMENTS. IT'S JUST GOING TO TAKE TWO MORE WEEKS TO RELOCATE EVERYTHING. UNFORESEEN CIRCUMSTANCES HAVE PUSHED BACK OUR TIMETABLE.
YOUR TIMETABLE, MS. SULLIVAN. NOT MINE.
YOU CAN'T JUST DESTROY ALL THESE BOOKS. THERE ARE HUNDREDS OF FIRST EDITIONS HERE.
THEN I SUGGEST YOU MOVE THEM.
I CAN'T MOVE THEM ALL. DO YOU KNOW HOW MUCH A FIRST EDITION IS WORTH?
NO, AND I DON'T CARE. I KNOW HOW MUCH A CONSTRUCTION FOREMAN COSTS PER HOUR.
WE'RE ON A SCHEDULE, MS. SULLIVAN. IF YOU DON'T HAVE THESE BOOKS OUT OF HERE BY MONDAY THEN I WILL.

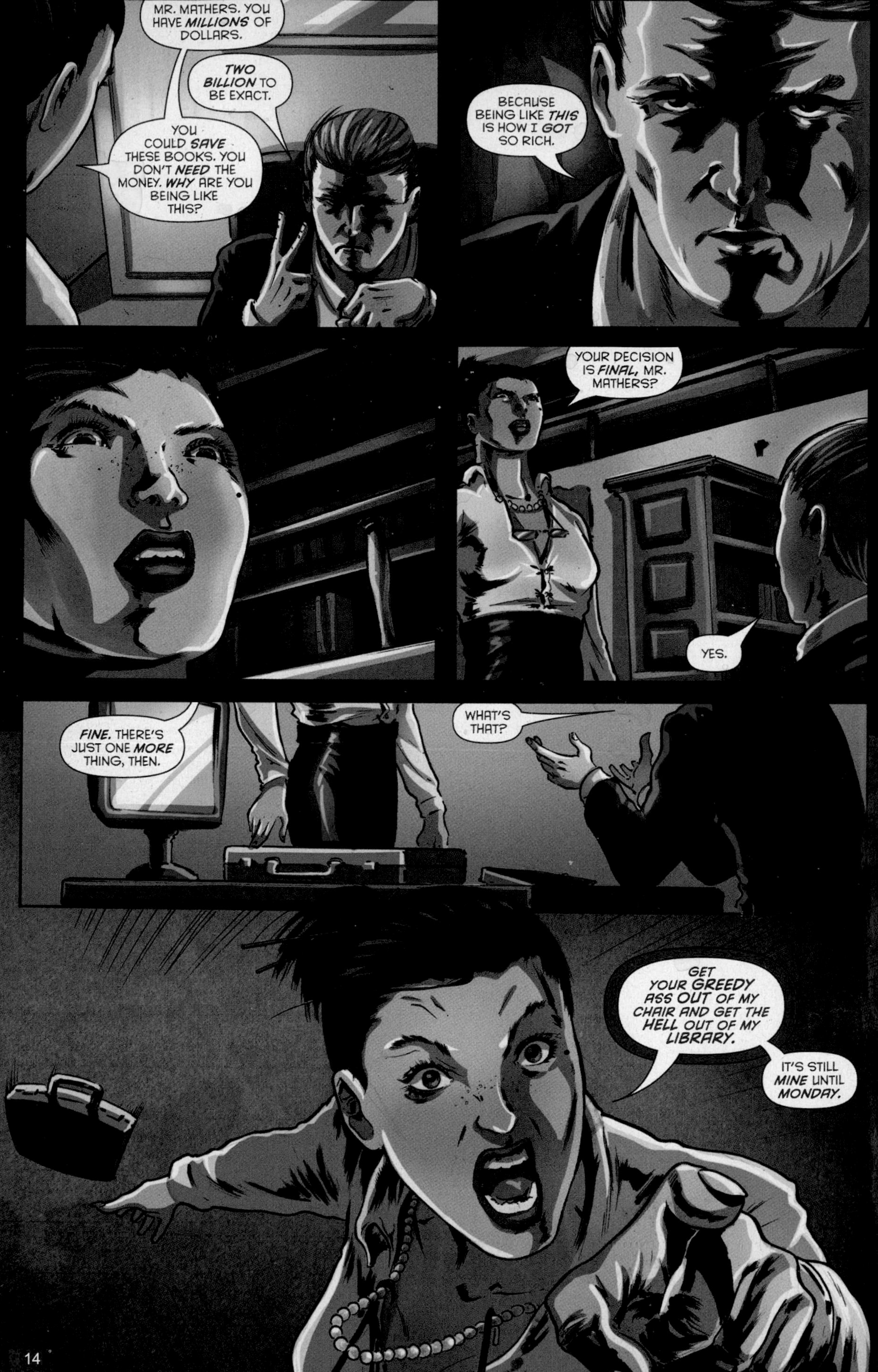
MR. MATHERS. YOU HAVE MILLIONS OF DOLLARS.
YOU COULD SAVE THESE BOOKS. YOU DON'T NEED THE MONEY. WHY ARE YOU BEING LIKE THIS?
TWO BILLION TO BE EXACT.
BECAUSE BEING LIKE THIS IS HOW I GOT SO RICH.
YOUR DECISION IS FINAL, MR. MATHERS?
YES.
FINE. THERE'S JUST ONE MORE THING, THEN.
WHAT'S THAT?
GET YOUR GREEDY ASS OUT OF MY CHAIR AND GET THE HELL OUT OF MY LIBRARY.
IT'S STILL MINE UNTIL MONDAY.

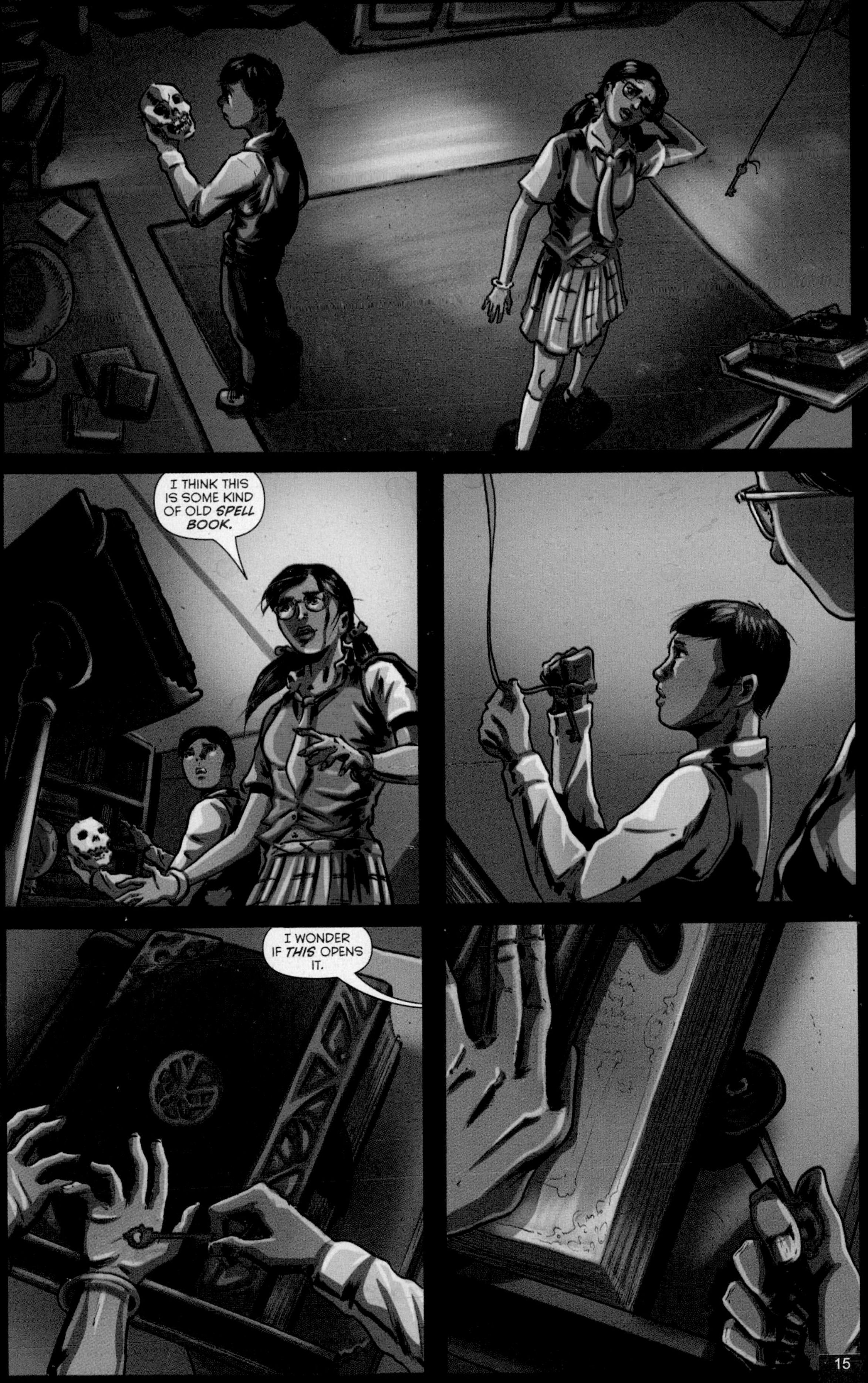
I THINK THIS IS SOME KIND OF OLD SPELL BOOK.
I WONDER IF THIS OPENS IT.

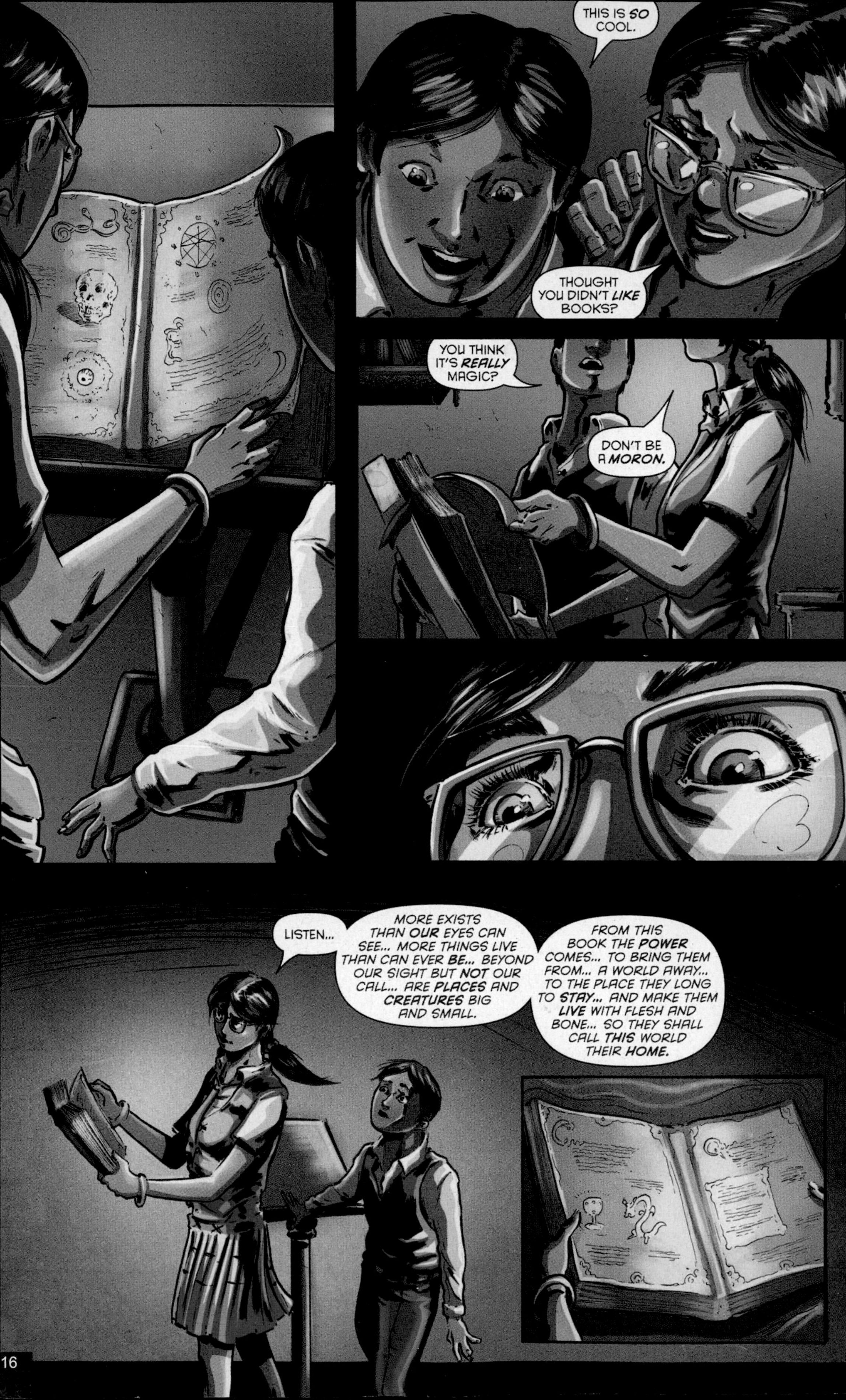
THIS IS SO COOL.
THOUGHT YOU DIDN'T LIKE BOOKS?
YOU THINK IT'S REALLY MAGIC?
DON'T BE A MORON.
LISTEN...
MORE EXISTS THAN OUR EYES CAN SEE... MORE THINGS LIVE THAN CAN EVER BE... BEYOND OUR SIGHT BUT NOT OUR CALL... ARE PLACES AND CREATURES BIG AND SMALL.
FROM THIS BOOK THE POWER COMES... TO BRING THEM FROM... A WORLD AWAY... TO THE PLACE THEY LONG TO STAY... AND MAKE THEM LIVE WITH FLESH AND BONE... SO THEY SHALL CALL THIS WORLD THEIR HOME.

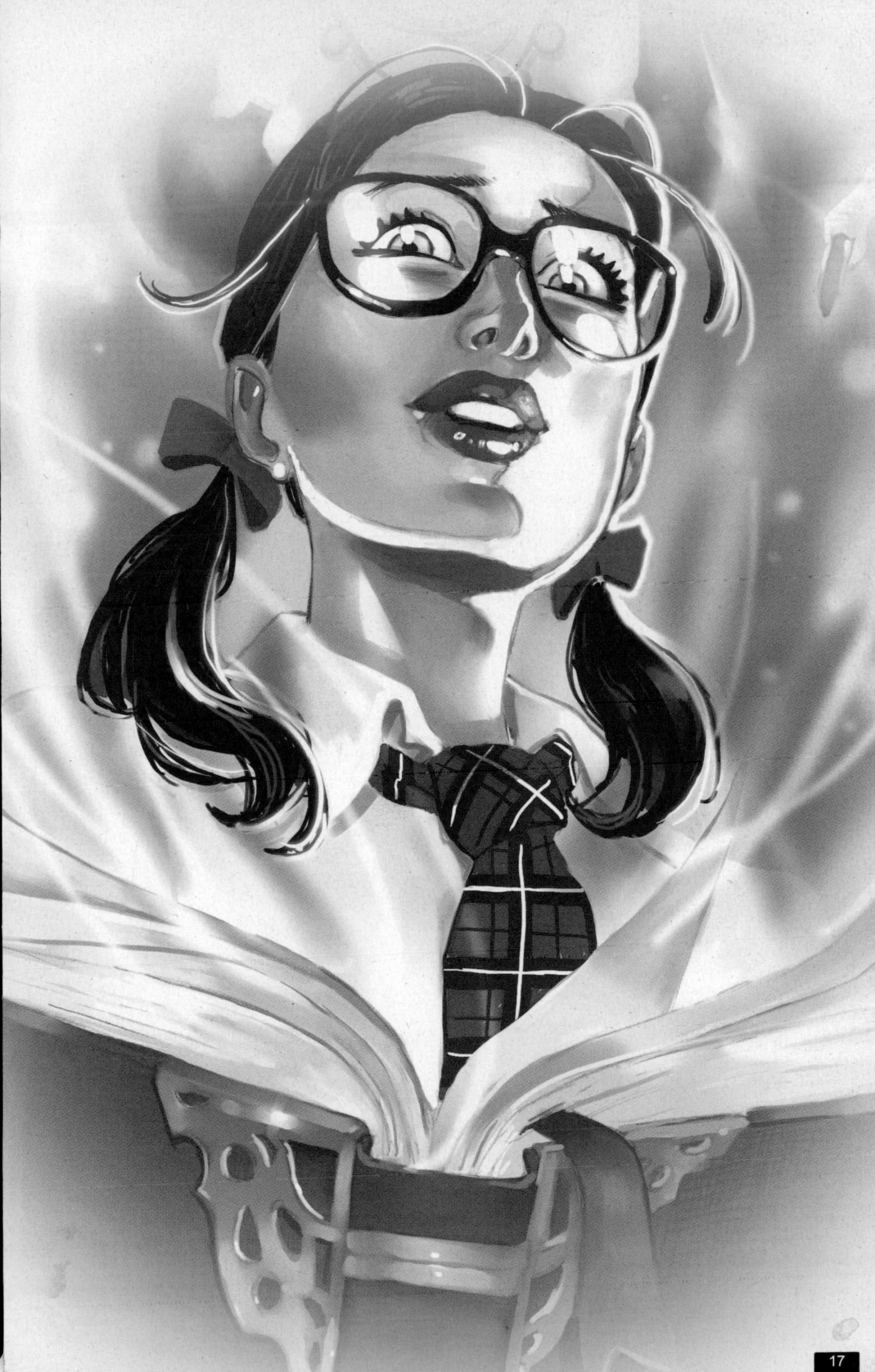

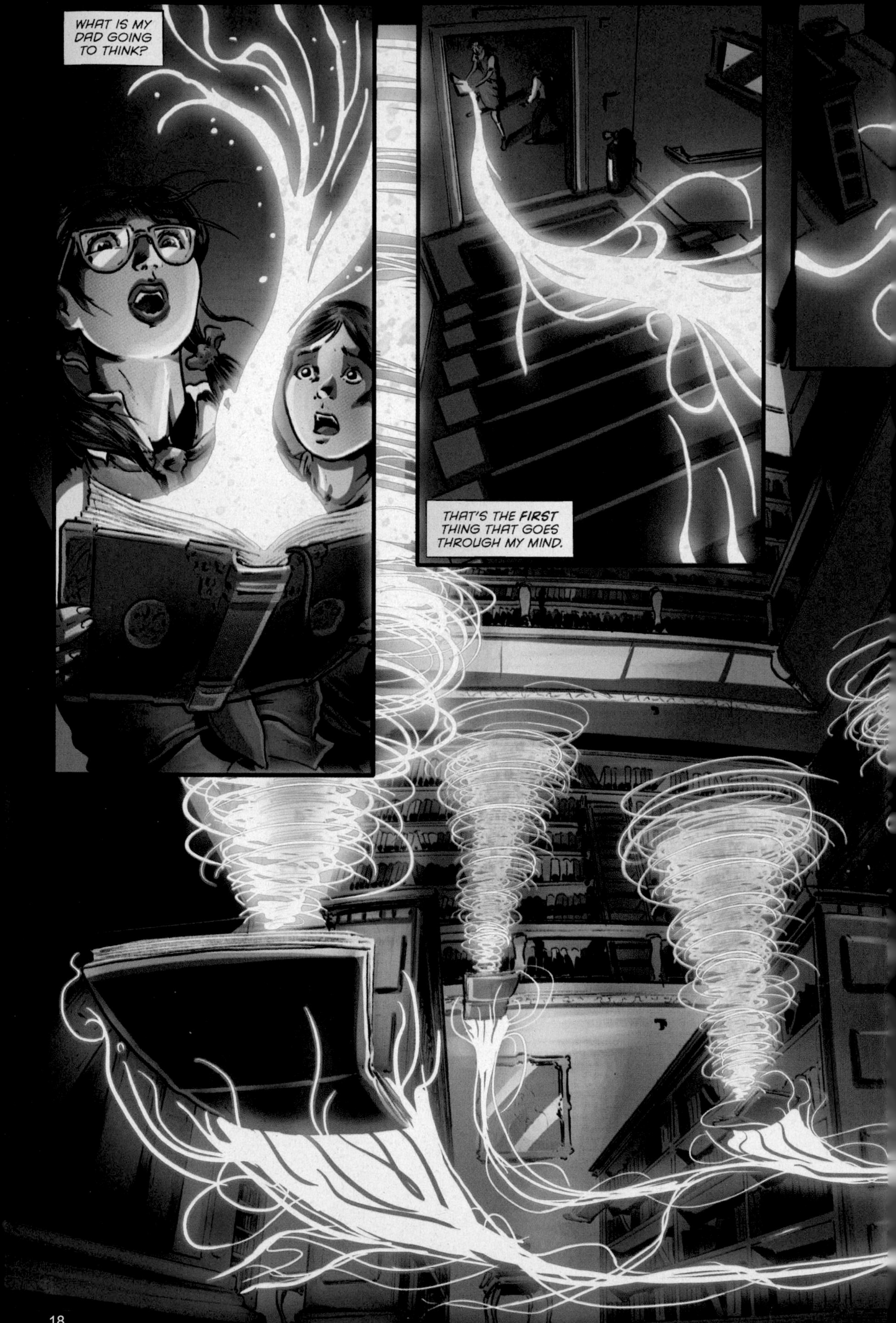
WHAT IS MY DAD GOING TO THINK?
THAT'S THE FIRST THING THAT GOES THROUGH MY MIND.

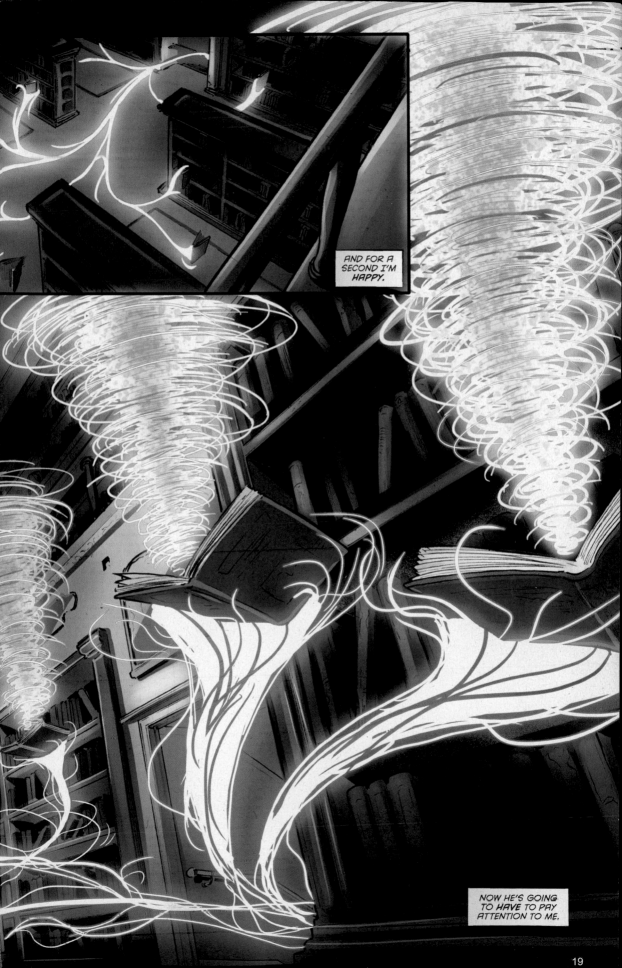

AND FOR A SECOND I'M HAPPY.

NOW HE'S GOING TO **HAVE** TO PAY ATTENTION TO ME.

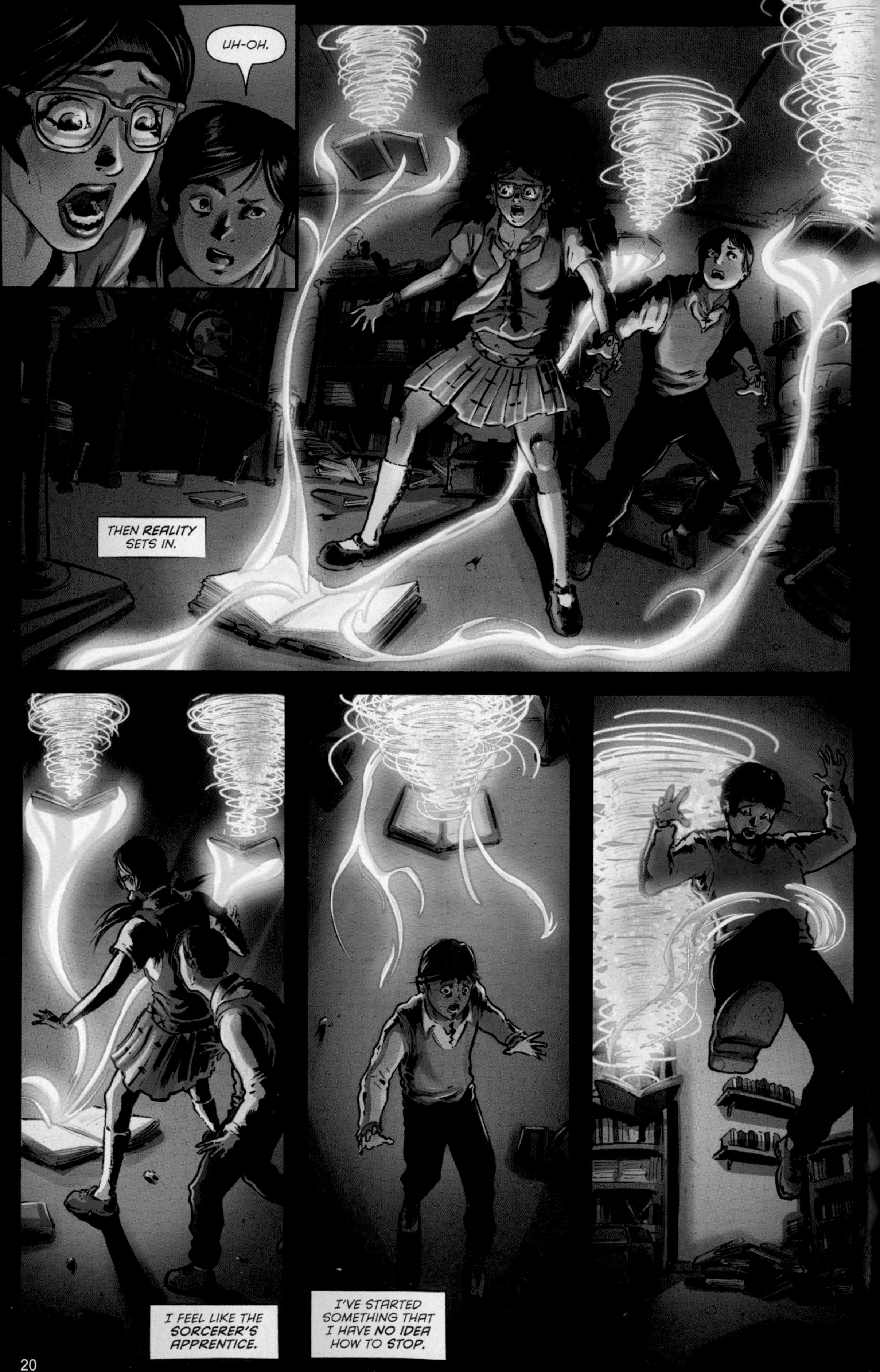
UH-OH.
THEN REALITY SETS IN.
I FEEL LIKE THE SORCERER'S APPRENTICE.
I'VE STARTED SOMETHING THAT I HAVE NO IDEA HOW TO STOP.

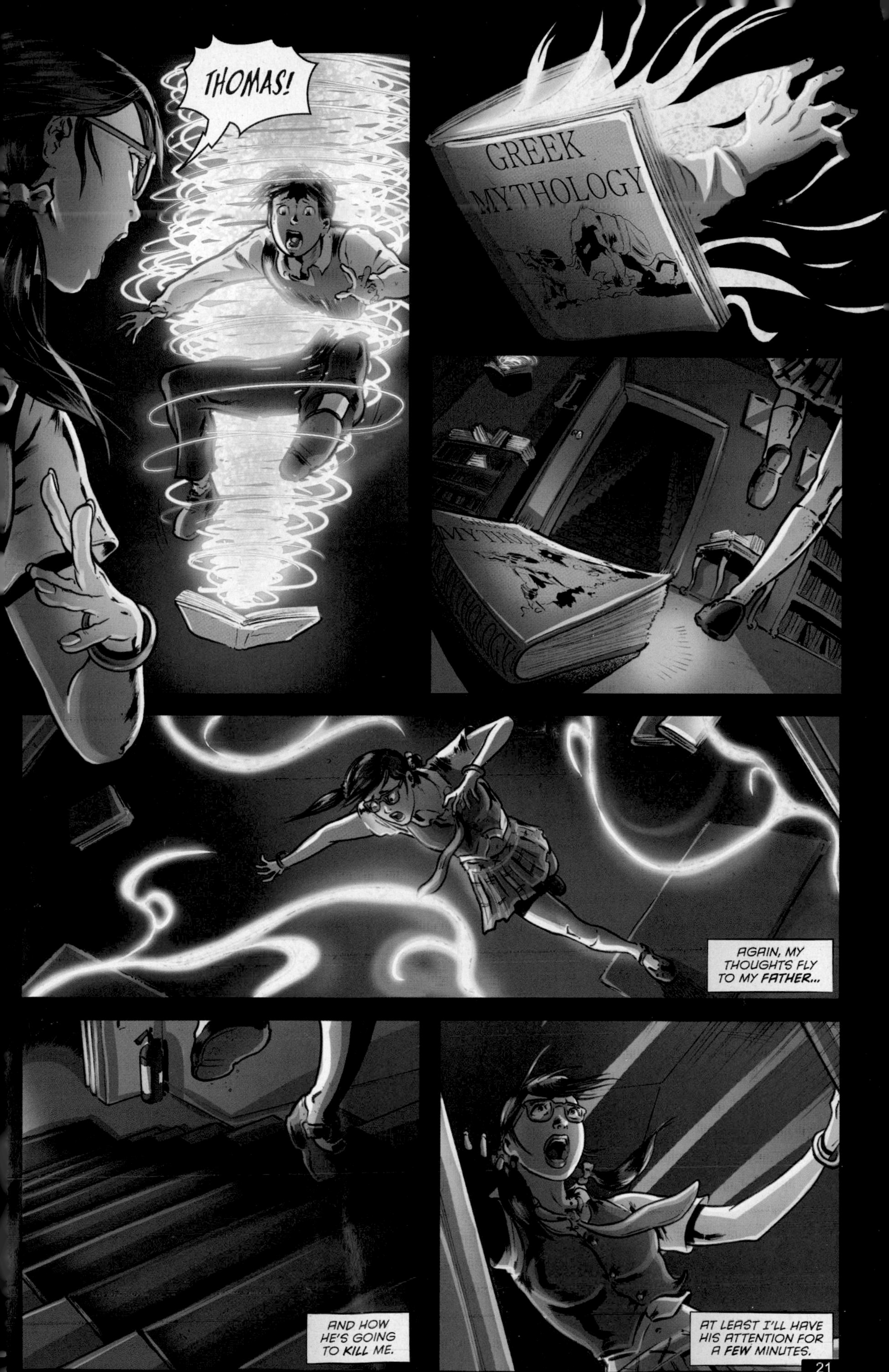
THOMAS!
GREEK MYTHOLOGY
AGAIN, MY THOUGHTS FLY TO MY FATHER...
AND HOW HE'S GOING TO KILL ME.
AT LEAST I'LL HAVE HIS ATTENTION FOR A FEW MINUTES.

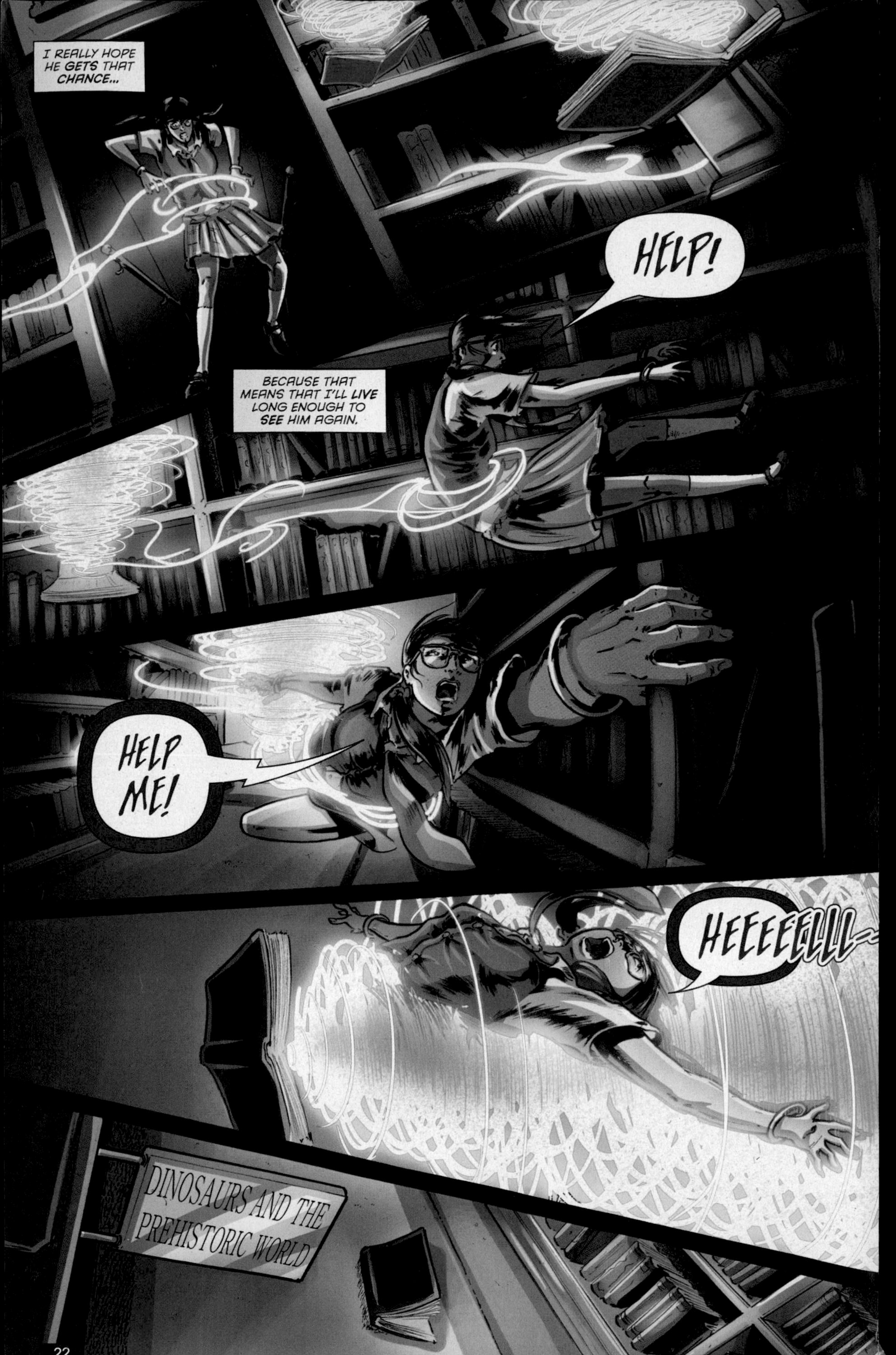
I REALLY HOPE HE GETS THAT CHANCE...
HELP!
BECAUSE THAT MEANS THAT I'LL LIVE LONG ENOUGH TO SEE HIM AGAIN.
HELP ME!
HEEEEELLL--
DINOSAURS AND THE PREHISTORIC WORLD

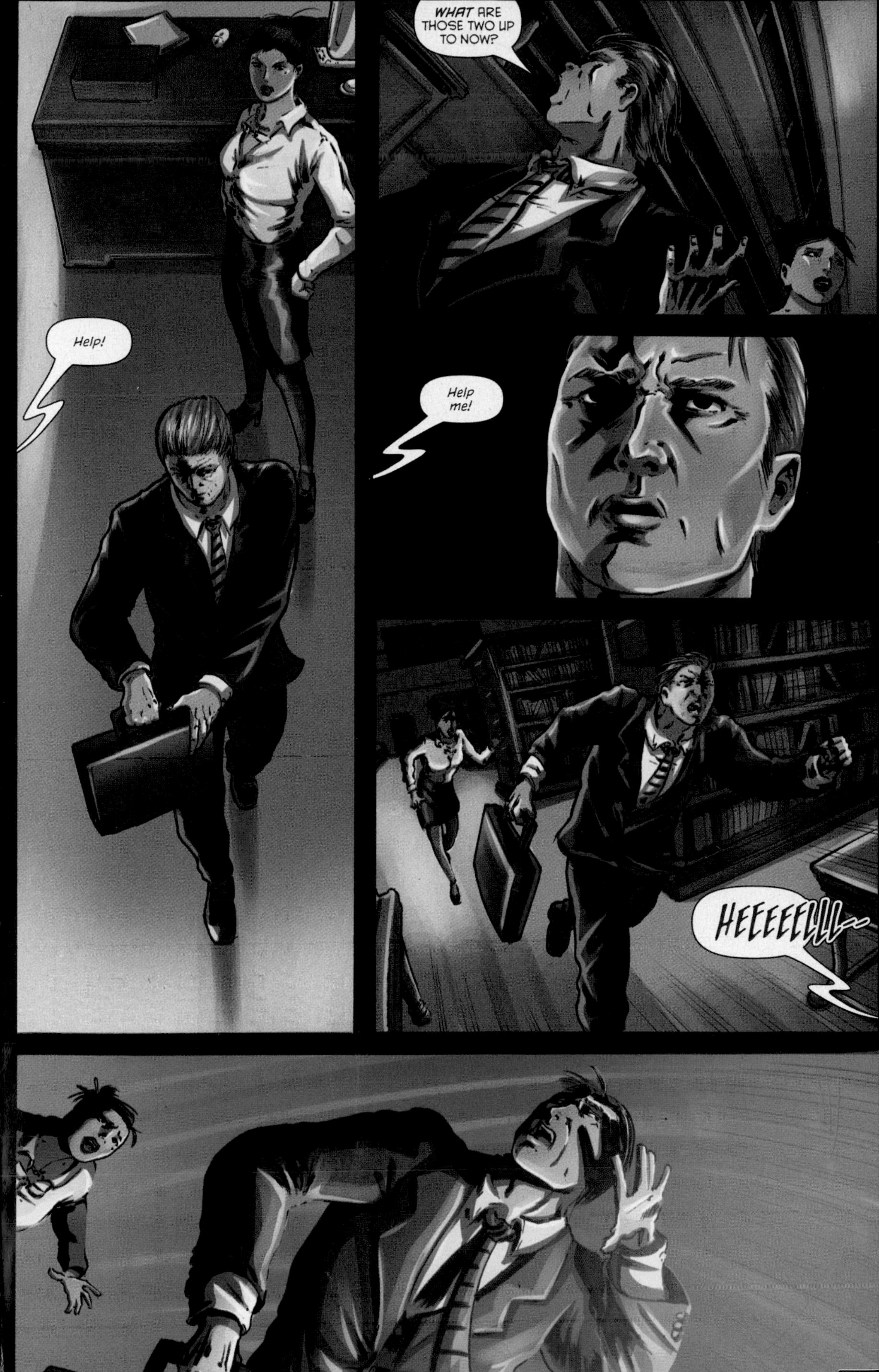
WHAT ARE THOSE TWO UP TO NOW?
Help!
Help me!
HEEEEELLL--

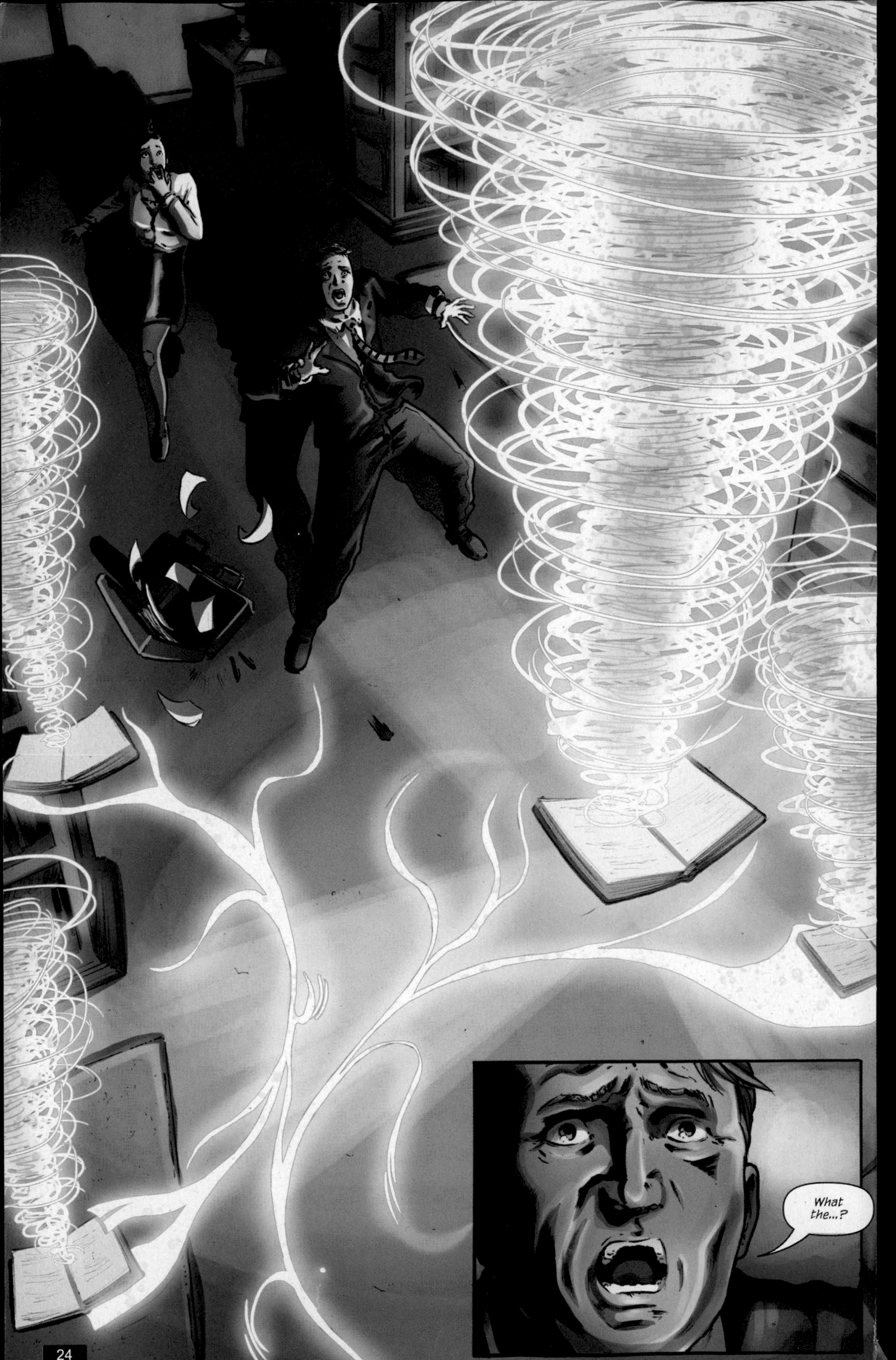
What the...?

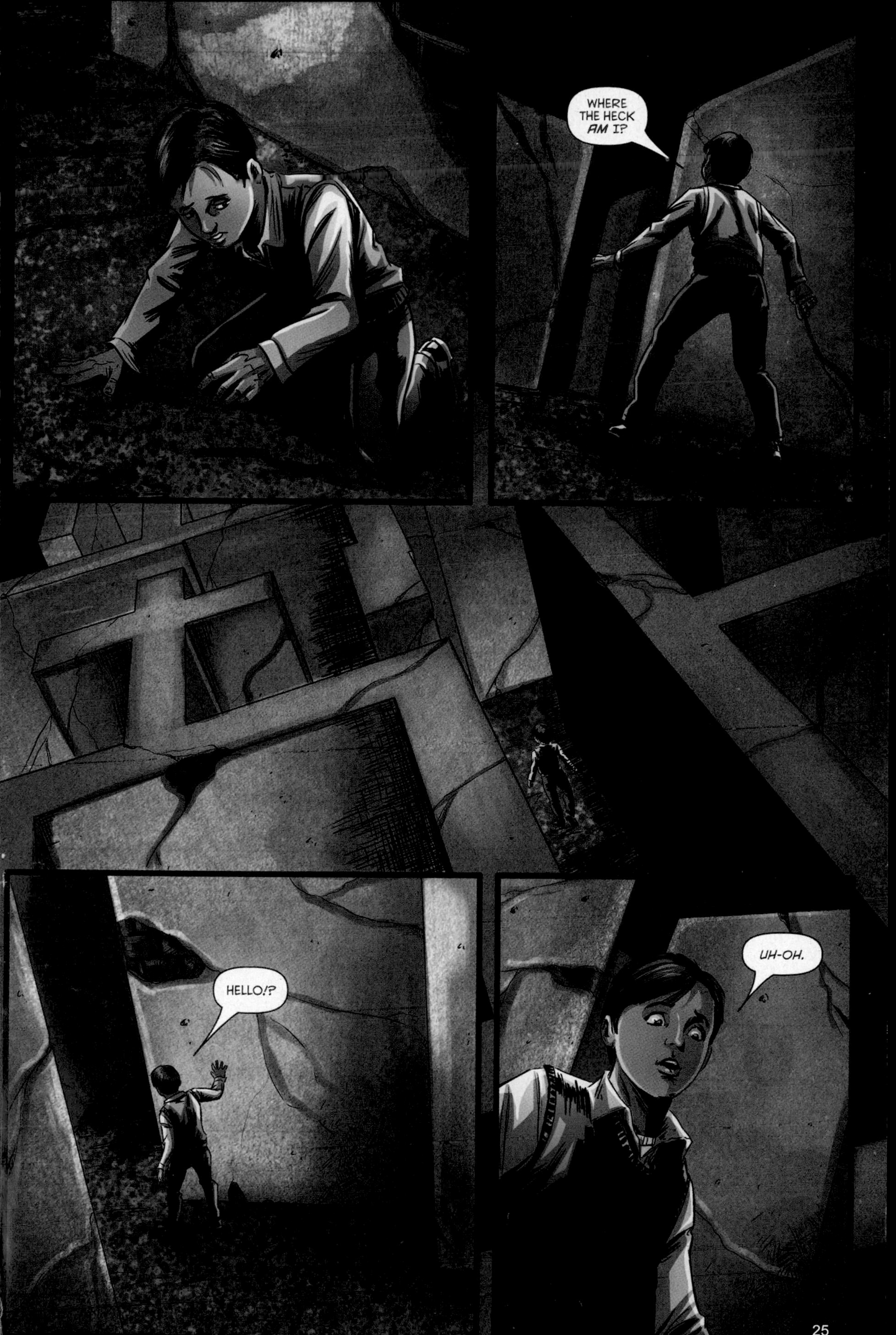
WHERE THE HECK *AM* I?
HELLO!?
UH-OH.

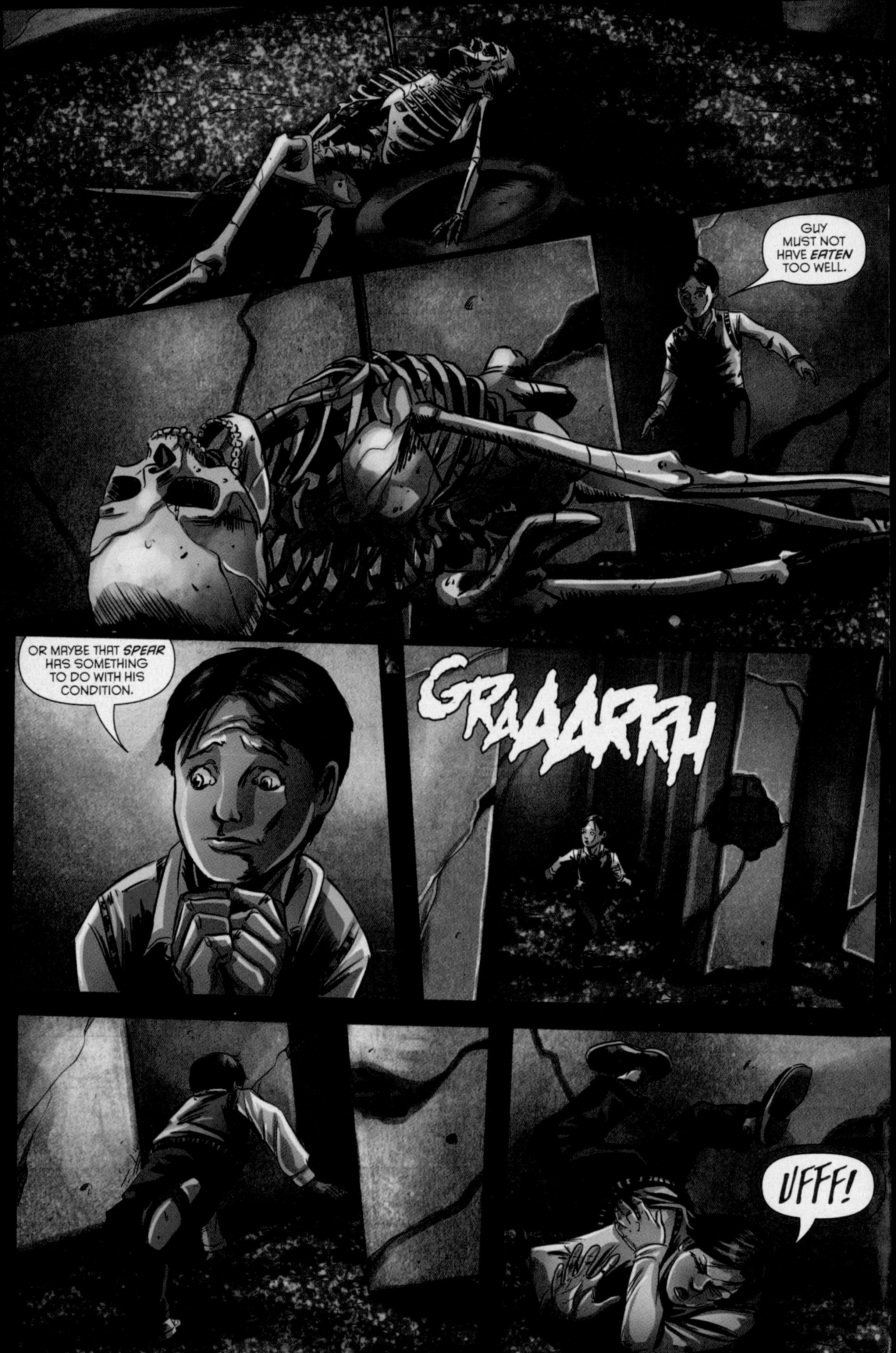
GUY MUST NOT HAVE EATEN TOO WELL.
OR MAYBE THAT SPEAR HAS SOMETHING TO DO WITH HIS CONDITION.
GRAAARRH
UFFF!

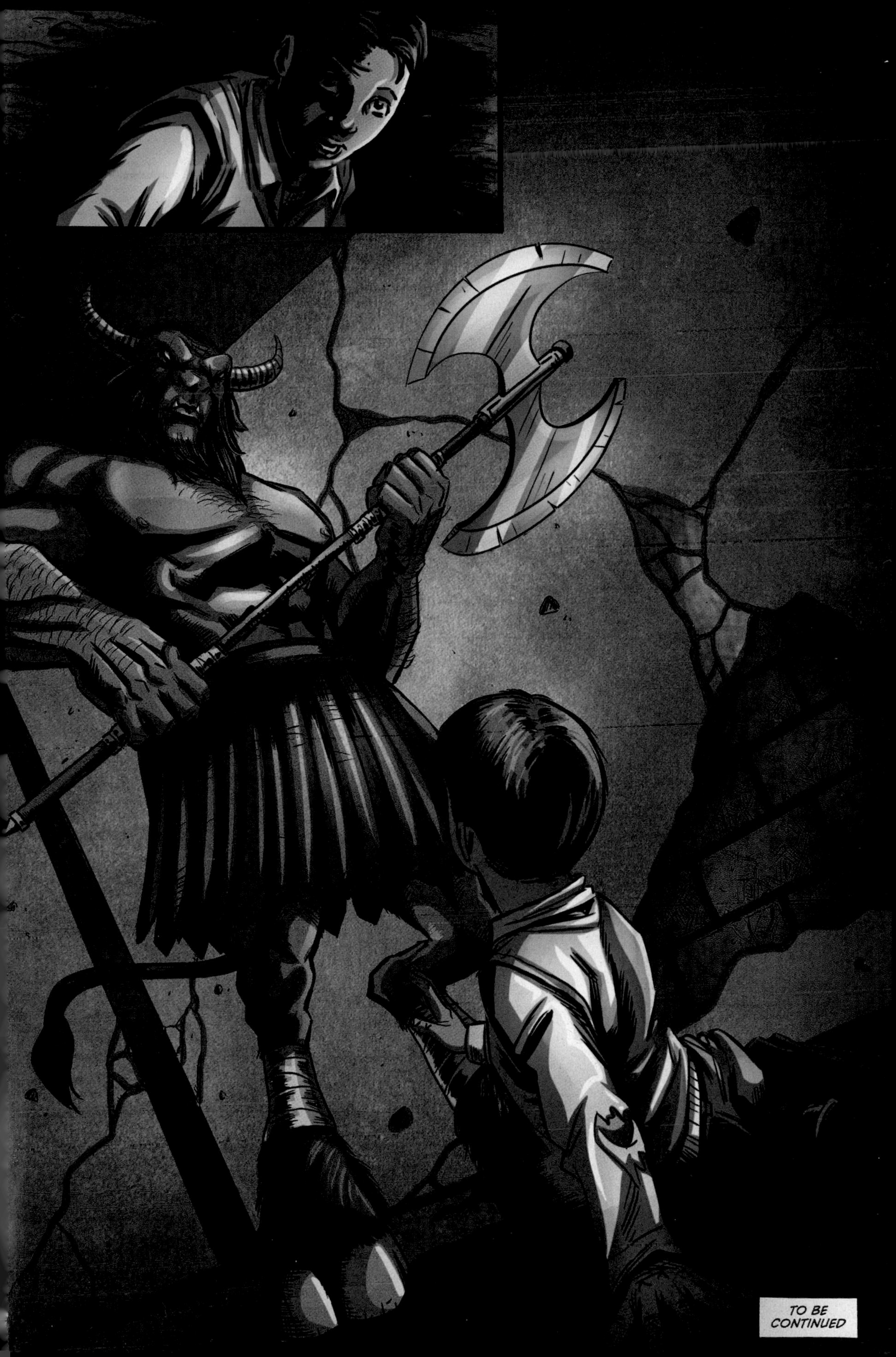
TO BE CONTINUED

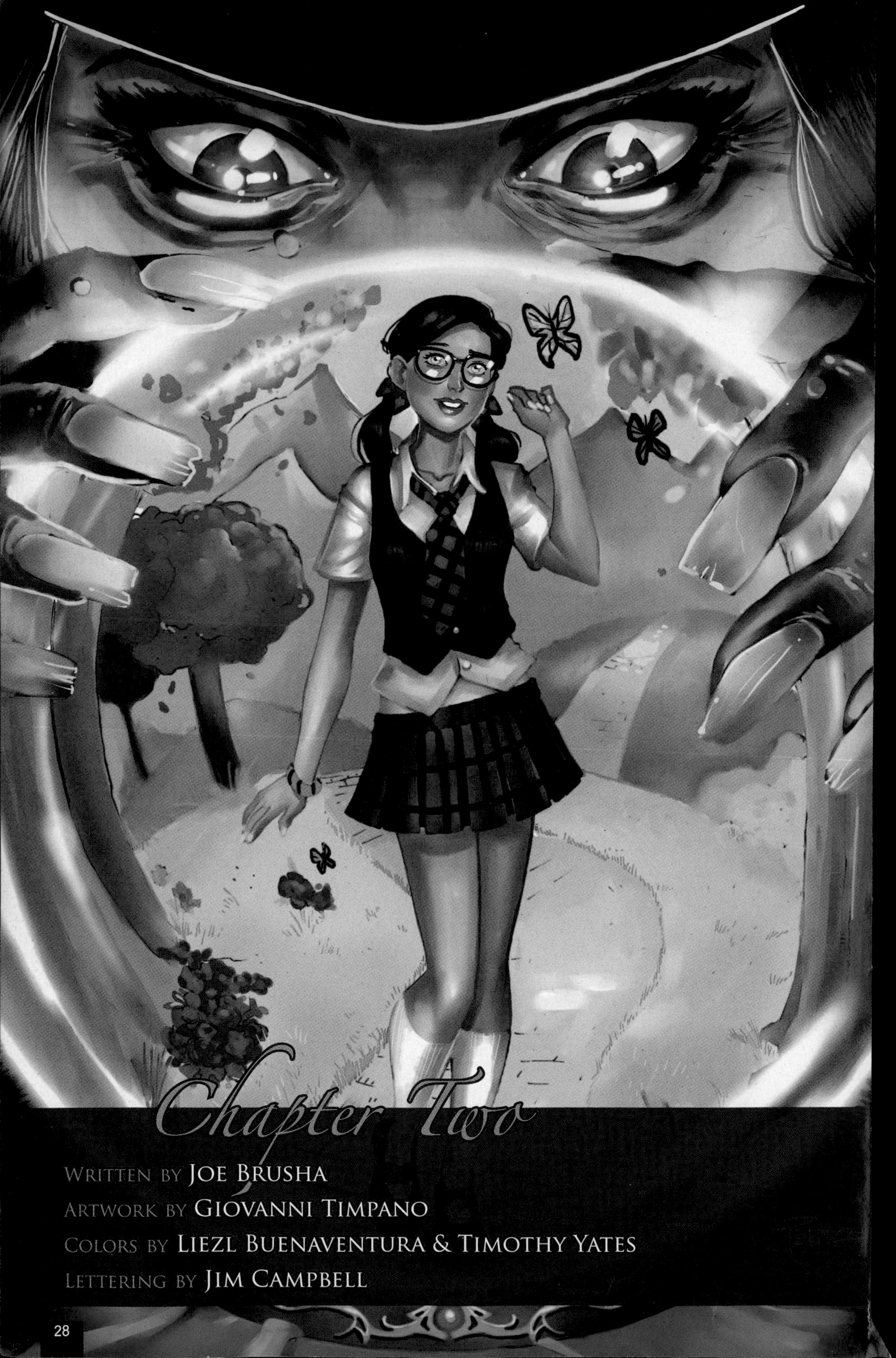

Chapter Two

WRITTEN BY JOE BRUSHA
ARTWORK BY GIOVANNI TIMPANO
COLORS BY LIEZL BUENAVENTURA & TIMOTHY YATES
LETTERING BY JIM CAMPBELL

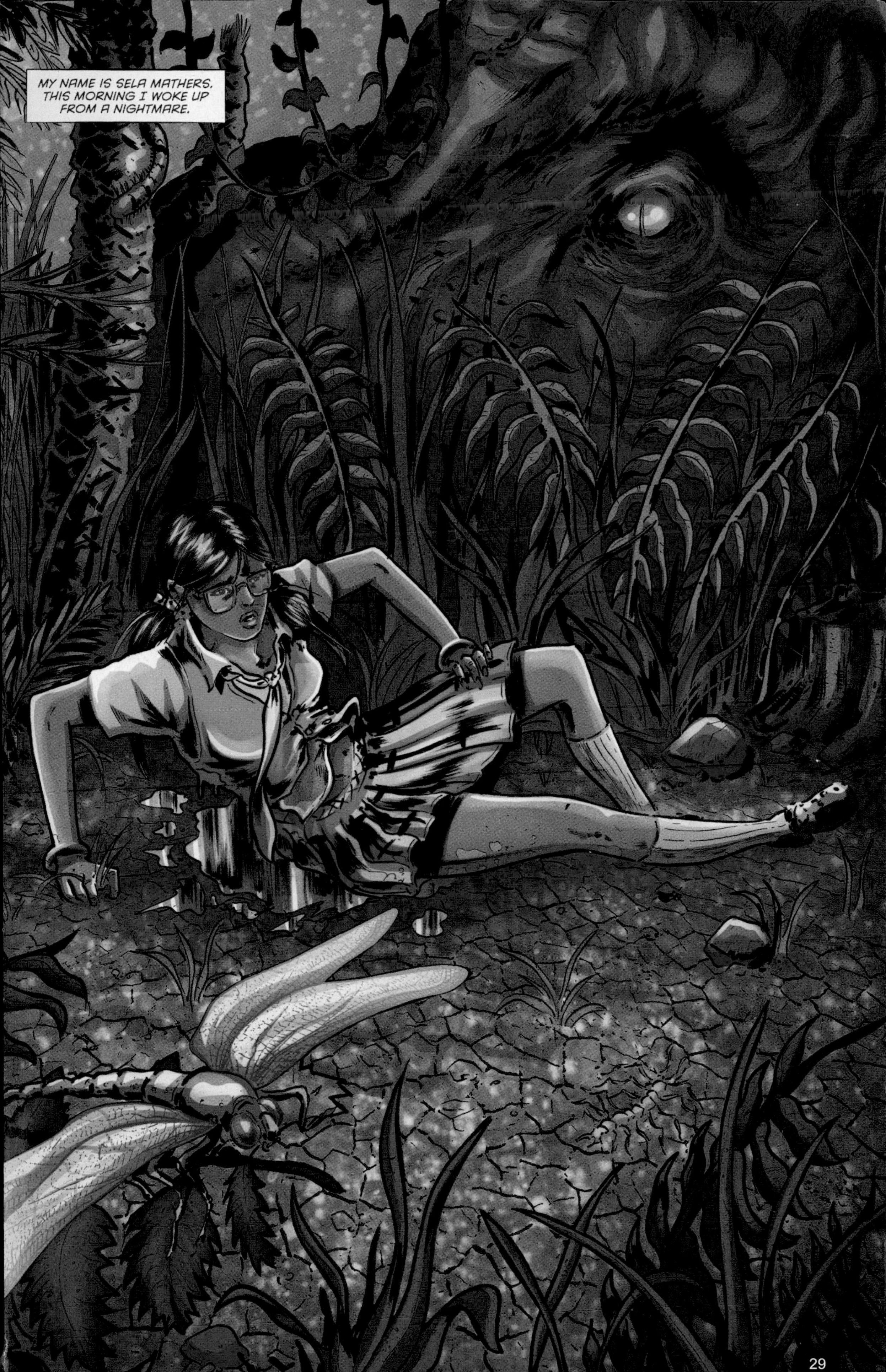
MY NAME IS SELA MATHERS. THIS MORNING I WOKE UP FROM A NIGHTMARE.

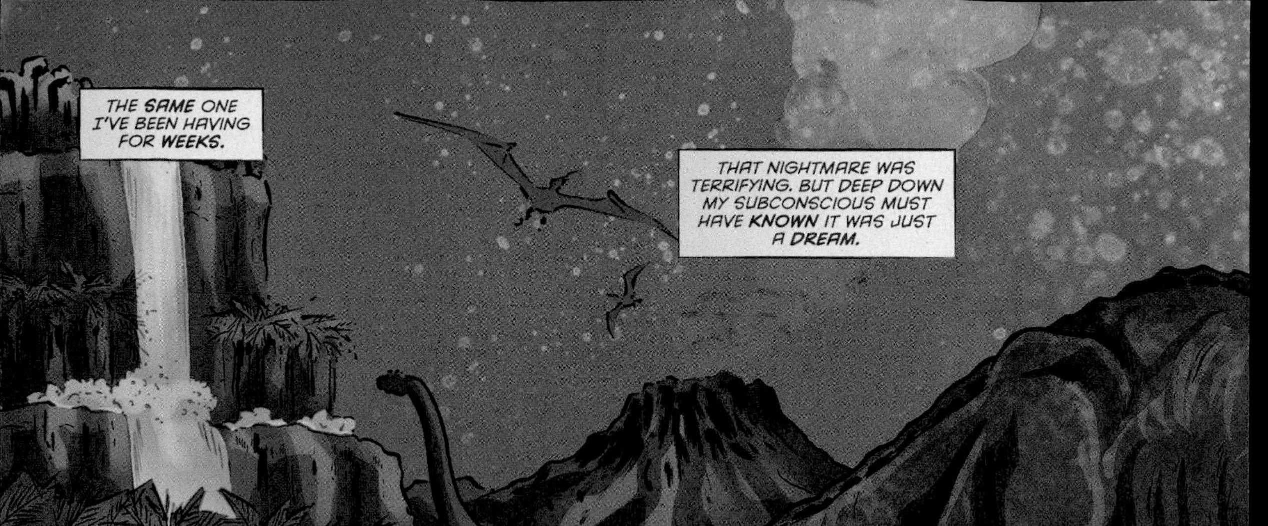
THE SAME ONE I'VE BEEN HAVING FOR WEEKS.
THAT NIGHTMARE WAS TERRIFYING. BUT DEEP DOWN MY SUBCONSCIOUS MUST HAVE KNOWN IT WAS JUST A DREAM.

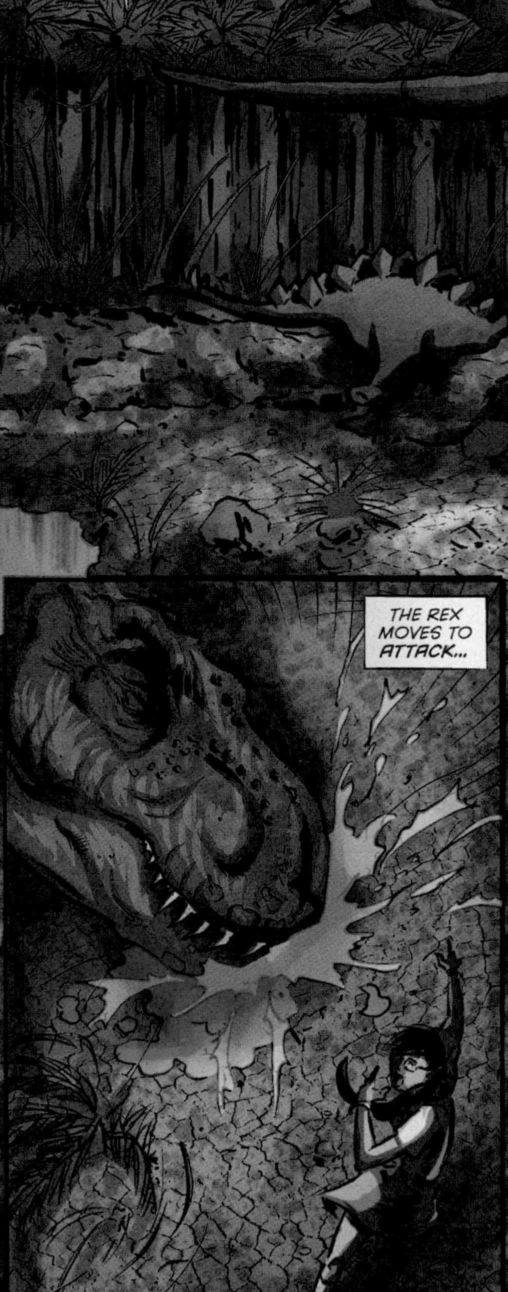
THE REX MOVES TO ATTACK...

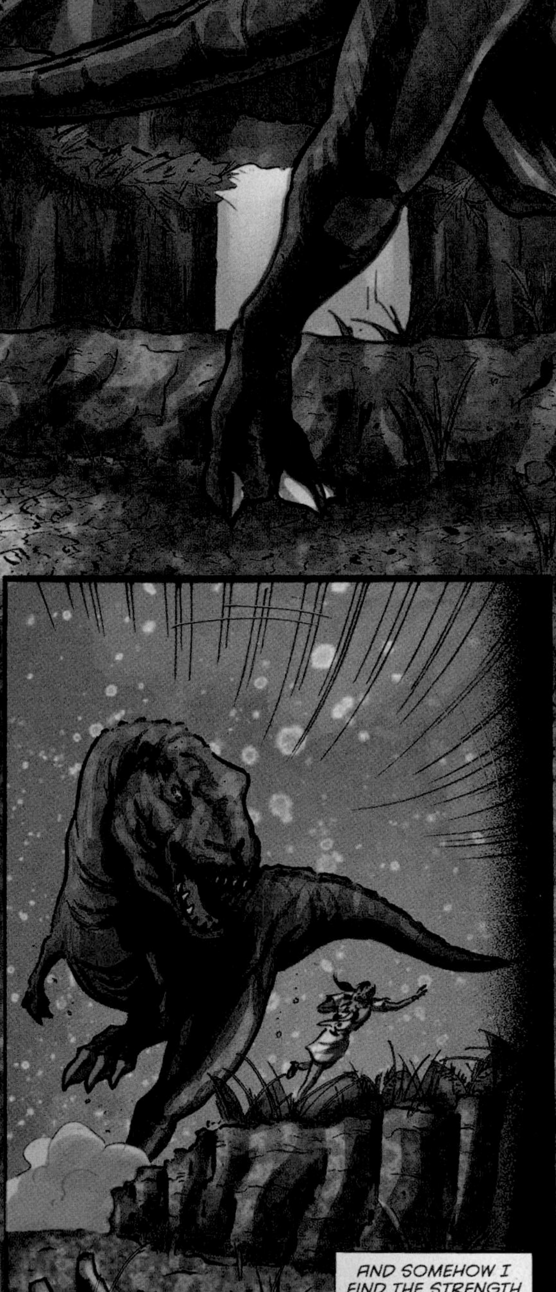
AND SOMEHOW I FIND THE STRENGTH TO MOVE... AND I RUN FOR MY LIFE.

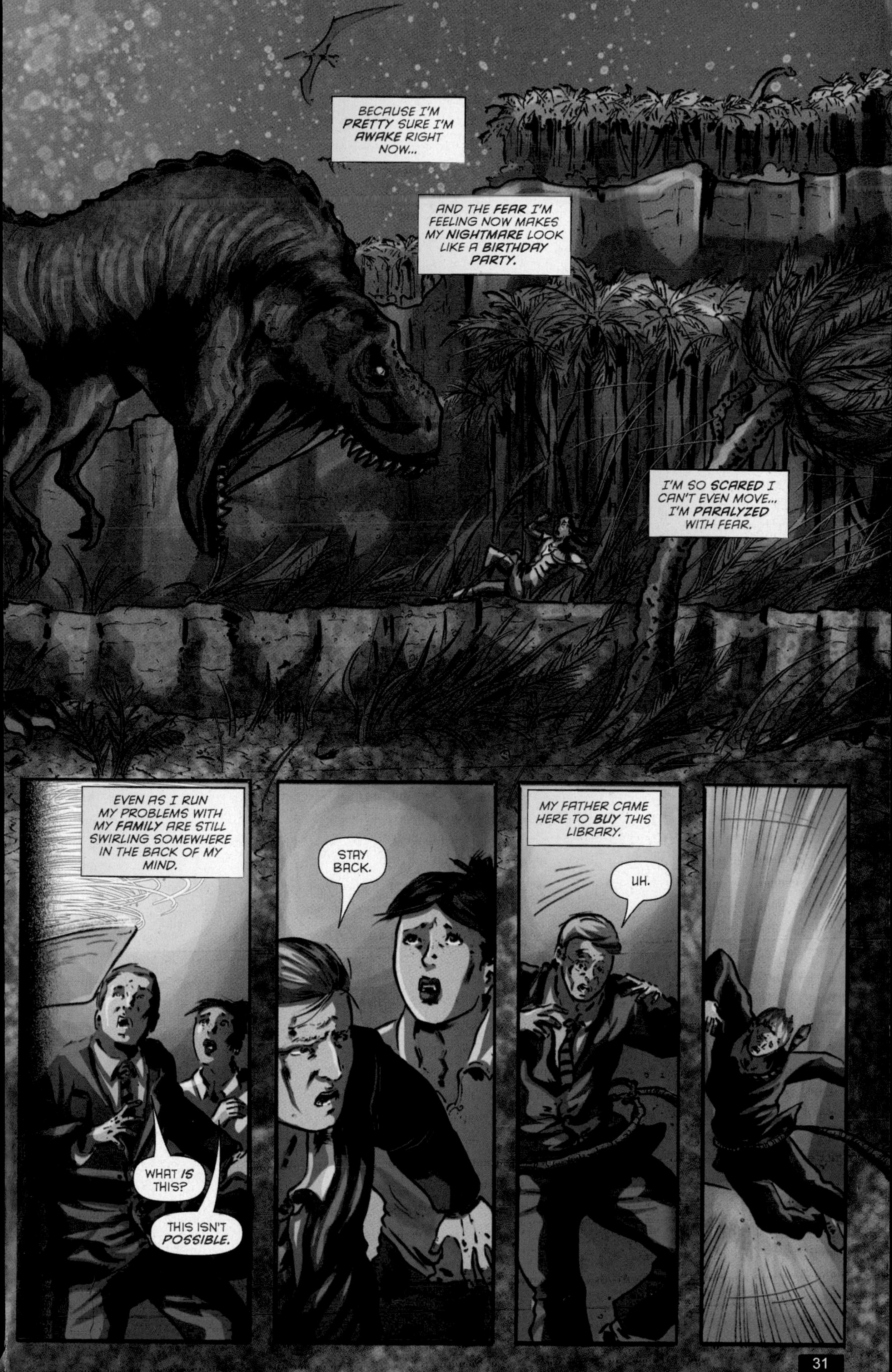

BECAUSE I'M PRETTY SURE I'M AWAKE RIGHT NOW...
AND THE FEAR I'M FEELING NOW MAKES MY NIGHTMARE LOOK LIKE A BIRTHDAY PARTY.
I'M SO SCARED I CAN'T EVEN MOVE... I'M PARALYZED WITH FEAR.
EVEN AS I RUN MY PROBLEMS WITH MY FAMILY ARE STILL SWIRLING SOMEWHERE IN THE BACK OF MY MIND.
WHAT IS THIS?
THIS ISN'T POSSIBLE.
STAY BACK.
MY FATHER CAME HERE TO BUY THIS LIBRARY.
UH.

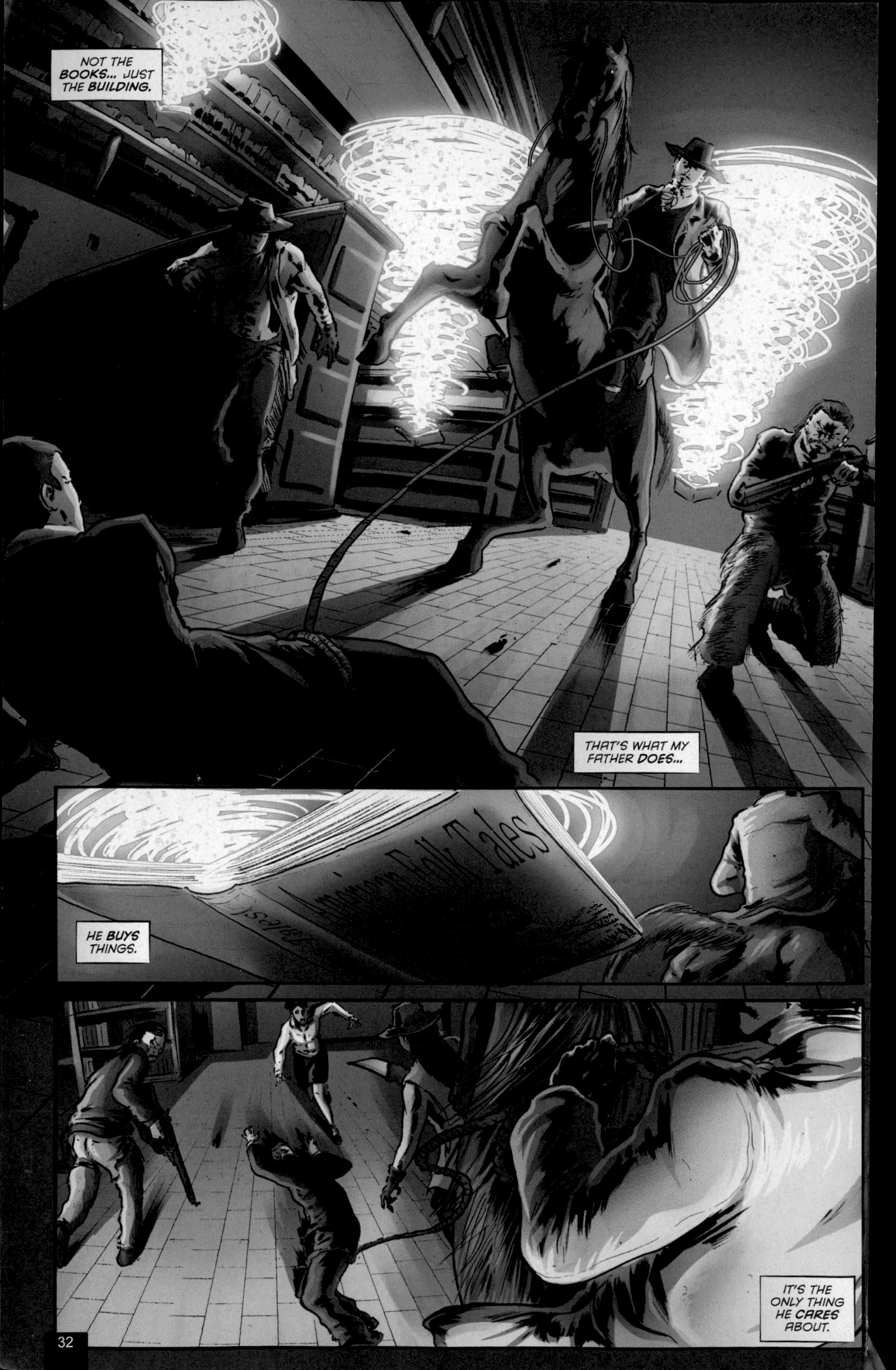
NOT THE BOOKS... JUST THE BUILDING.
THAT'S WHAT MY FATHER DOES...
HE BUYS THINGS.
IT'S THE ONLY THING HE CARES ABOUT.

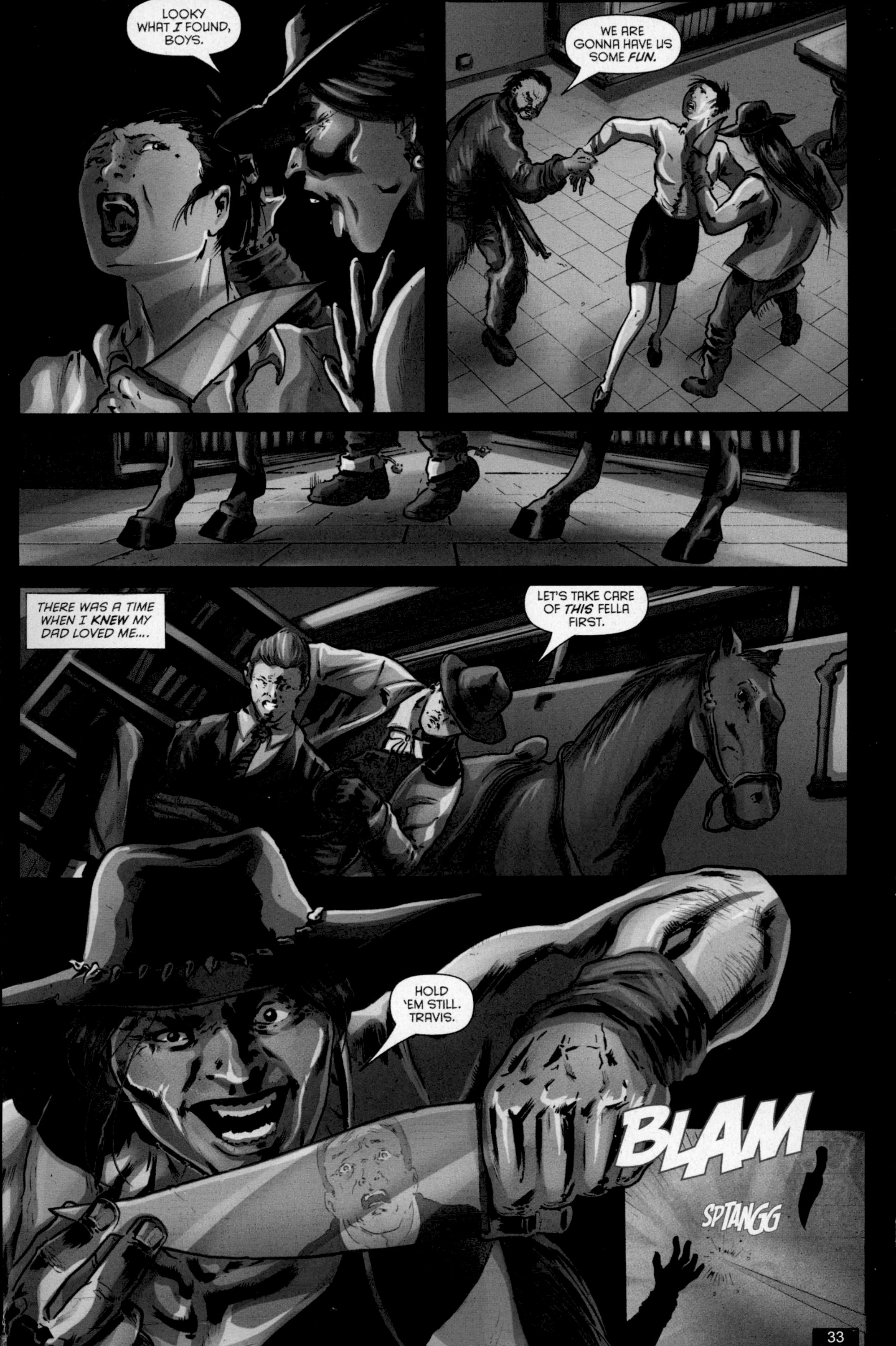
LOOKY WHAT *I* FOUND, BOYS.
WE ARE GONNA HAVE US SOME ***FUN.***
THERE WAS A TIME WHEN I **KNEW** MY DAD LOVED ME....
LET'S TAKE CARE OF ***THIS*** FELLA FIRST.
HOLD 'EM STILL. TRAVIS.
BLAM
SPTANGG

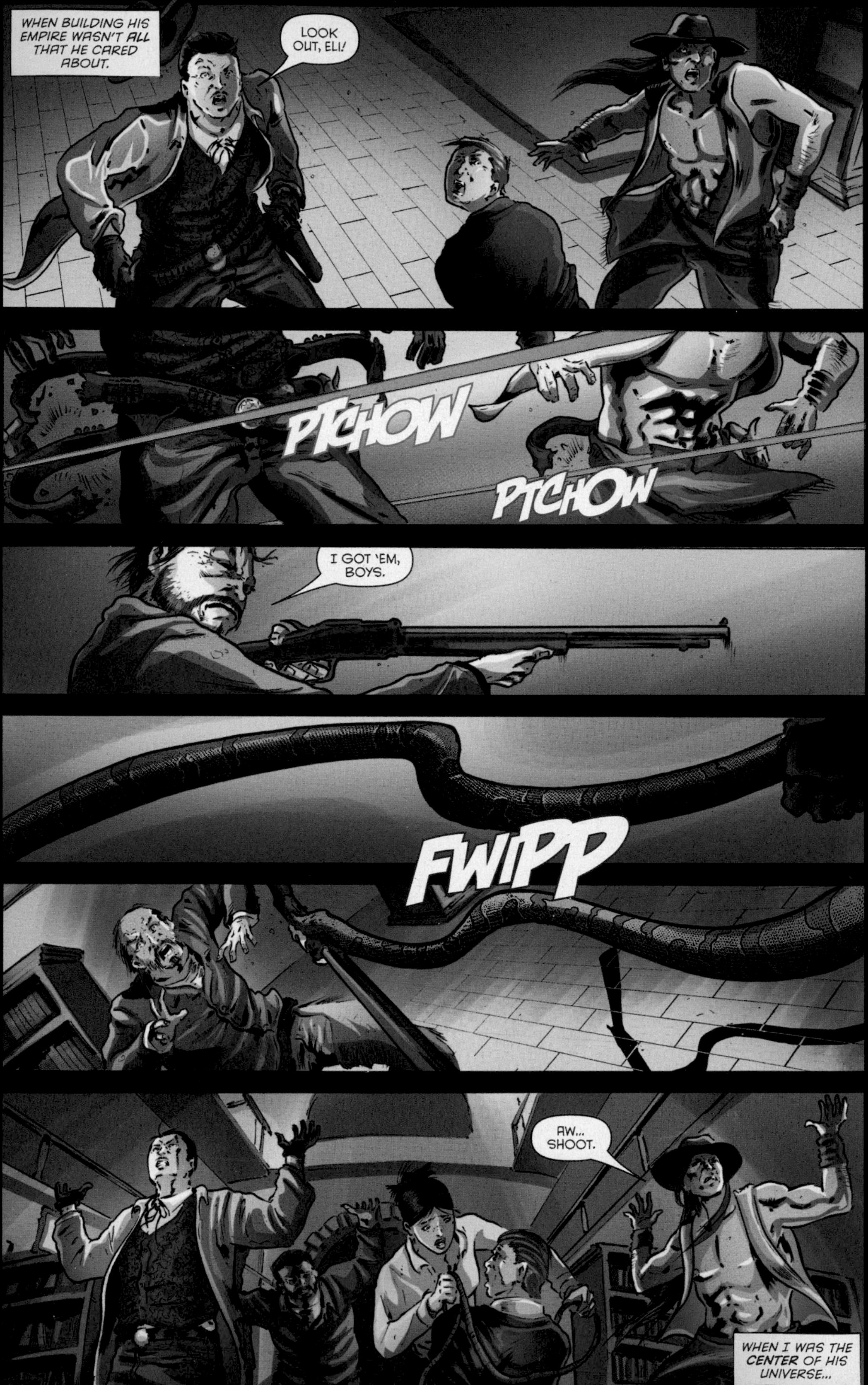
WHEN BUILDING HIS EMPIRE WASN'T ALL THAT HE CARED ABOUT.
LOOK OUT, ELI!
PTCHOW
PTCHOW
I GOT 'EM, BOYS.
FWIPP
AW... SHOOT.
WHEN I WAS THE CENTER OF HIS UNIVERSE...

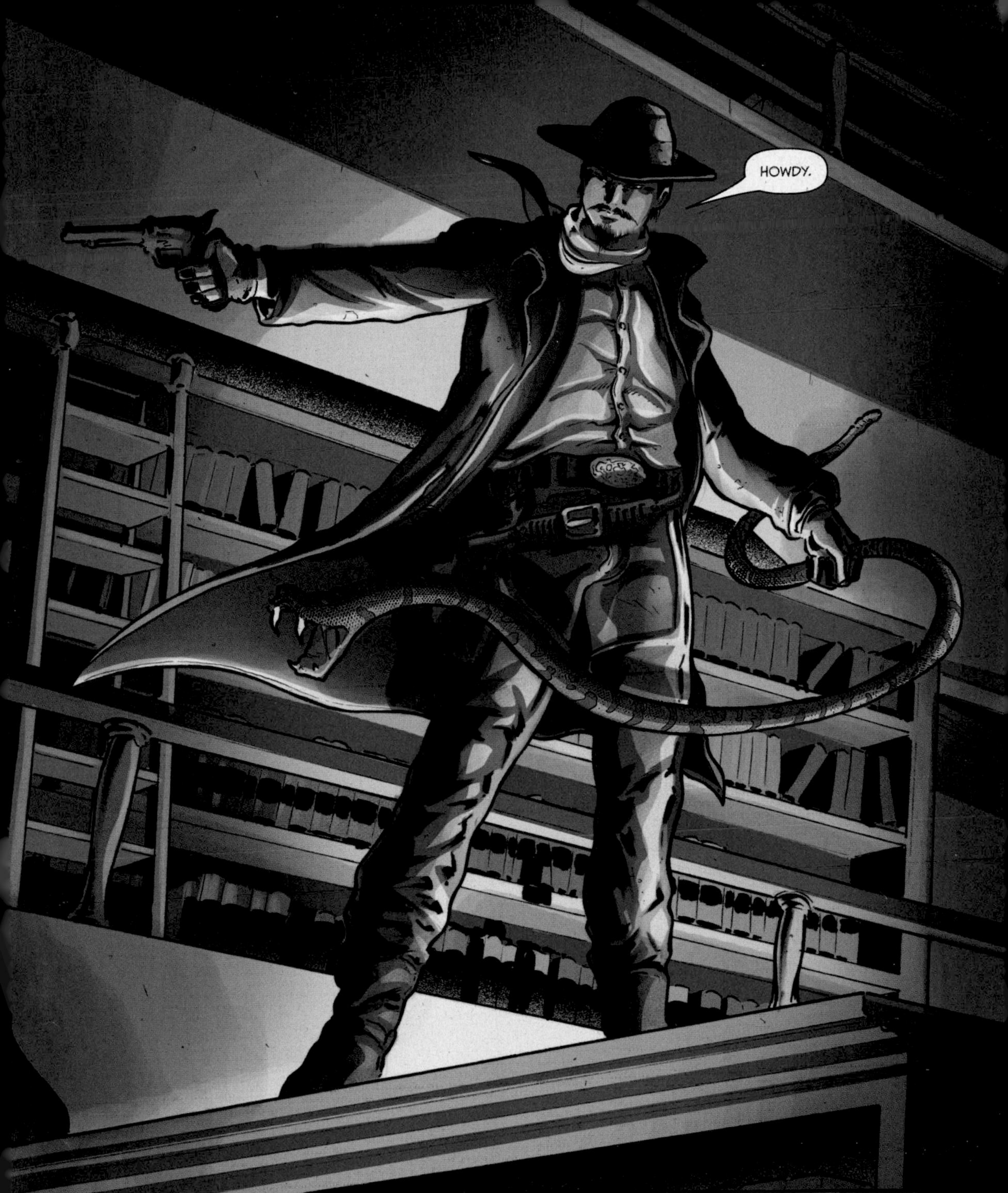
HOWDY.

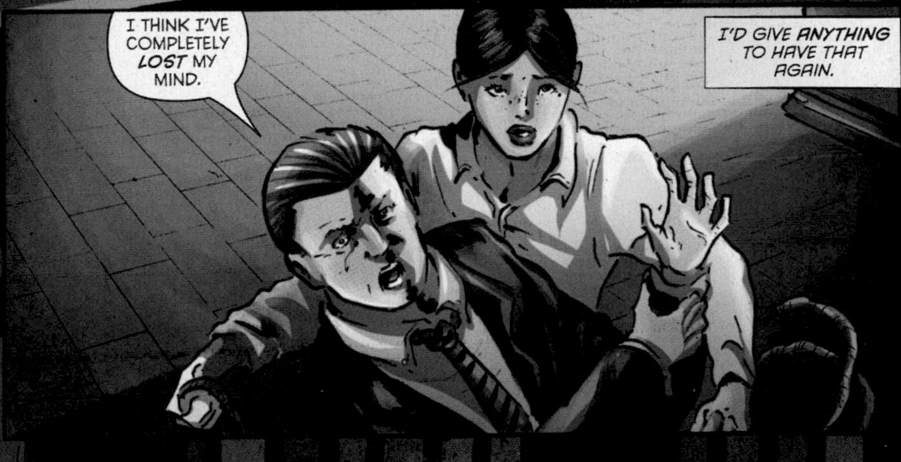
I THINK I'VE COMPLETELY *LOST* MY MIND.
I'D GIVE ***ANYTHING*** *TO HAVE THAT AGAIN.*

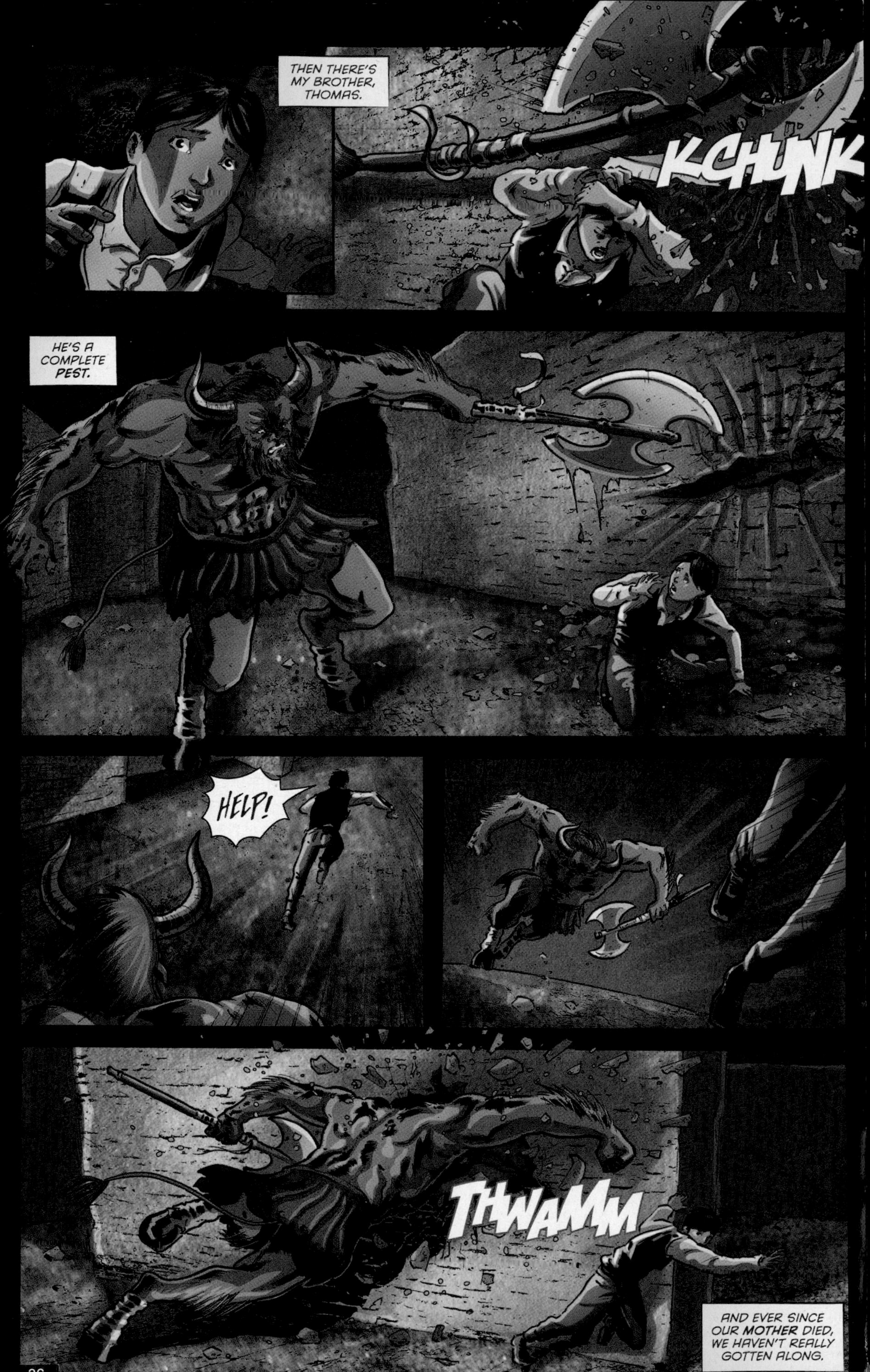
THEN THERE'S MY BROTHER, THOMAS.
KCHUNK
HE'S A COMPLETE PEST.
HELP!
THWAMM
AND EVER SINCE OUR MOTHER DIED, WE HAVEN'T REALLY GOTTEN ALONG.

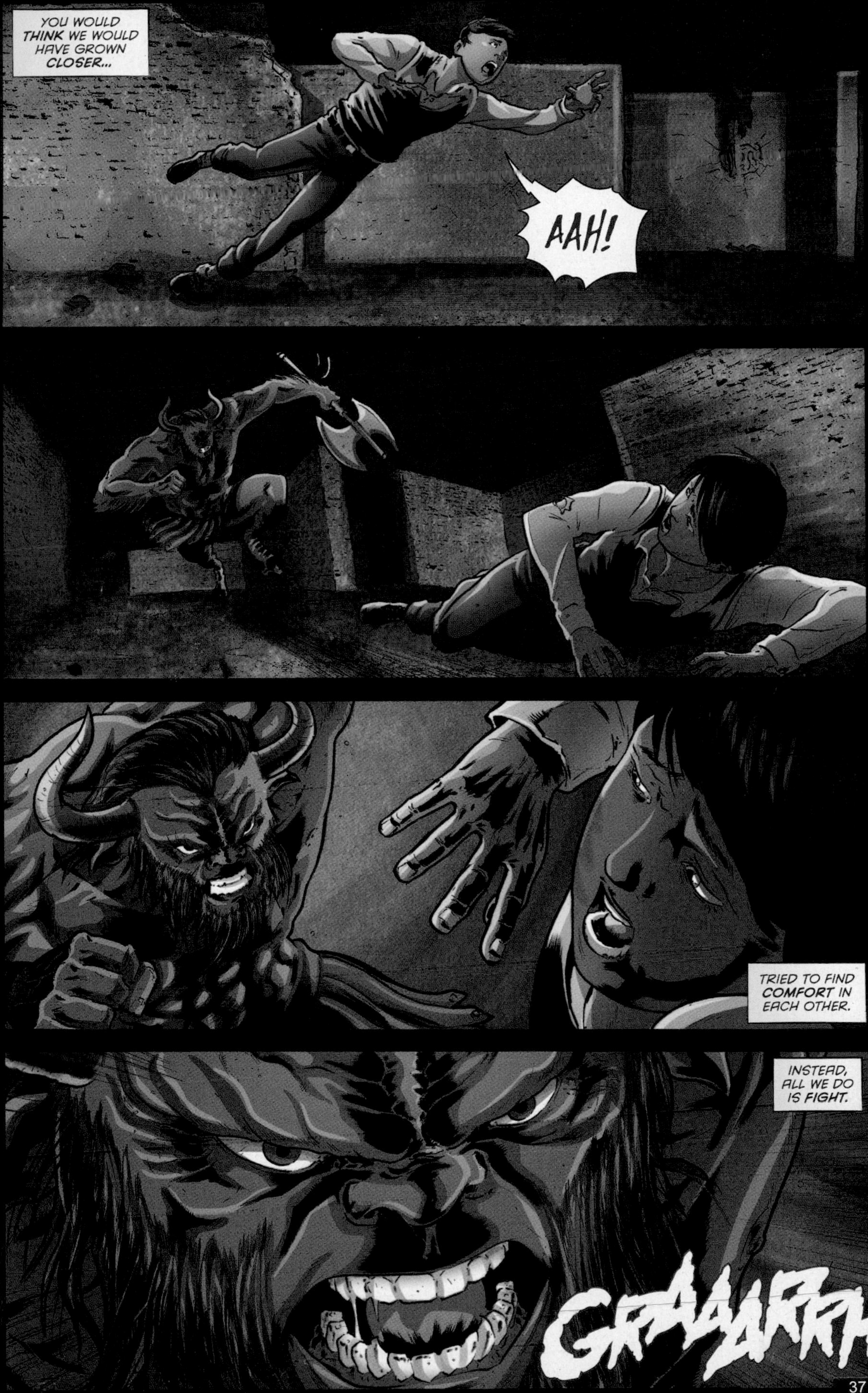
YOU WOULD THINK WE WOULD HAVE GROWN CLOSER...
AAH!
TRIED TO FIND COMFORT IN EACH OTHER.
INSTEAD, ALL WE DO IS FIGHT.
GRAAARRH

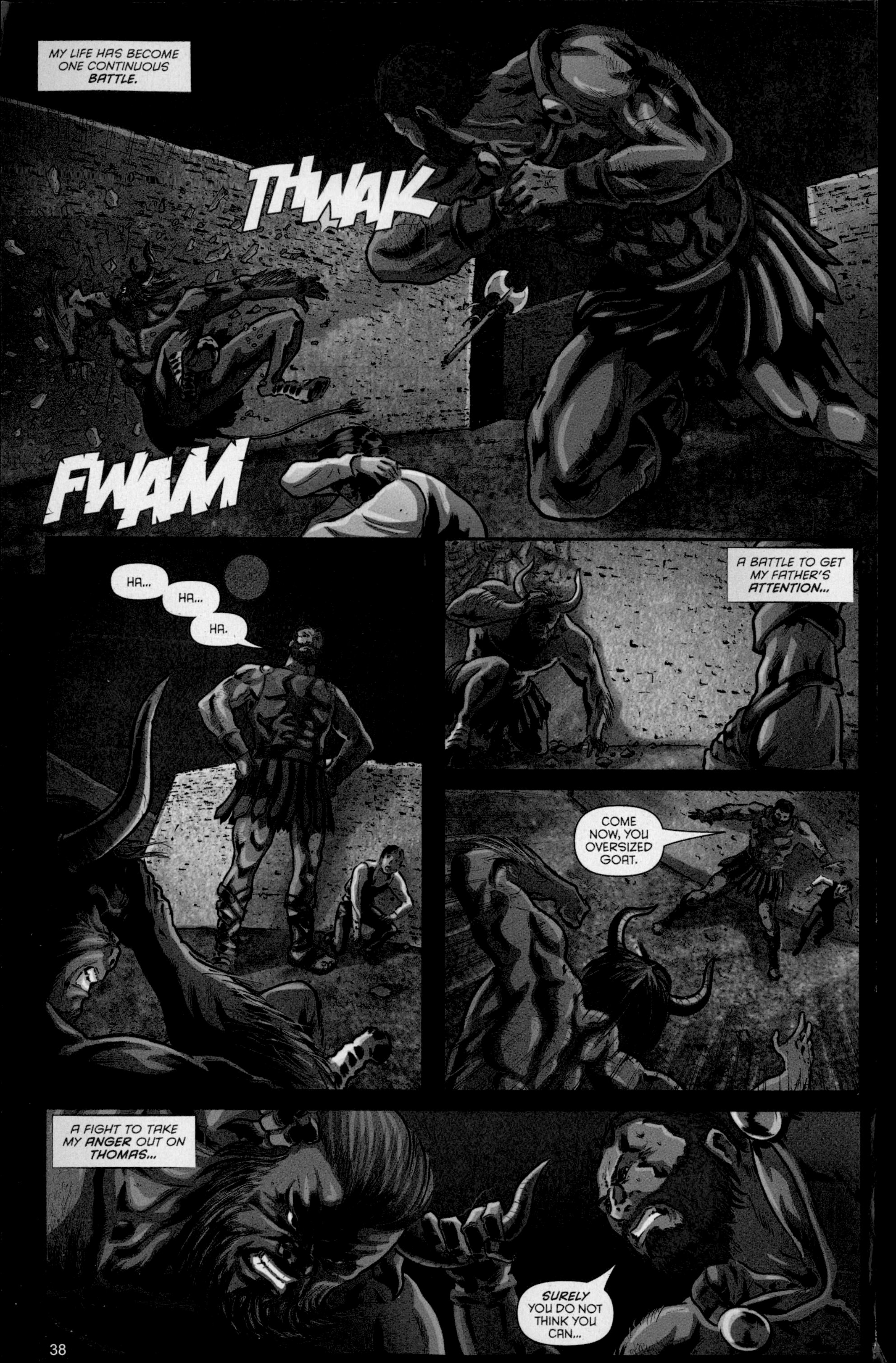
MY LIFE HAS BECOME ONE CONTINUOUS BATTLE.
THWAK
FWAM
HA...
HA...
HA.
A BATTLE TO GET MY FATHER'S ATTENTION...
COME NOW, YOU OVERSIZED GOAT.
A FIGHT TO TAKE MY ANGER OUT ON THOMAS...
SURELY YOU DO NOT THINK YOU CAN...

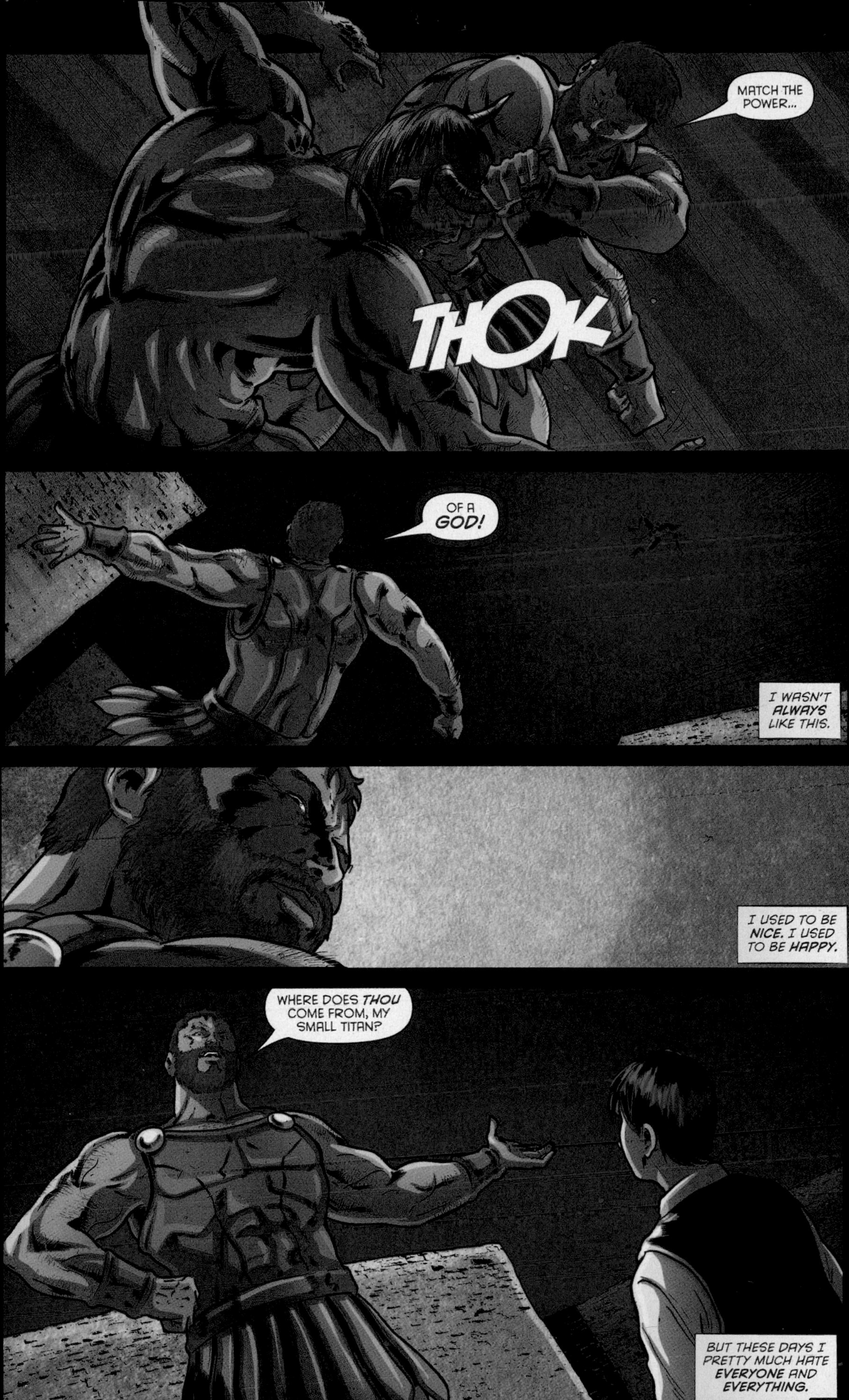
MATCH THE POWER...
THOK
OF A GOD!
I WASN'T ALWAYS LIKE THIS.
I USED TO BE NICE. I USED TO BE HAPPY.
WHERE DOES THOU COME FROM, MY SMALL TITAN?
BUT THESE DAYS I PRETTY MUCH HATE EVERYONE AND EVERYTHING.

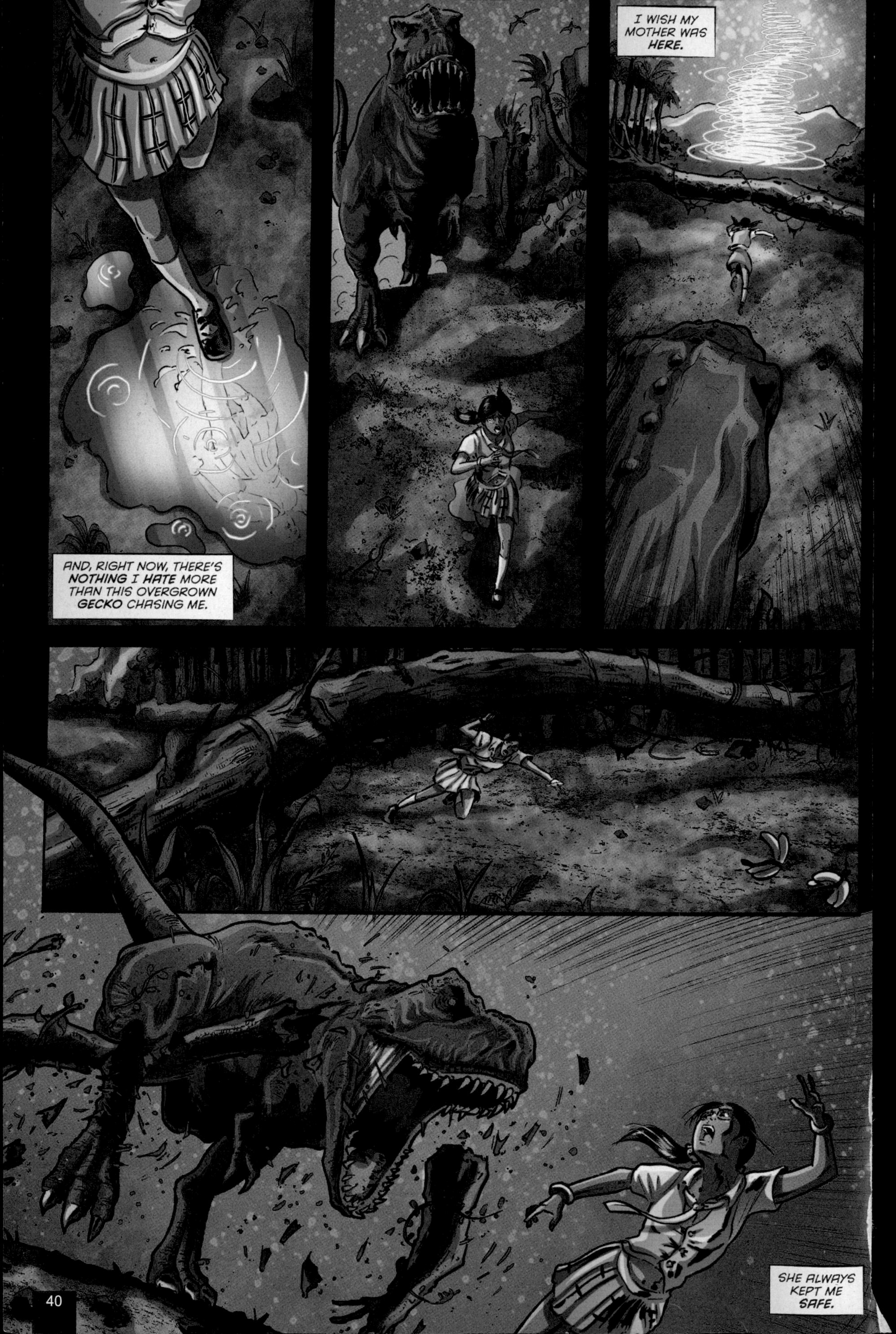
AND, RIGHT NOW, THERE'S NOTHING I HATE MORE THAN THIS OVERGROWN GECKO CHASING ME.
I WISH MY MOTHER WAS HERE.
SHE ALWAYS KEPT ME SAFE.

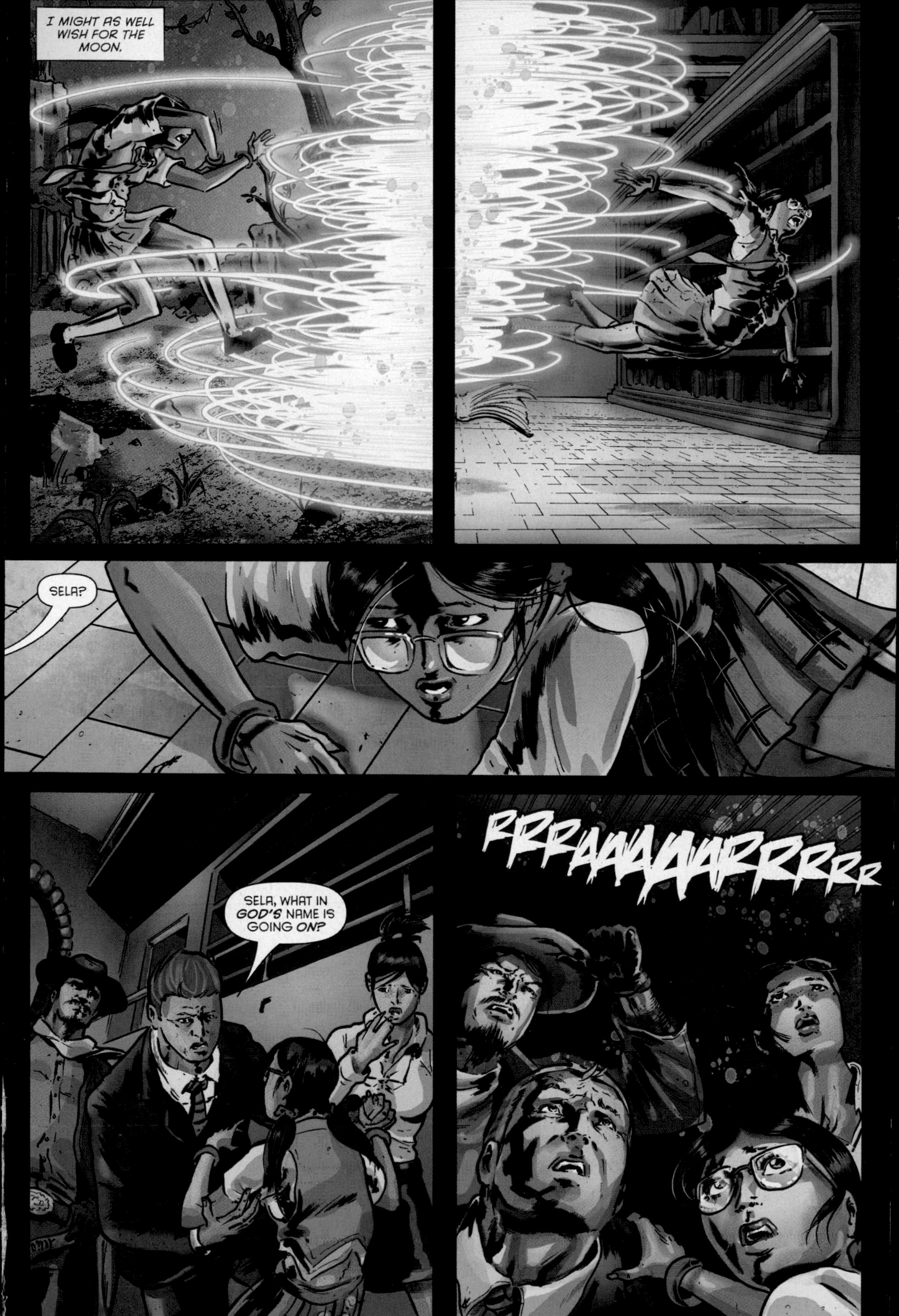
I MIGHT AS WELL WISH FOR THE MOON.
SELA?
SELA, WHAT IN GOD'S NAME IS GOING ON?
RRRAAAAARRRRR

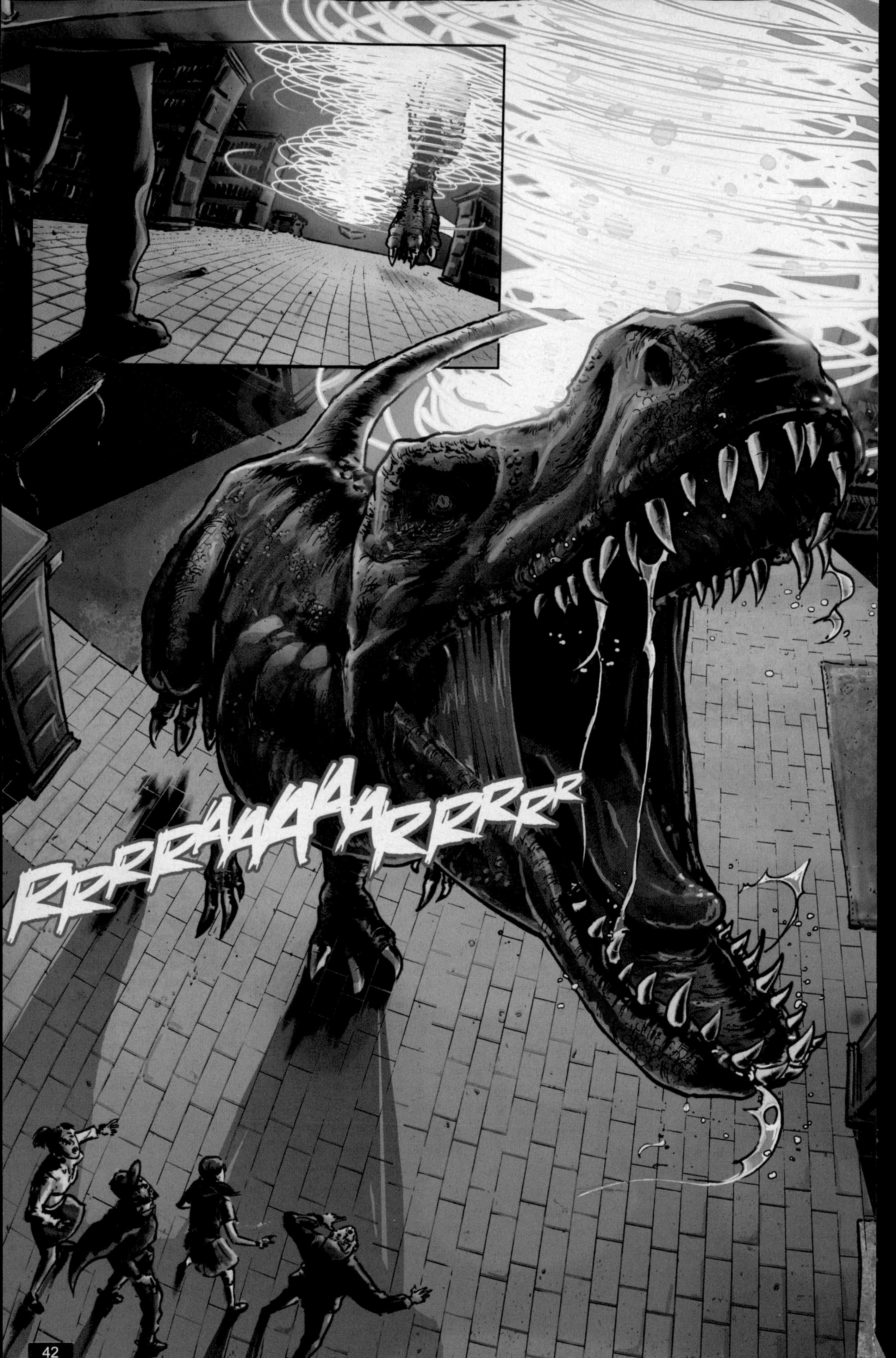
RRRRAAAAARRRRR

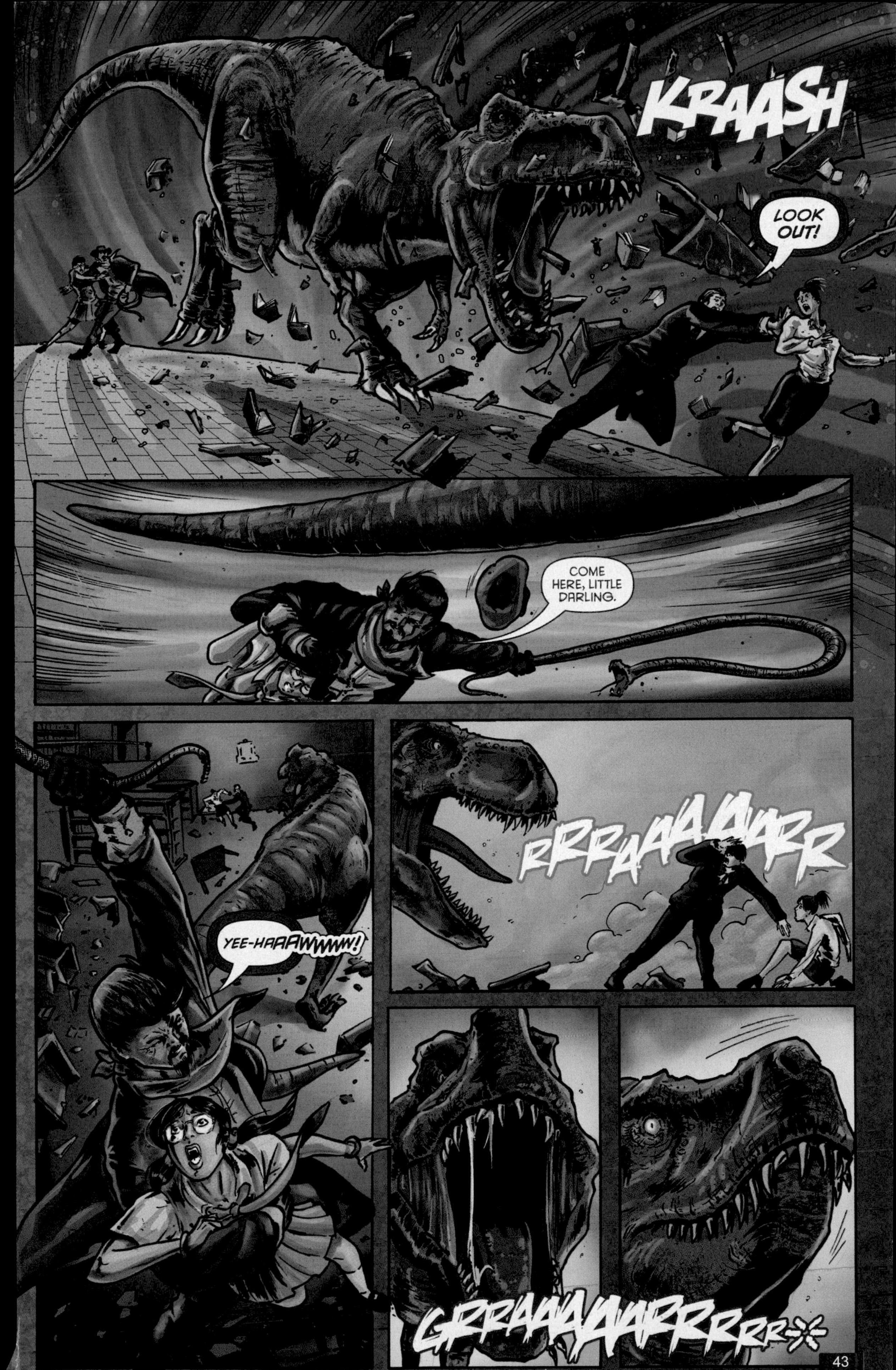
KRAASH
LOOK OUT!
COME HERE, LITTLE DARLING.
YEE-HAAAWWWW!
RRRAAAAAARR
GRRAAAAAARRRRRR

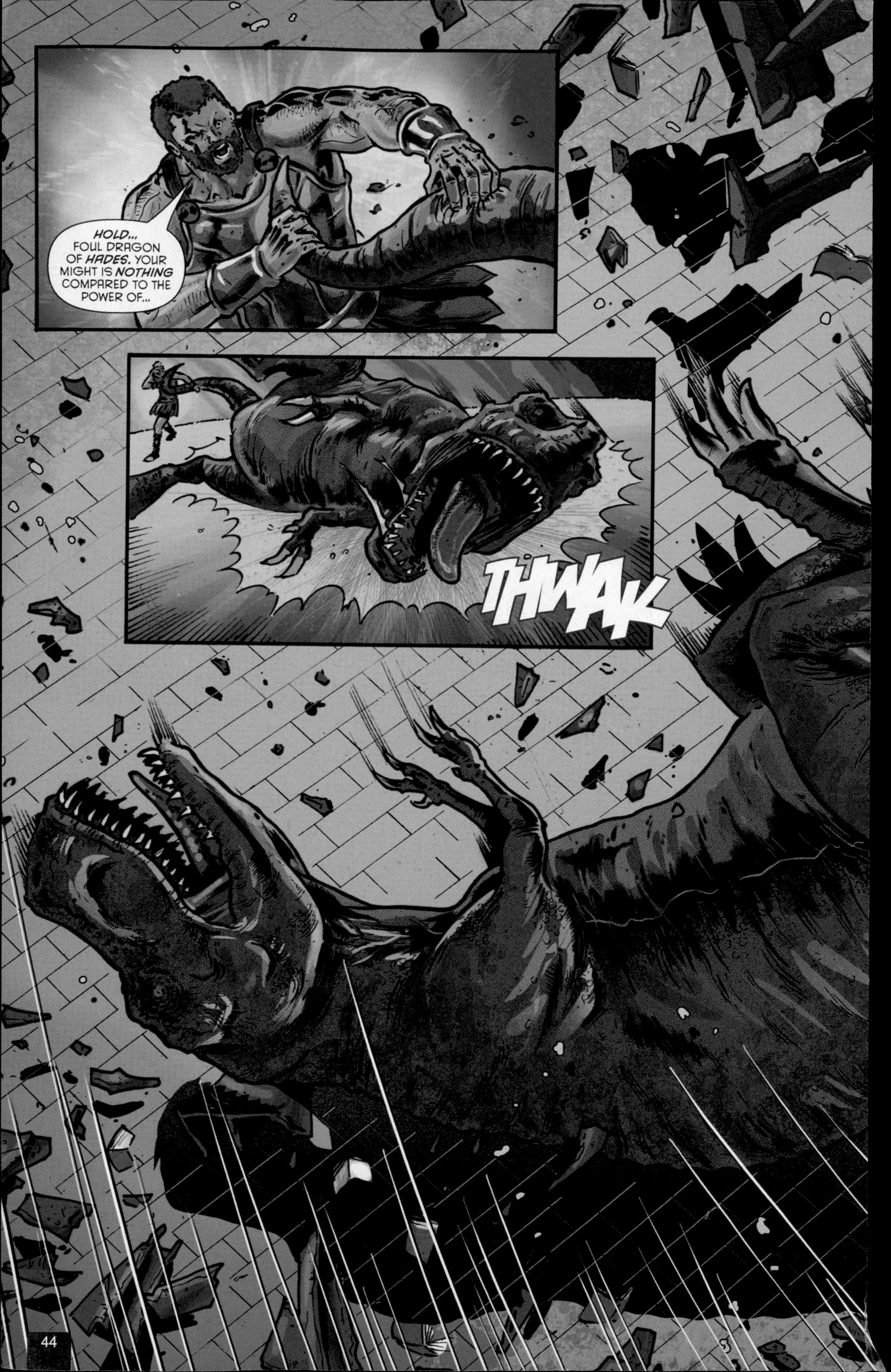
HOLD... FOUL DRAGON OF HADES. YOUR MIGHT IS NOTHING COMPARED TO THE POWER OF...
THWAK

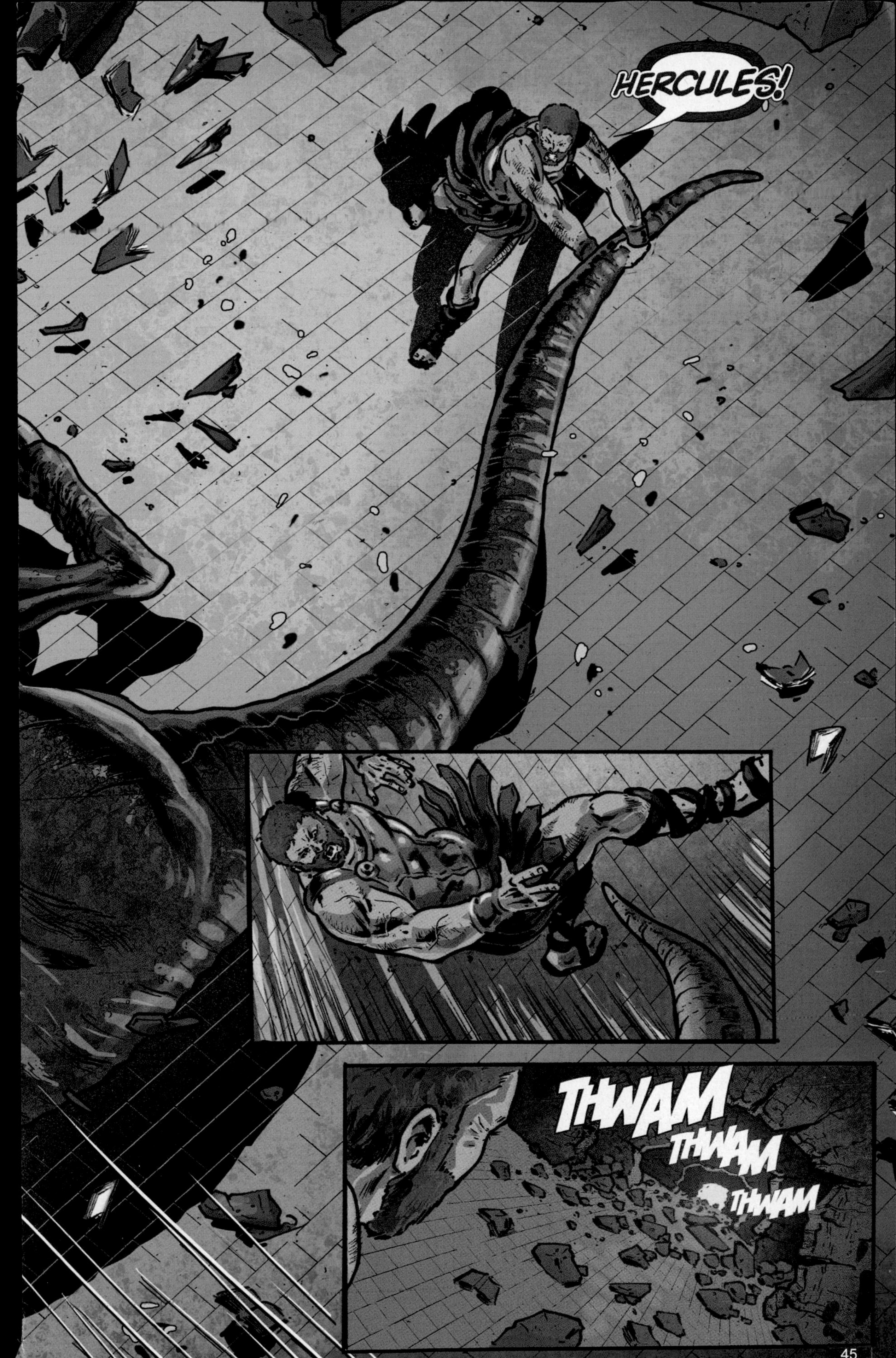
HERCULES!
THWAM
THWAM
THWAM

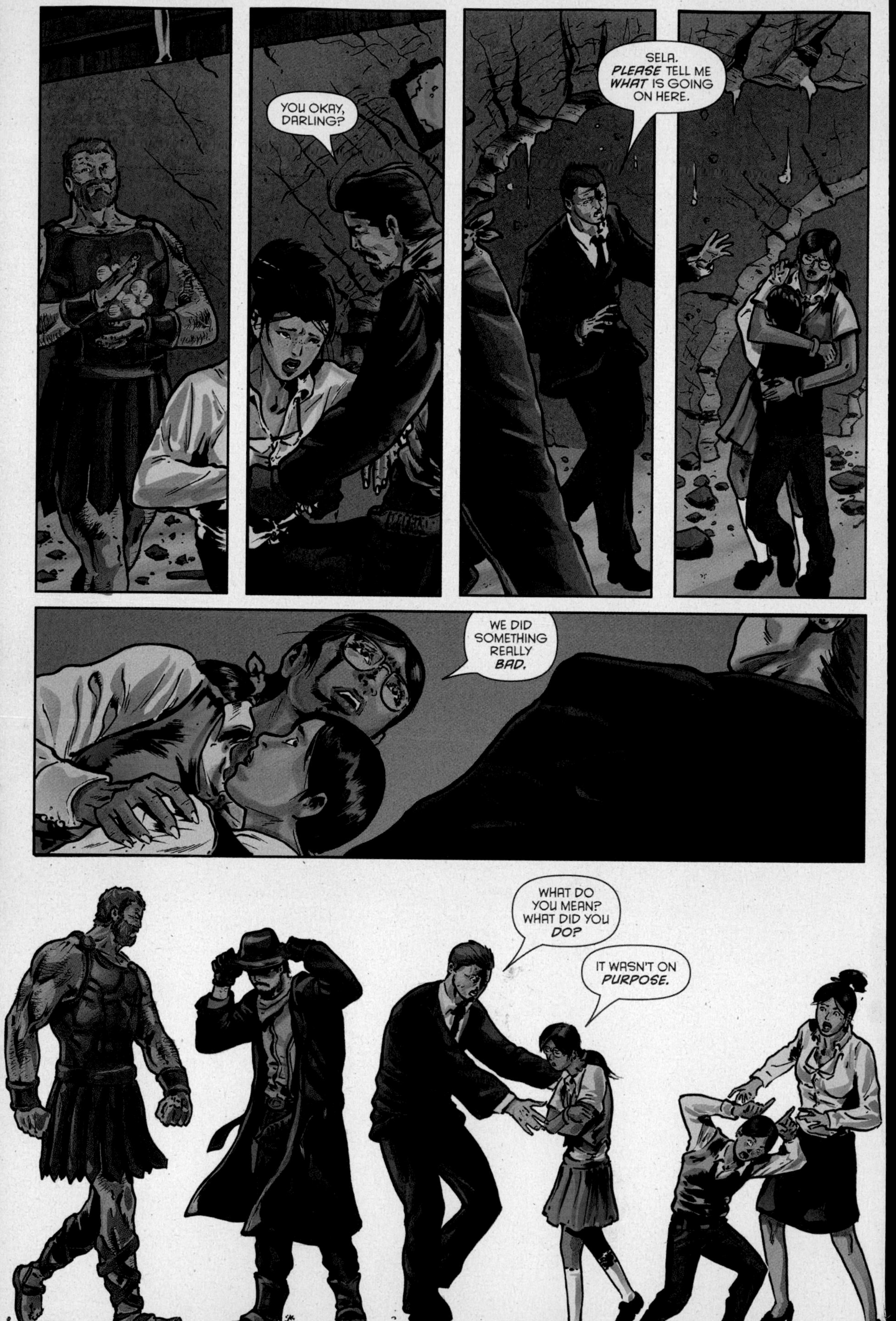
YOU OKAY, DARLING?
SELA. PLEASE TELL ME WHAT IS GOING ON HERE.
WE DID SOMETHING REALLY BAD.
WHAT DO YOU MEAN? WHAT DID YOU DO?
IT WASN'T ON PURPOSE.

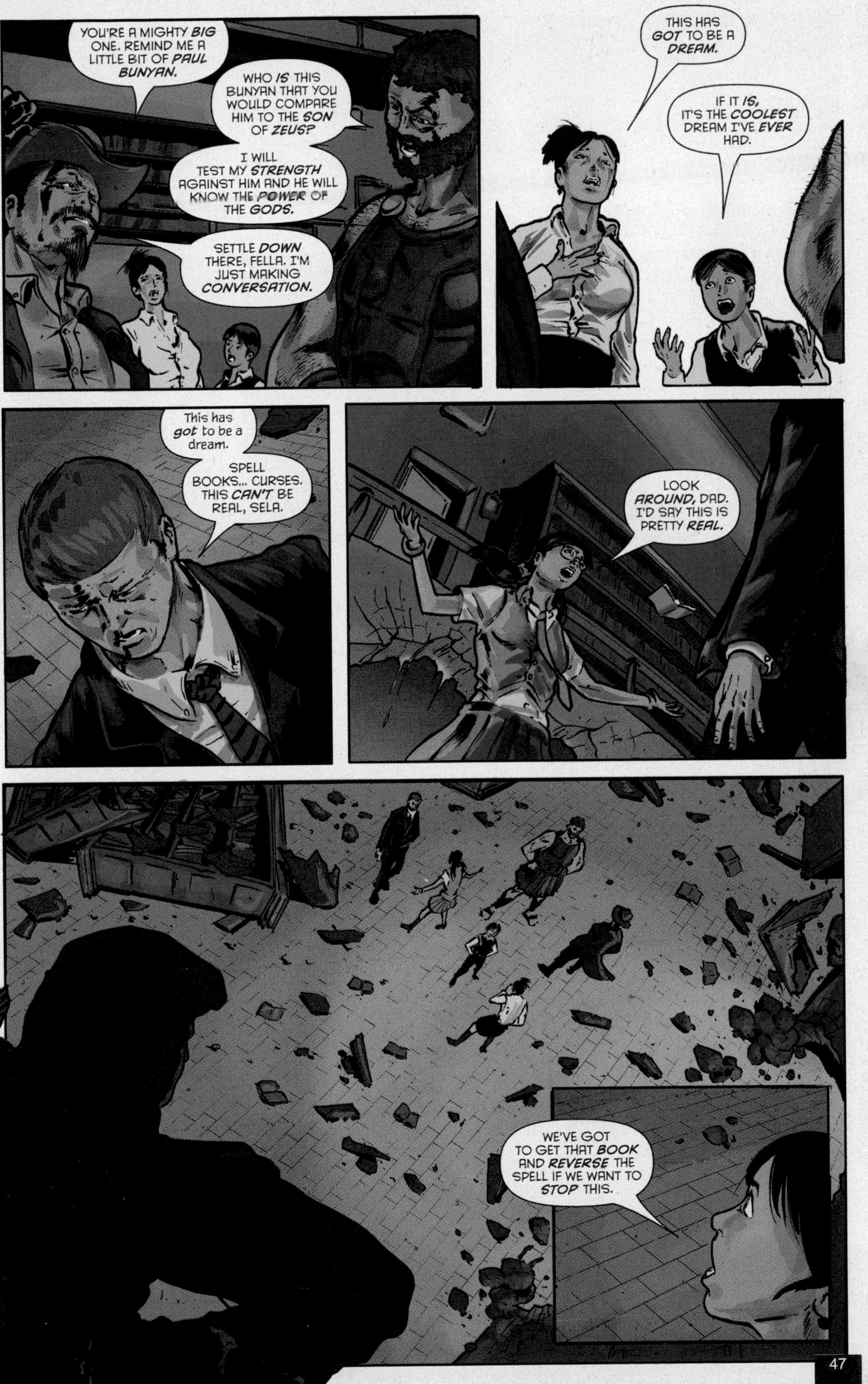

YOU'RE A MIGHTY BIG ONE. REMIND ME A LITTLE BIT OF PAUL BUNYAN.
WHO IS THIS BUNYAN THAT YOU WOULD COMPARE HIM TO THE SON OF ZEUS?
I WILL TEST MY STRENGTH AGAINST HIM AND HE WILL KNOW THE POWER OF THE GODS.
SETTLE DOWN THERE, FELLA. I'M JUST MAKING CONVERSATION.
THIS HAS GOT TO BE A DREAM.
IF IT IS, IT'S THE COOLEST DREAM I'VE EVER HAD.
This has got to be a dream.
SPELL BOOKS... CURSES. THIS CAN'T BE REAL, SELA.
LOOK AROUND, DAD. I'D SAY THIS IS PRETTY REAL.
WE'VE GOT TO GET THAT BOOK AND REVERSE THE SPELL IF WE WANT TO STOP THIS.

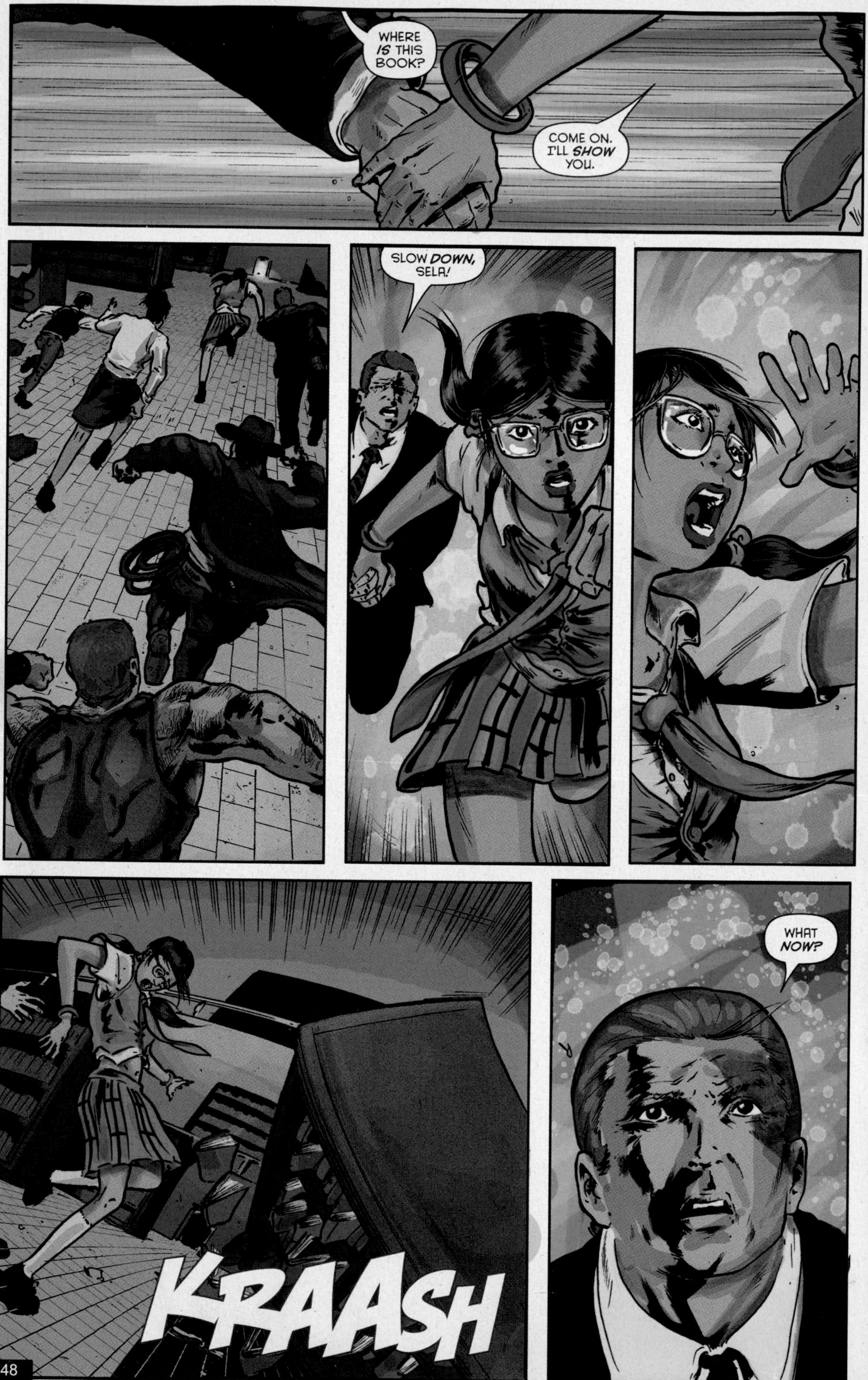
WHERE IS THIS BOOK?
COME ON. I'LL SHOW YOU.
SLOW DOWN, SELA!
KRAASH
WHAT NOW?

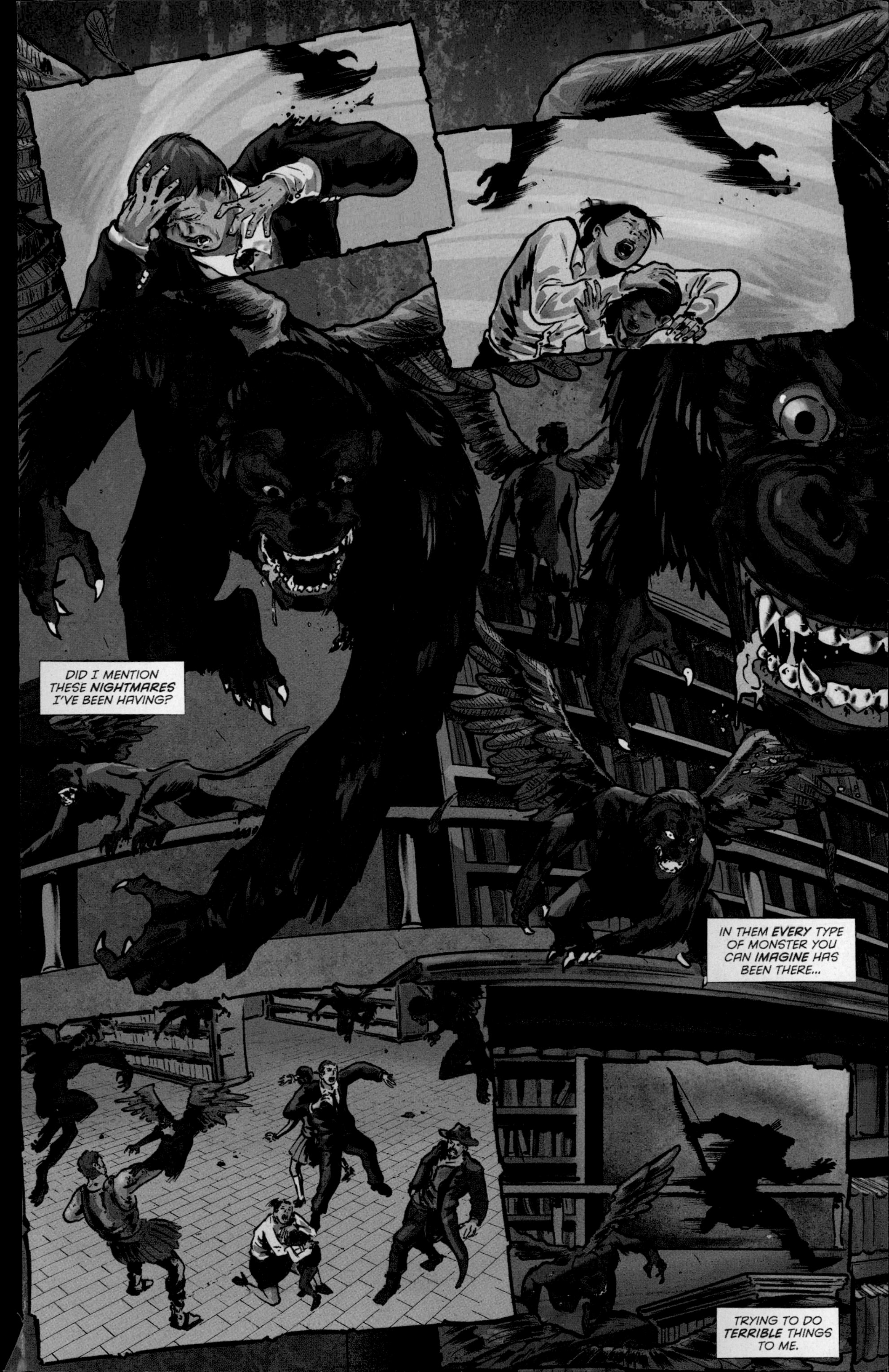
DID I MENTION THESE NIGHTMARES I'VE BEEN HAVING?
IN THEM EVERY TYPE OF MONSTER YOU CAN IMAGINE HAS BEEN THERE...
TRYING TO DO TERRIBLE THINGS TO ME.

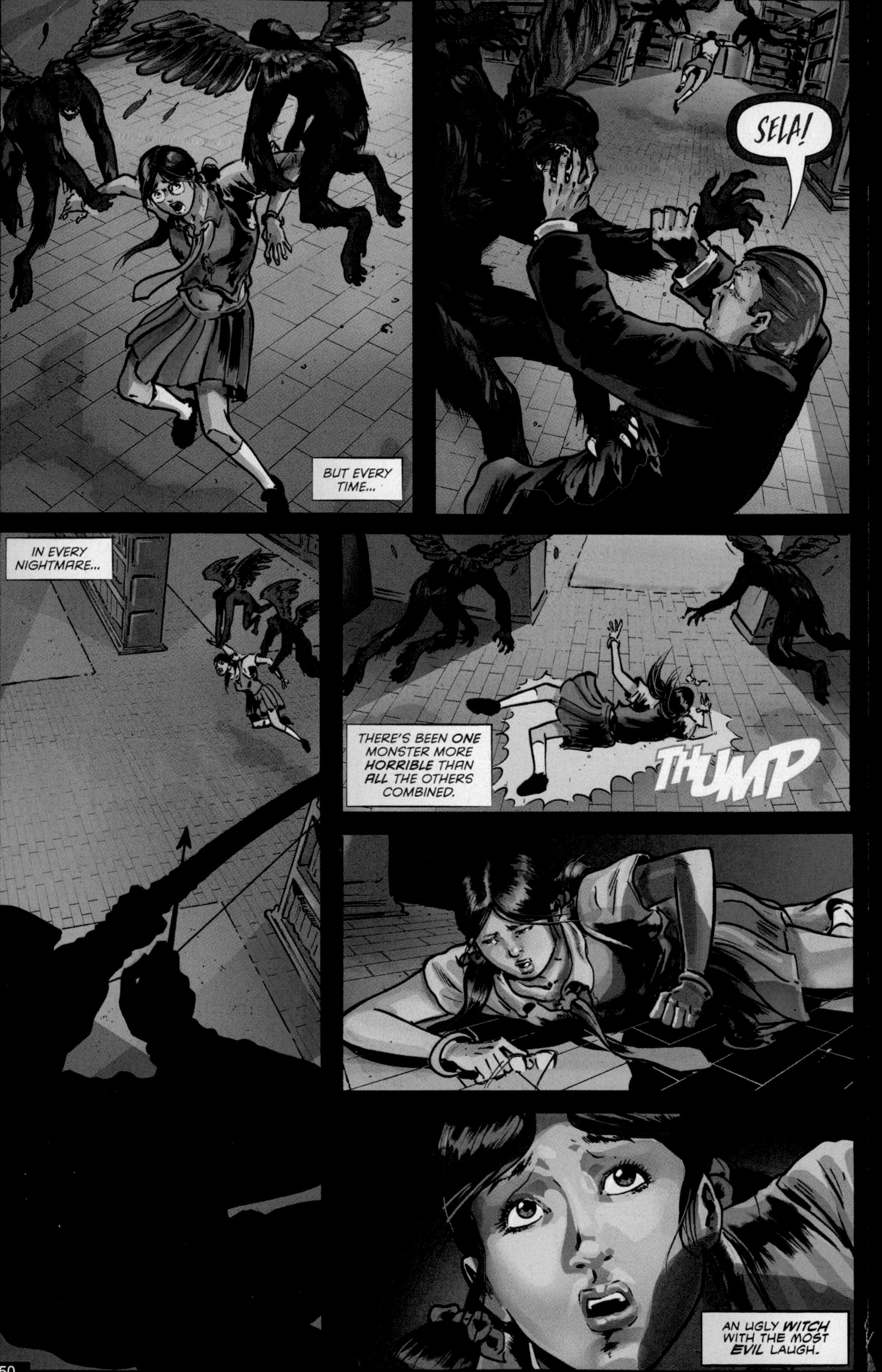
BUT EVERY TIME...
SELA!
IN EVERY NIGHTMARE...
THERE'S BEEN ONE MONSTER MORE HORRIBLE THAN ALL THE OTHERS COMBINED.
THUMP
AN UGLY WITCH WITH THE MOST EVIL LAUGH.

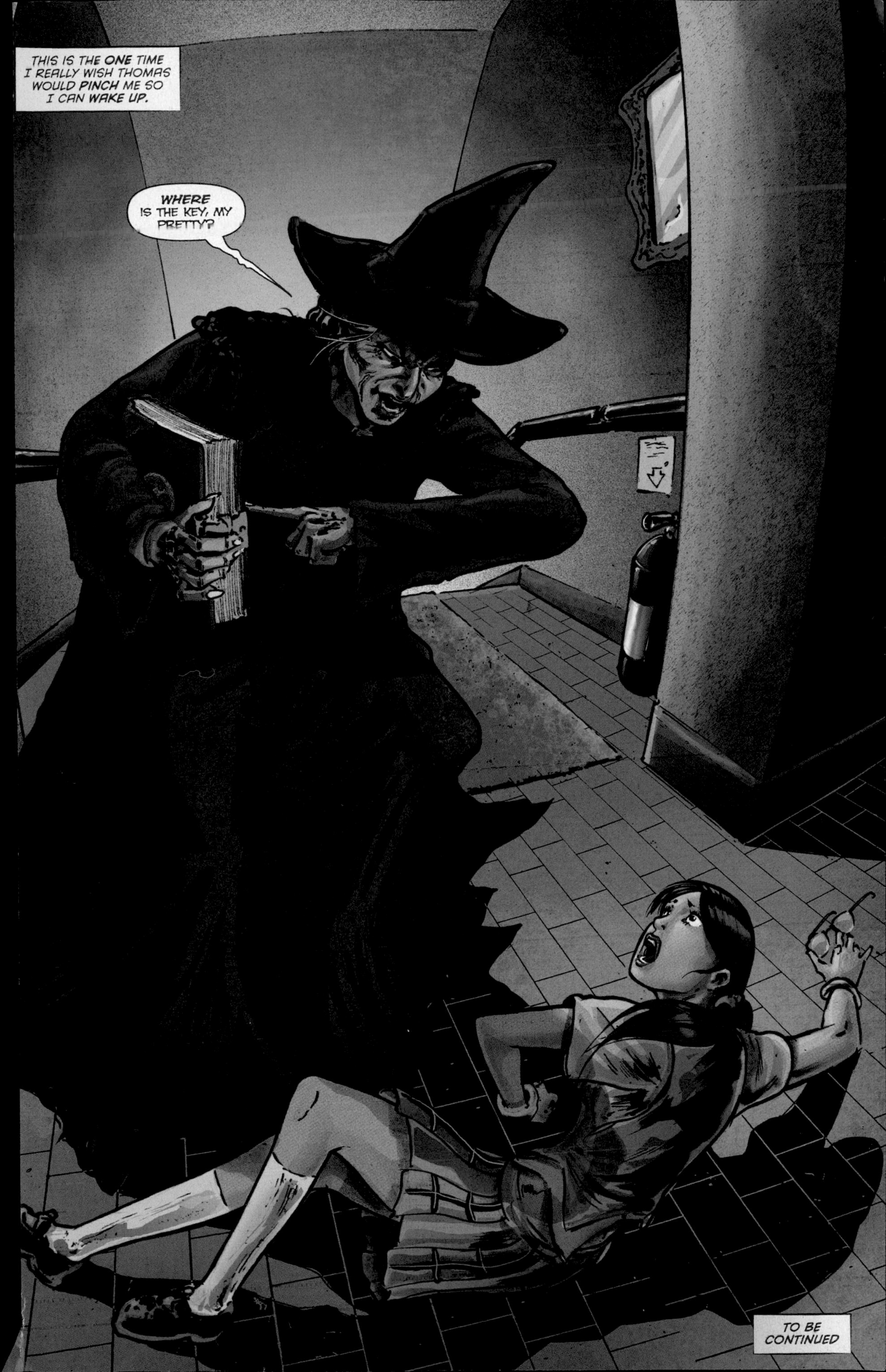
THIS IS THE ONE TIME I REALLY WISH THOMAS WOULD PINCH ME SO I CAN WAKE UP.
WHERE IS THE KEY, MY PRETTY?
TO BE CONTINUED

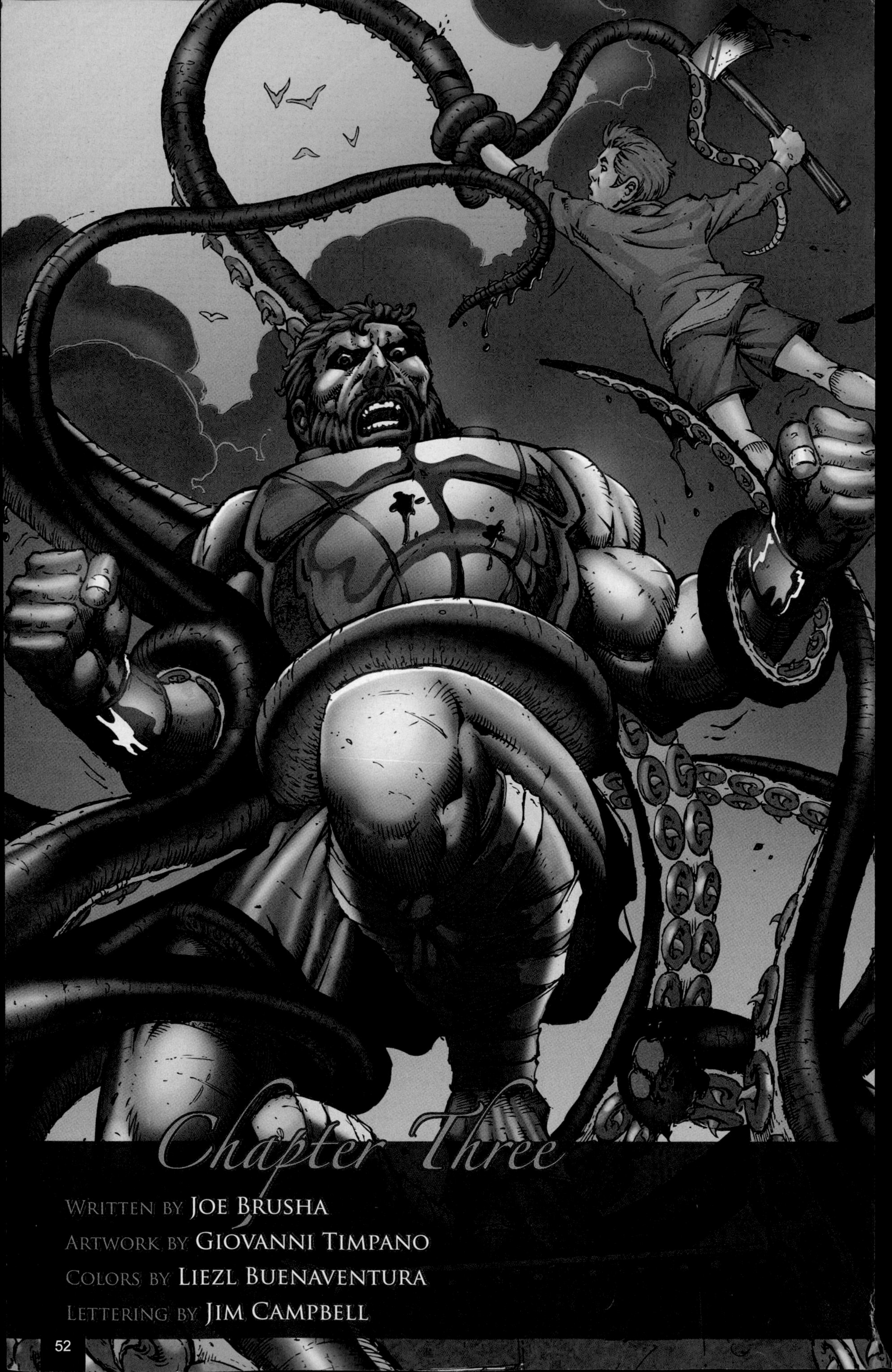

Chapter Three

WRITTEN BY JOE BRUSHA
ARTWORK BY GIOVANNI TIMPANO
COLORS BY LIEZL BUENAVENTURA
LETTERING BY JIM CAMPBELL

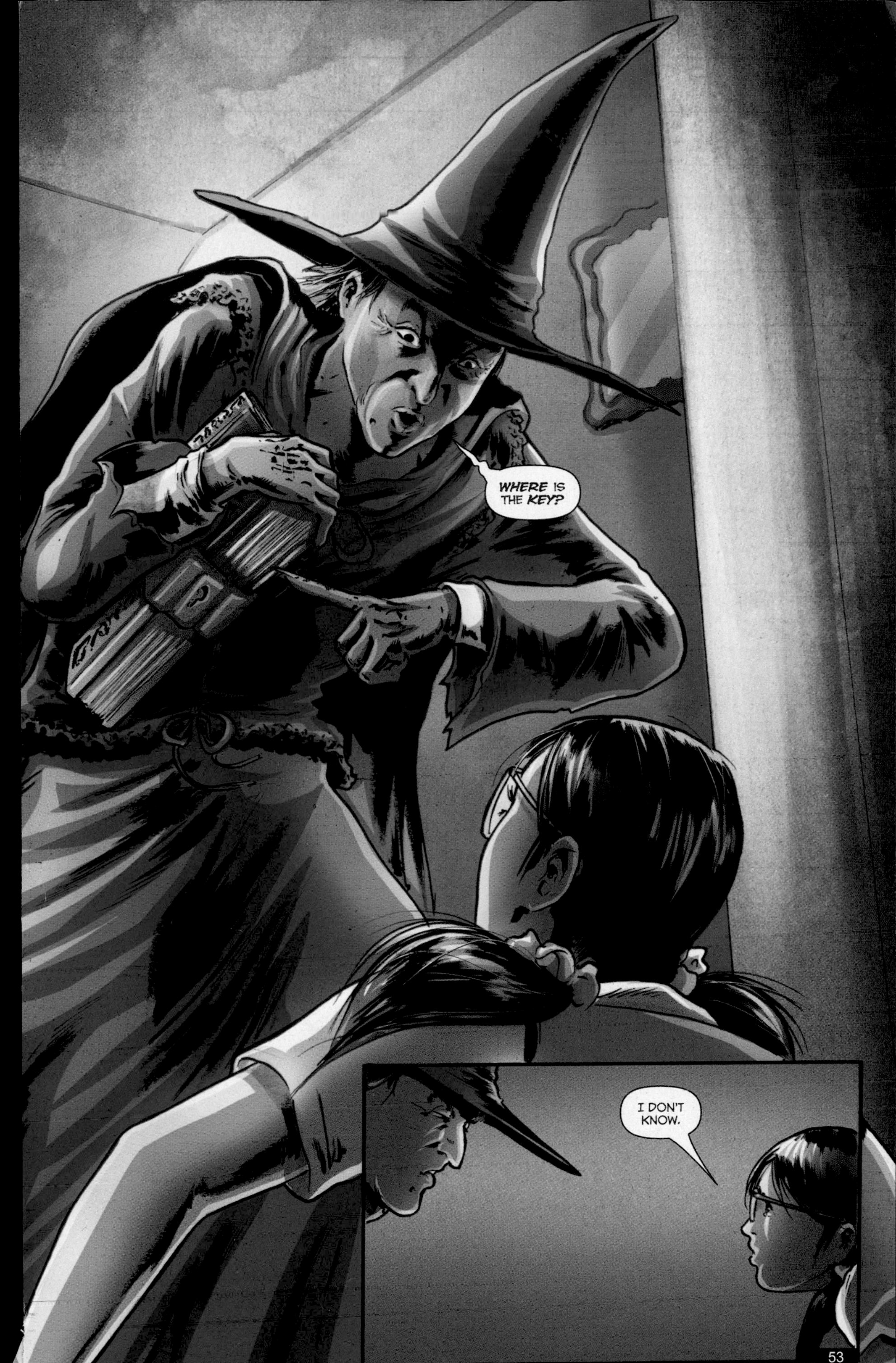
WHERE IS THE KEY?
I DON'T KNOW.

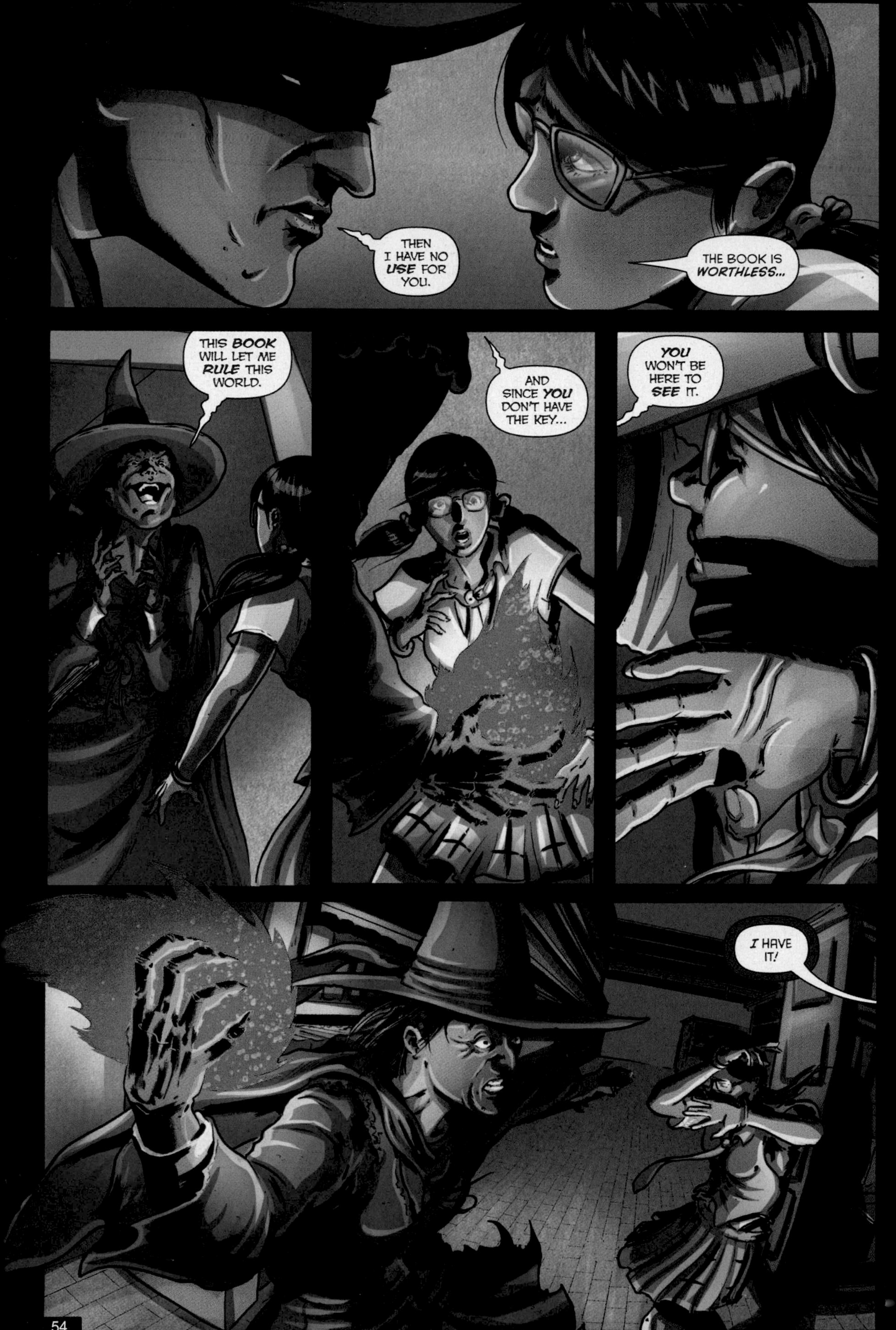
THE BOOK IS WORTHLESS...
THEN I HAVE NO USE FOR YOU.
THIS BOOK WILL LET ME RULE THIS WORLD.
AND SINCE YOU DON'T HAVE THE KEY...
YOU WON'T BE HERE TO SEE IT.
I HAVE IT!

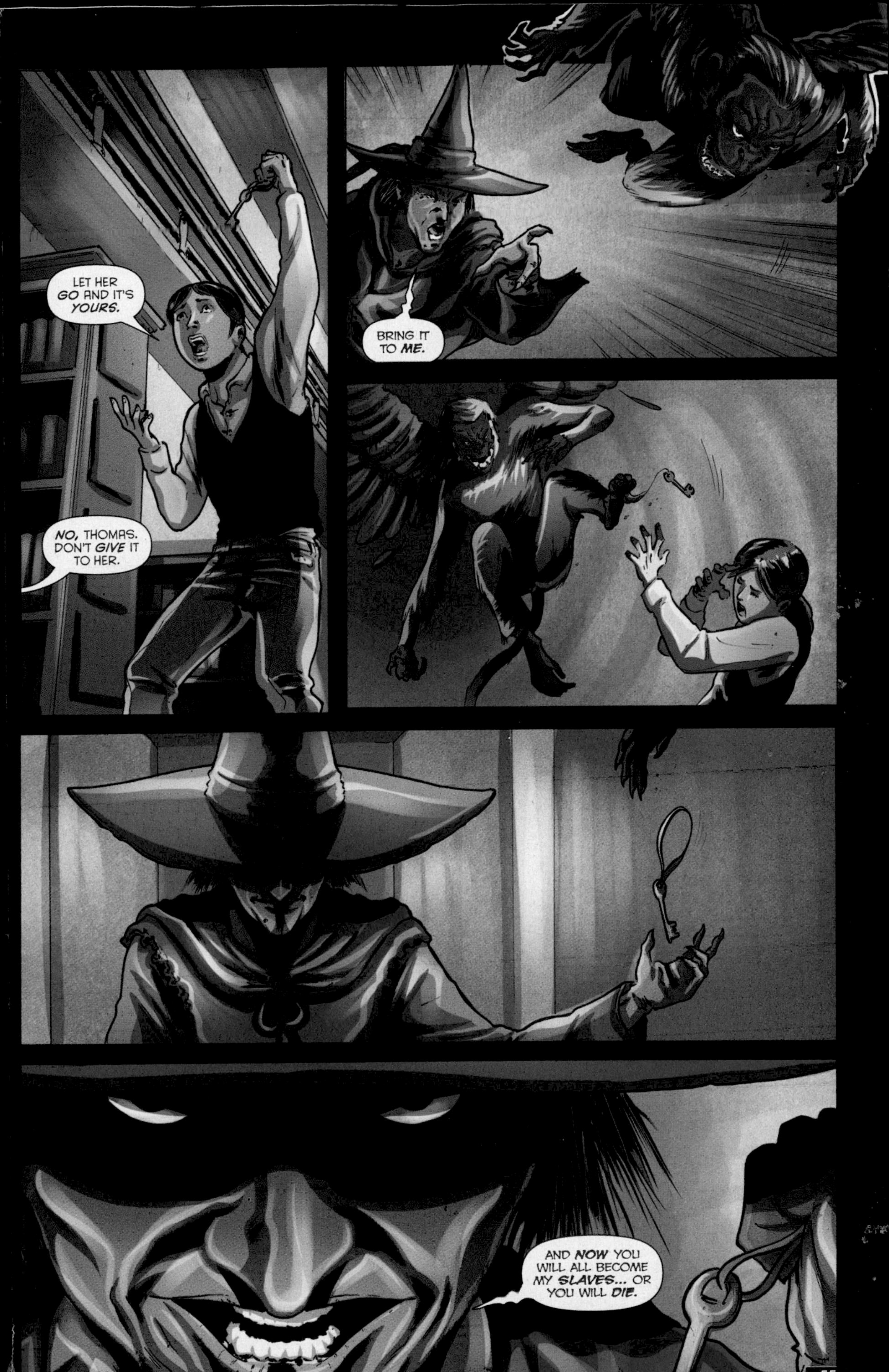
LET HER GO AND IT'S YOURS.
NO, THOMAS. DON'T GIVE IT TO HER.
BRING IT TO ME.
AND NOW YOU WILL ALL BECOME MY SLAVES... OR YOU WILL DIE.

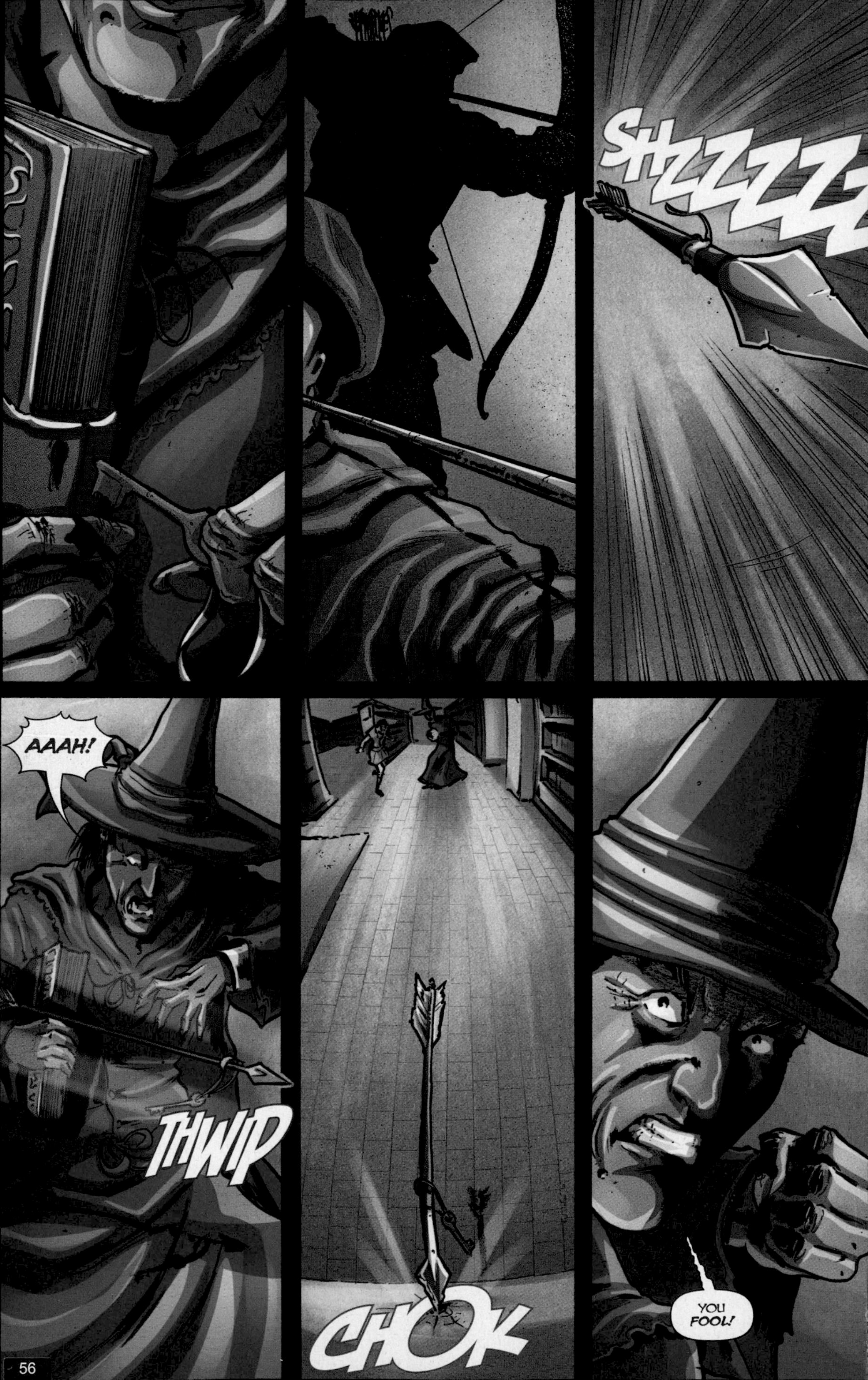
SHZZZZ
AAAH!
THWIP
CHOK
YOU FOOL!

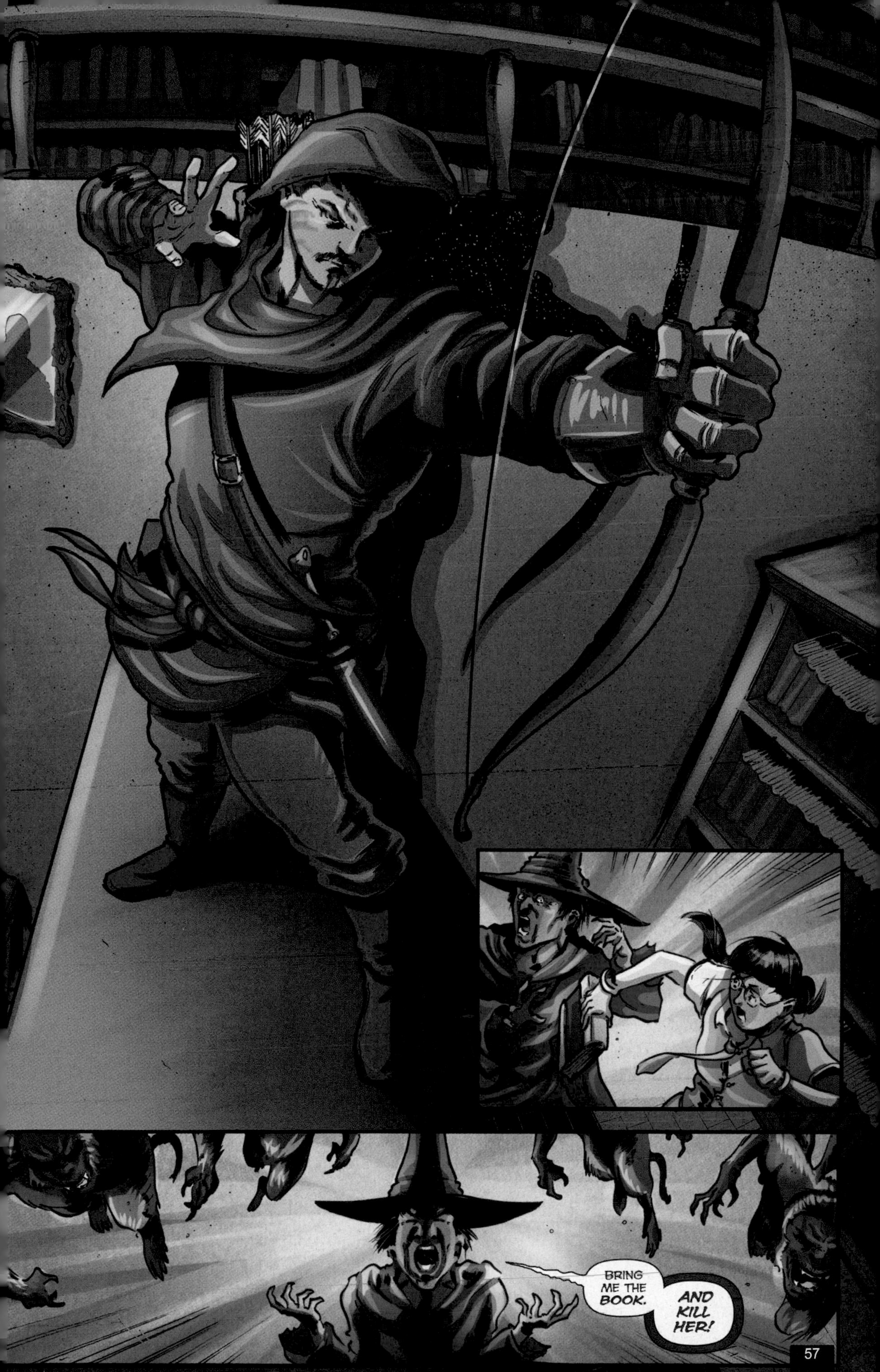
BRING ME THE BOOK.
AND KILL HER!

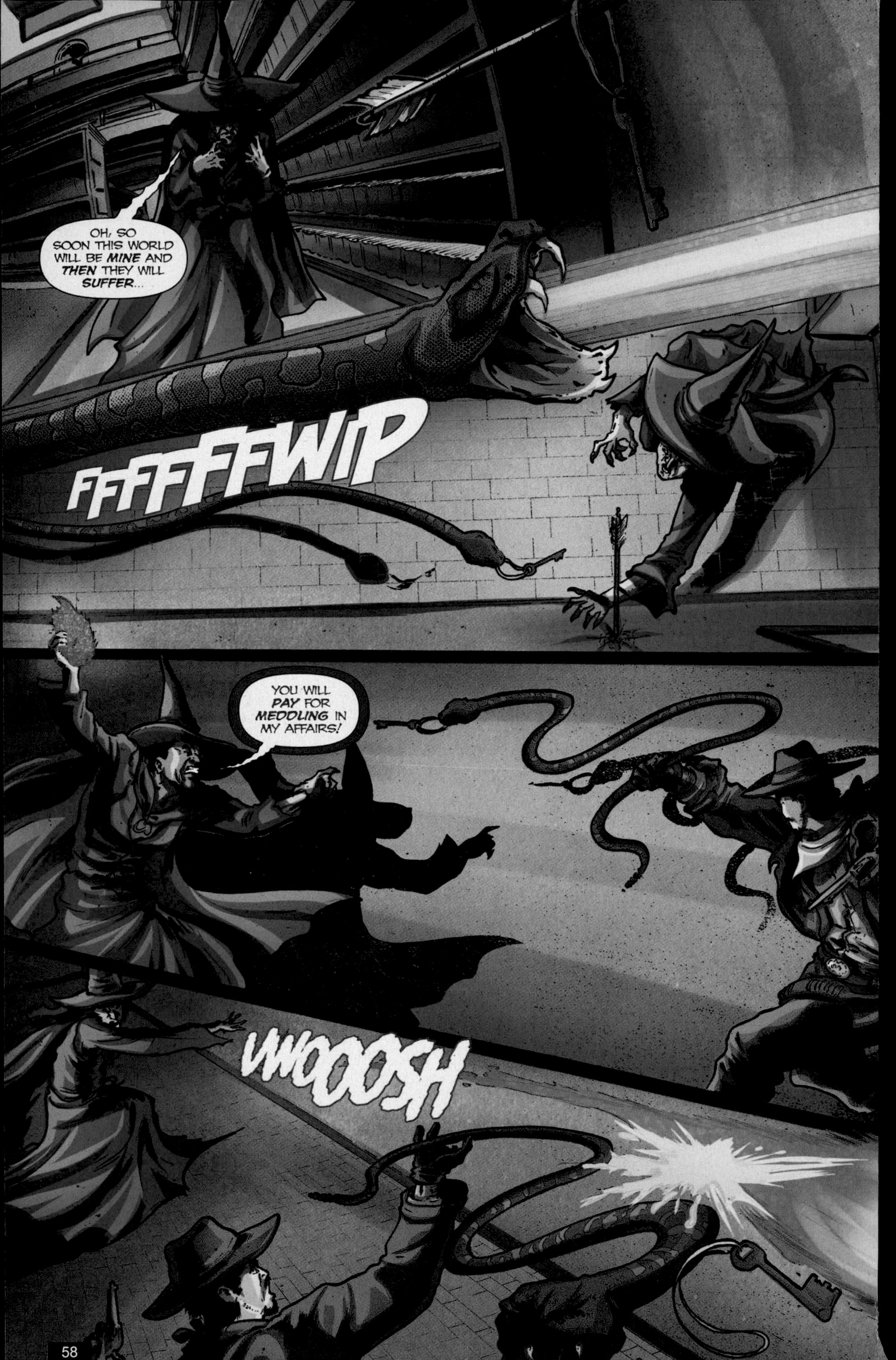
OH, SO SOON THIS WORLD WILL BE MINE AND THEN THEY WILL SUFFER...
FFFFFFWIP
YOU WILL PAY FOR MEDDLING IN MY AFFAIRS!
VWOOOSH

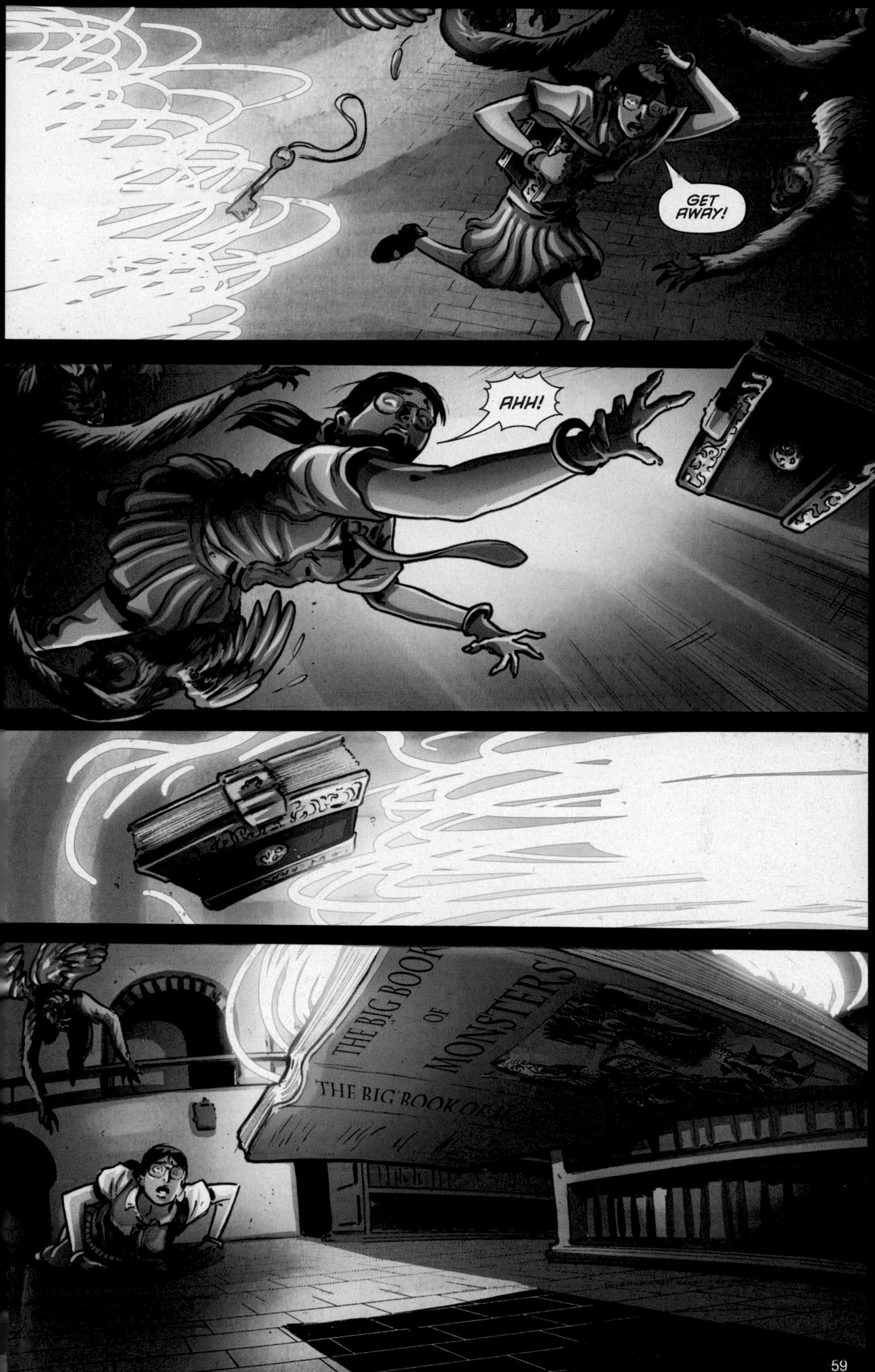
GET AWAY!
AHH!
THE BIG BOOK OF MONSTERS
THE BIG BOOK OF

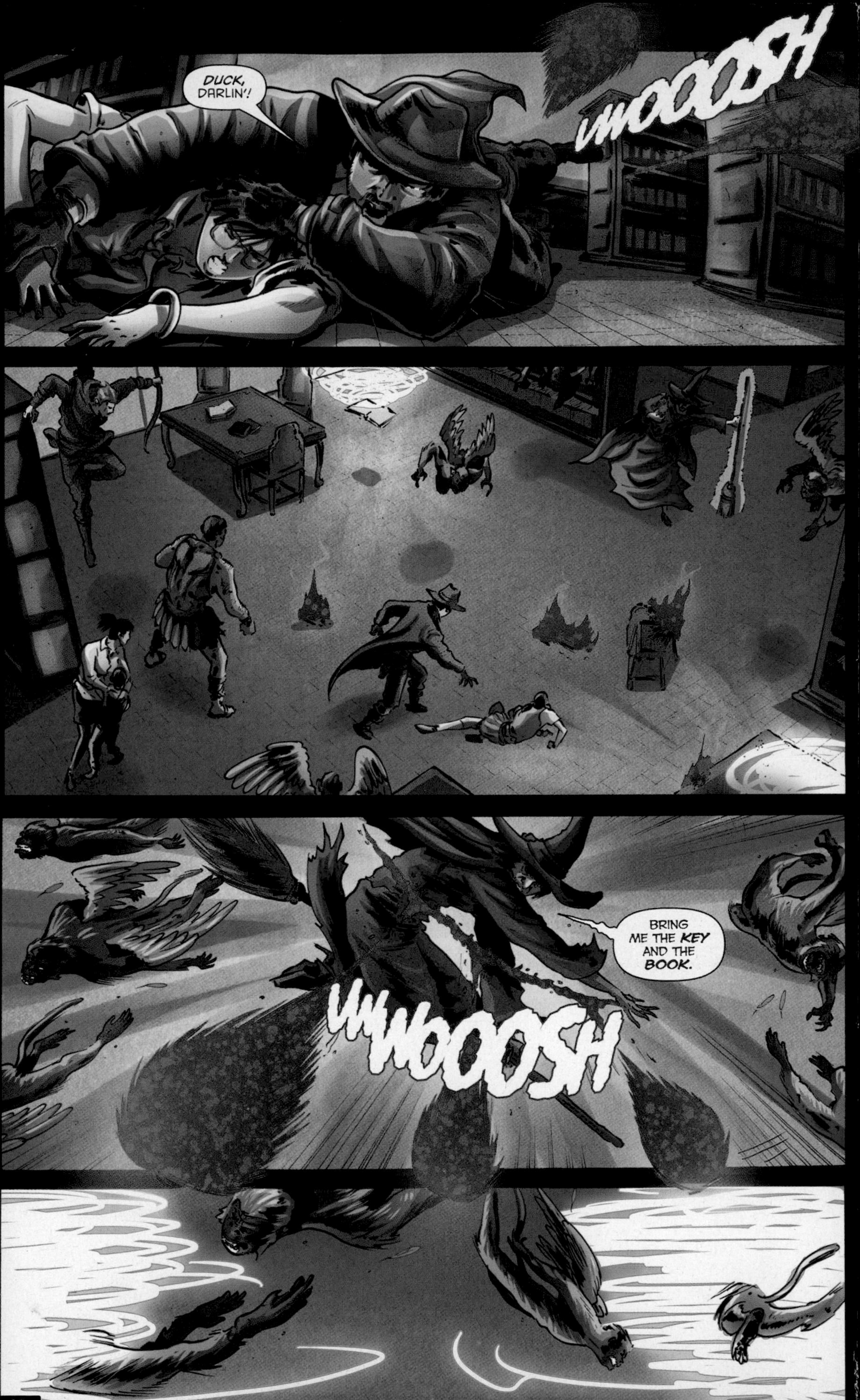
DUCK, DARLIN'!
WWOOOSH
BRING ME THE KEY AND THE BOOK.
WWOOOSH

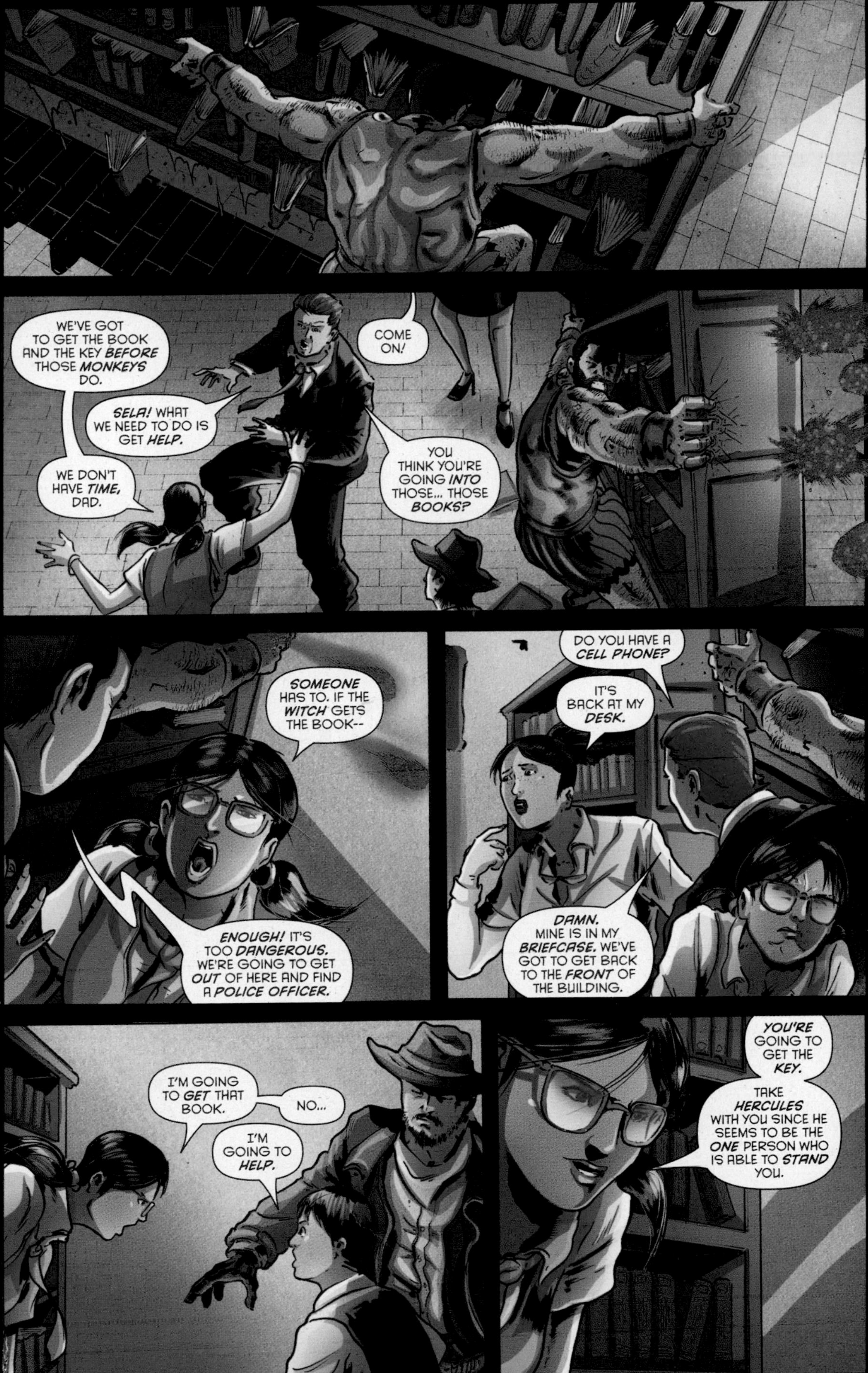
WE'VE GOT TO GET THE BOOK AND THE KEY BEFORE THOSE MONKEYS DO.
COME ON!
SELA! WHAT WE NEED TO DO IS GET HELP.
WE DON'T HAVE TIME, DAD.
YOU THINK YOU'RE GOING INTO THOSE... THOSE BOOKS?
SOMEONE HAS TO. IF THE WITCH GETS THE BOOK--
ENOUGH! IT'S TOO DANGEROUS. WE'RE GOING TO GET OUT OF HERE AND FIND A POLICE OFFICER.
DO YOU HAVE A CELL PHONE?
IT'S BACK AT MY DESK.
DAMN. MINE IS IN MY BRIEFCASE. WE'VE GOT TO GET BACK TO THE FRONT OF THE BUILDING.
I'M GOING TO GET THAT BOOK.
NO...
I'M GOING TO HELP.
YOU'RE GOING TO GET THE KEY.
TAKE HERCULES WITH YOU SINCE HE SEEMS TO BE THE ONE PERSON WHO IS ABLE TO STAND YOU.

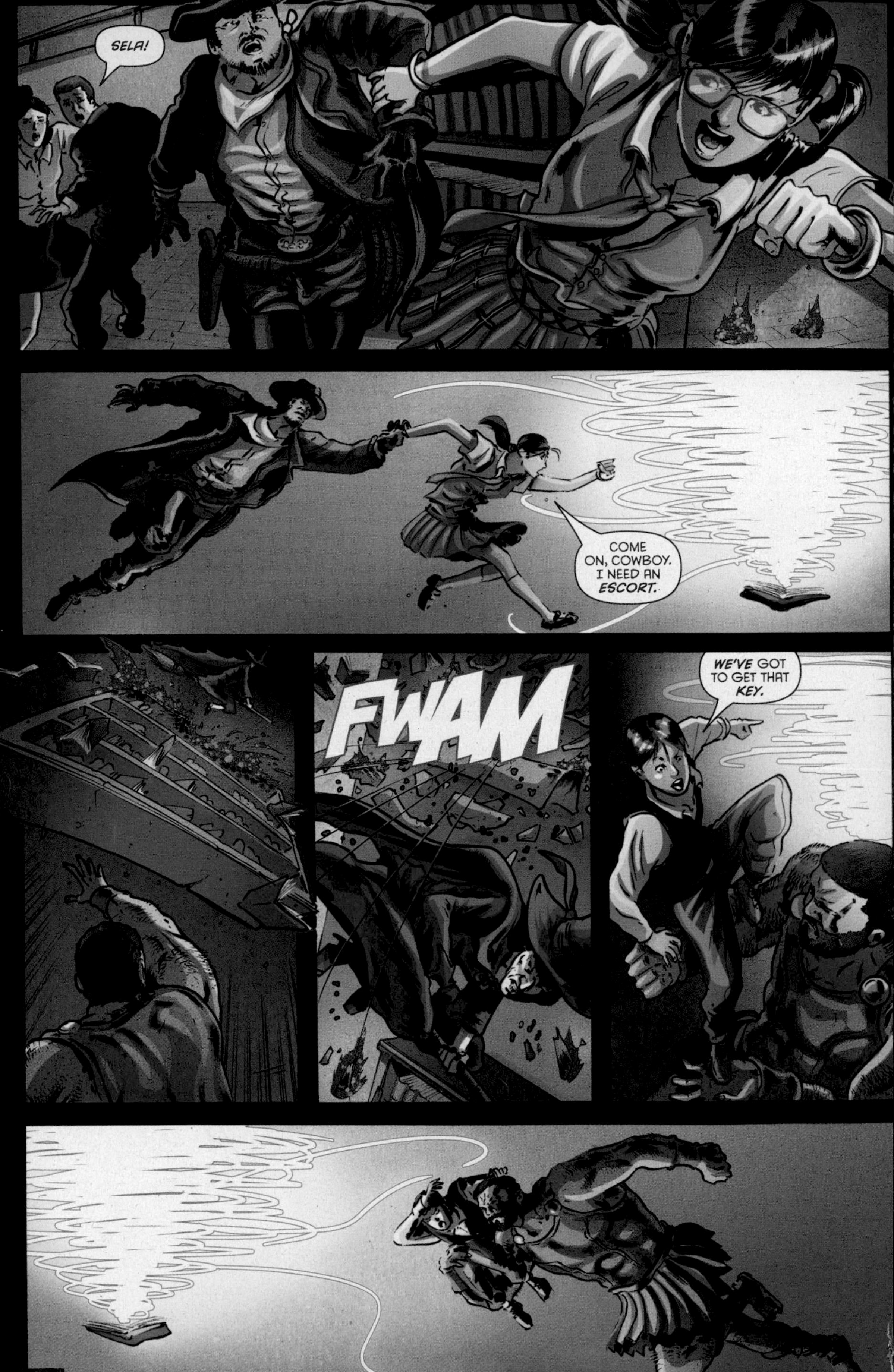
SELA!
COME ON, COWBOY. I NEED AN ESCORT.
FWAM
WE'VE GOT TO GET THAT KEY.

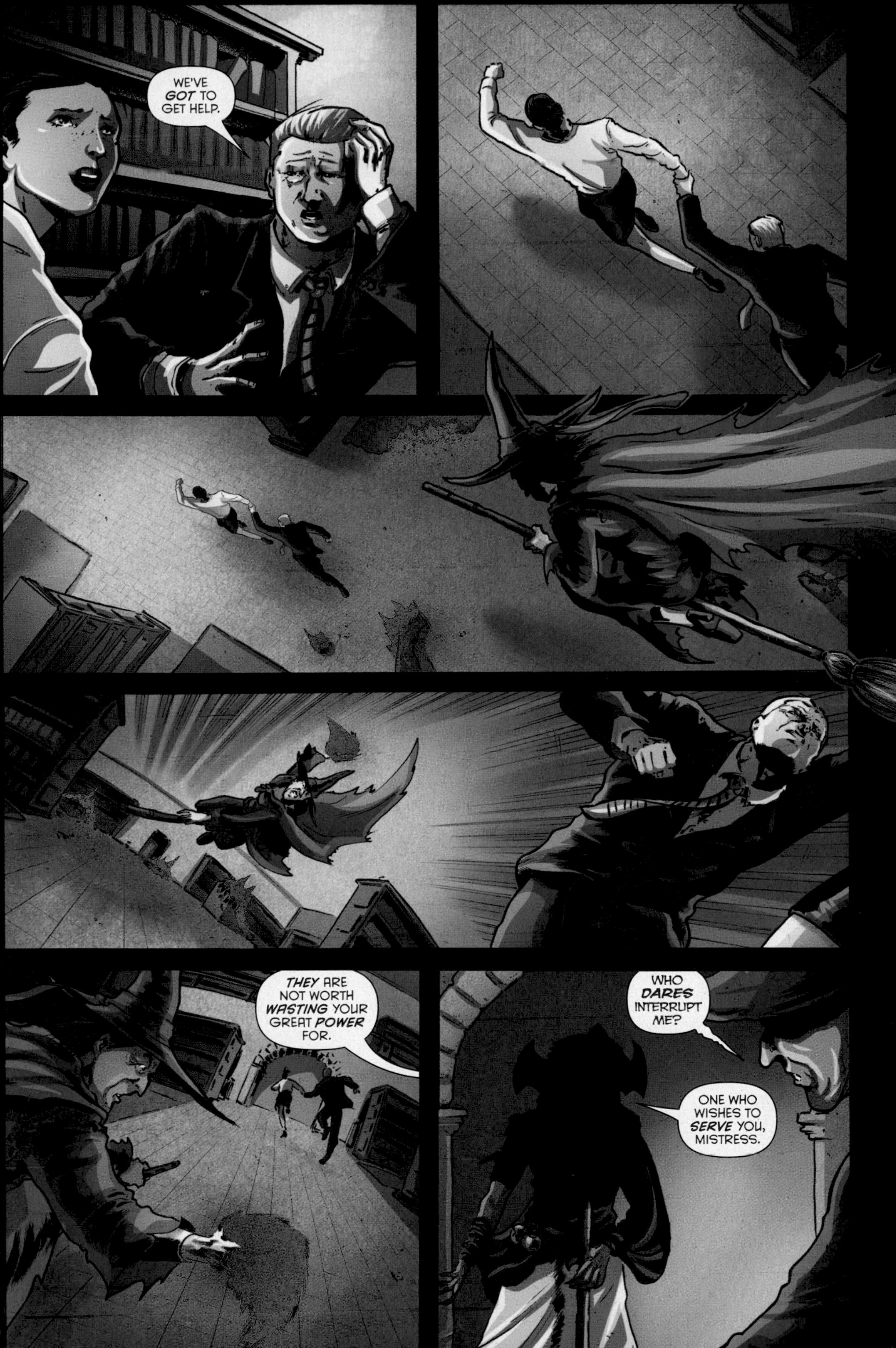
WE'VE GOT TO GET HELP.
THEY ARE NOT WORTH WASTING YOUR GREAT POWER FOR.
WHO DARES INTERRUPT ME?
ONE WHO WISHES TO SERVE YOU, MISTRESS.

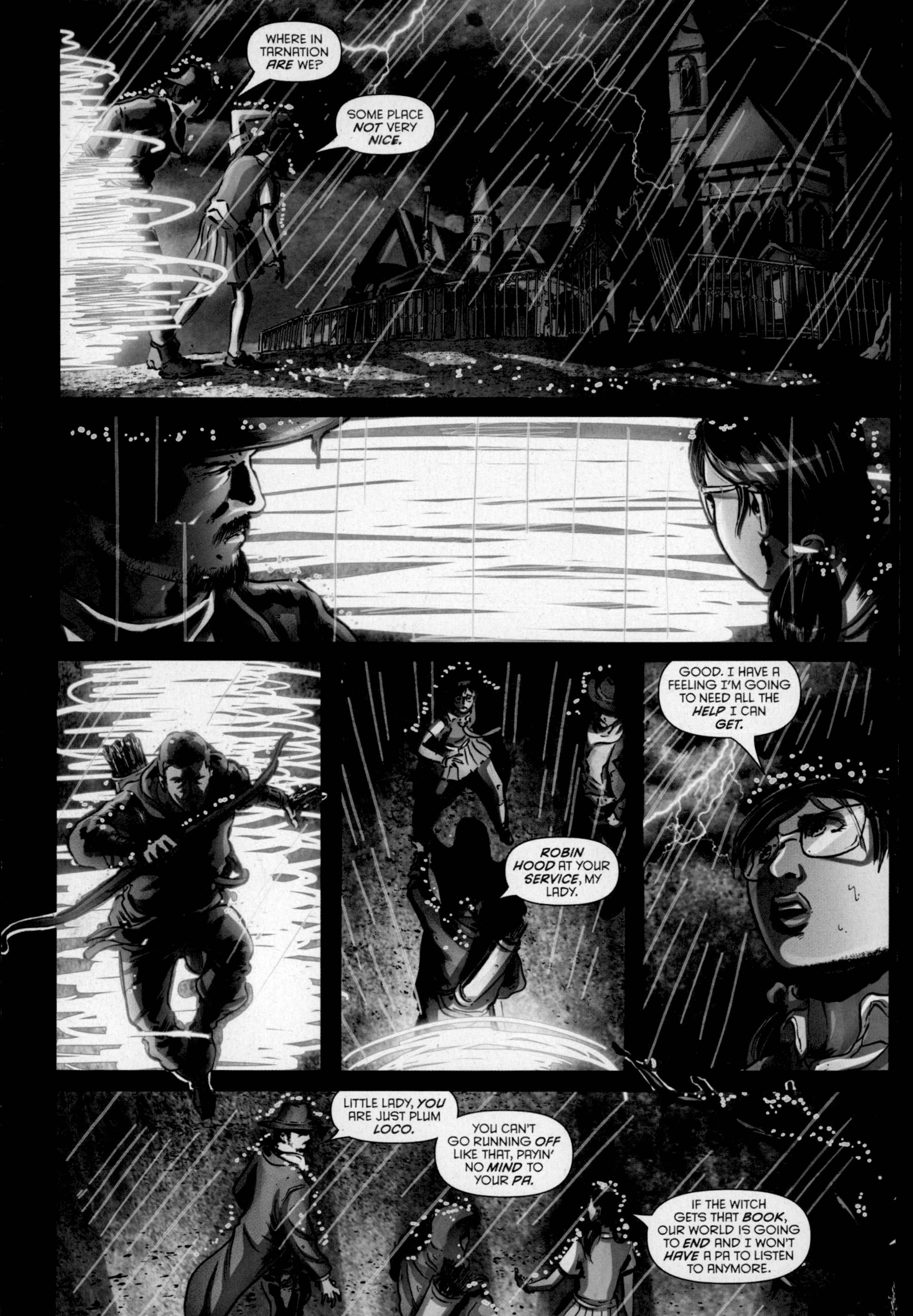
WHERE IN TARNATION ARE WE?
SOME PLACE NOT VERY NICE.
ROBIN HOOD AT YOUR SERVICE, MY LADY.
GOOD. I HAVE A FEELING I'M GOING TO NEED ALL THE HELP I CAN GET.
LITTLE LADY, YOU ARE JUST PLUM LOCO.
YOU CAN'T GO RUNNING OFF LIKE THAT, PAYIN' NO MIND TO YOUR PA.
IF THE WITCH GETS THAT BOOK, OUR WORLD IS GOING TO END AND I WON'T HAVE A PA TO LISTEN TO ANYMORE.

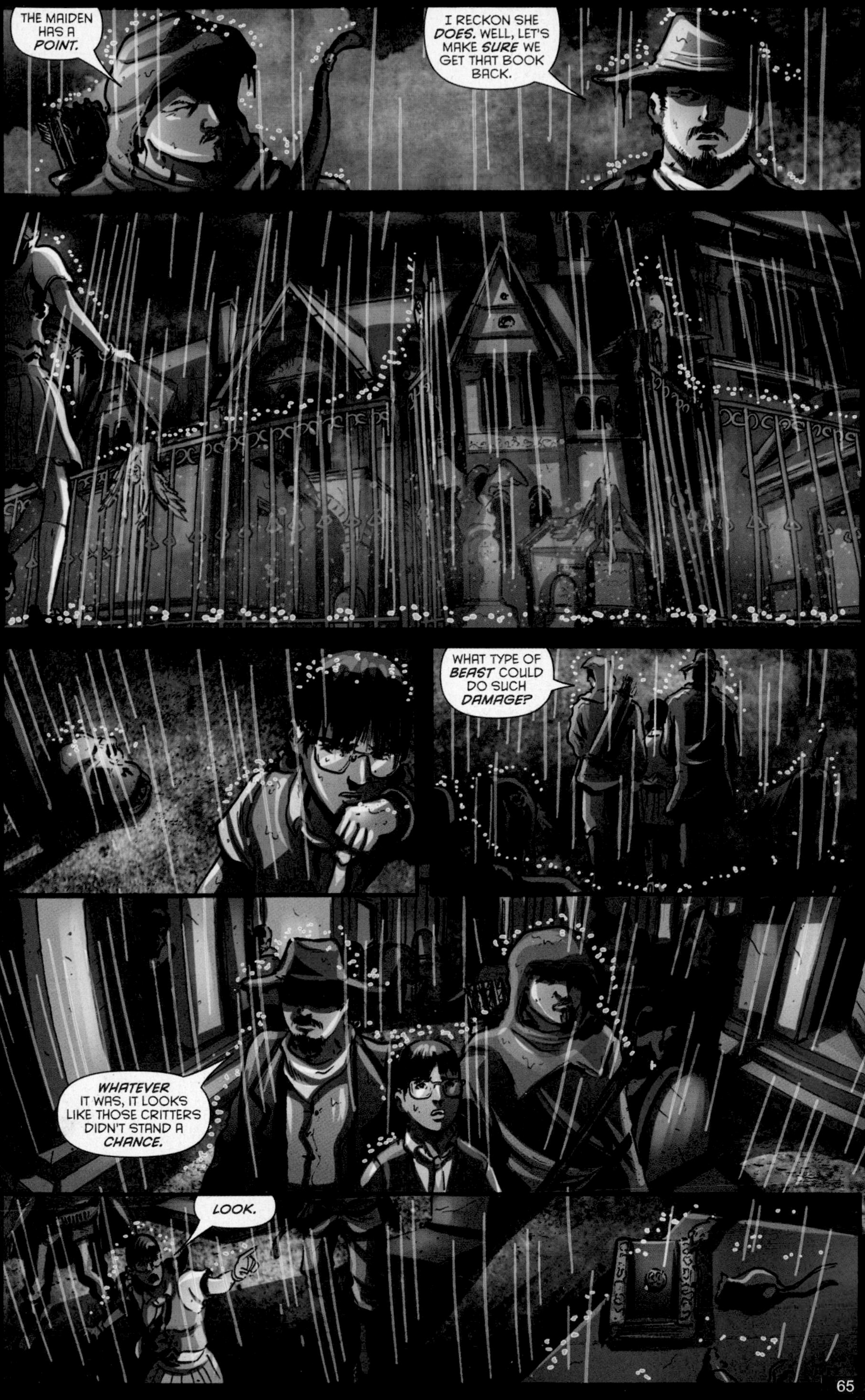
THE MAIDEN HAS A POINT.
I RECKON SHE DOES. WELL, LET'S MAKE SURE WE GET THAT BOOK BACK.
WHAT TYPE OF BEAST COULD DO SUCH DAMAGE?
WHATEVER IT WAS, IT LOOKS LIKE THOSE CRITTERS DIDN'T STAND A CHANCE.
LOOK.

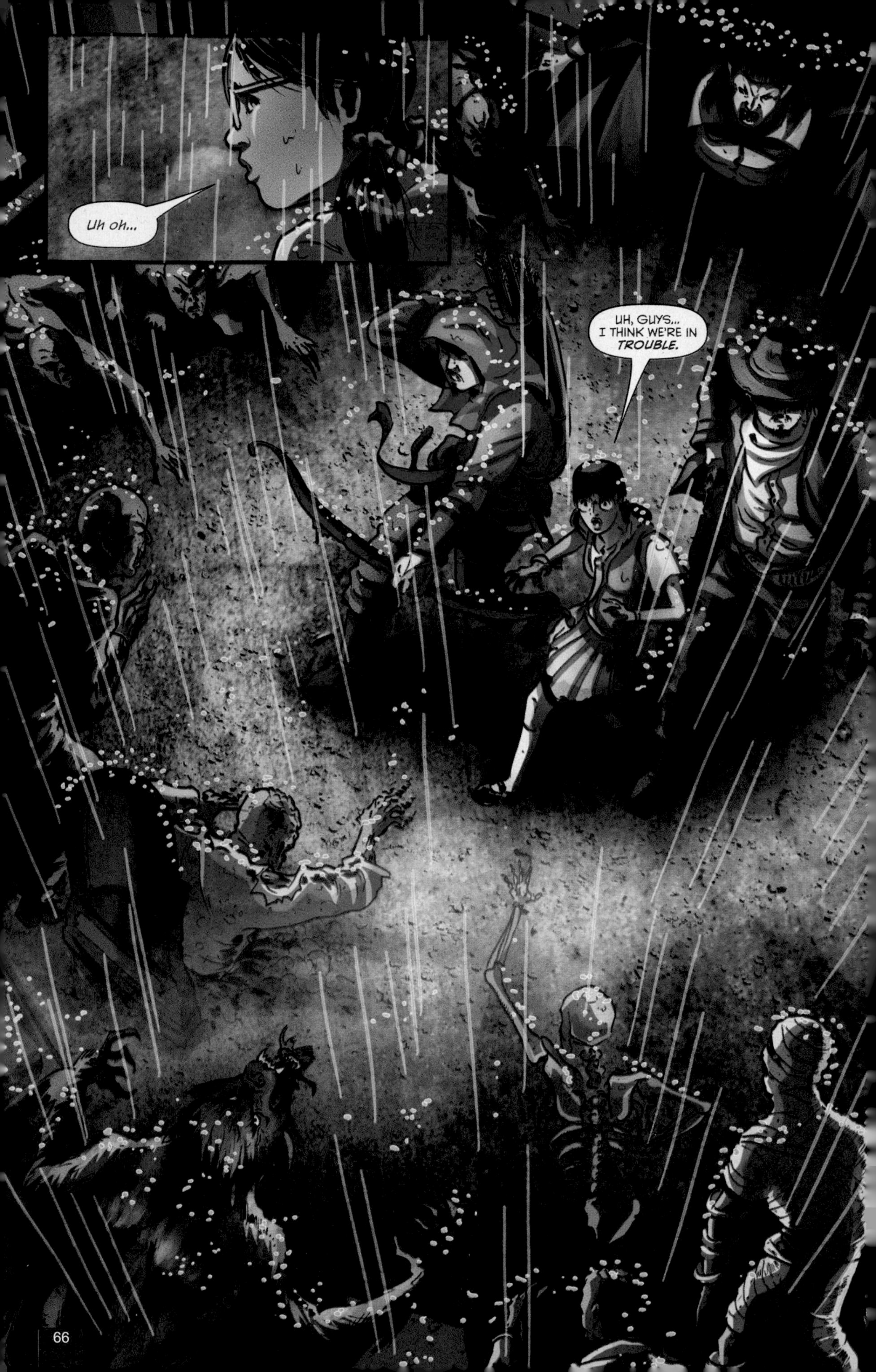
Uh oh...
UH, GUYS... I THINK WE'RE IN *TROUBLE.*

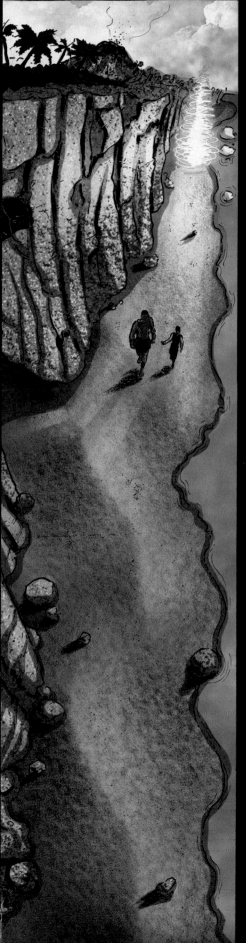

HOW ARE WE GOING TO FIND THIS KEY? IT'S LIKE LOOKING FOR A *NEEDLE* IN A *HAYSTACK.*

DO NOT DISTRESS, YOUNG TITAN. THIS SHALL PROVE *NO* OBSTACLE FOR THE SON OF *ZEUS.* FOR I HAVE COMPLETED THE *TWELVE LABORS!*

LISTEN.

LOOK.

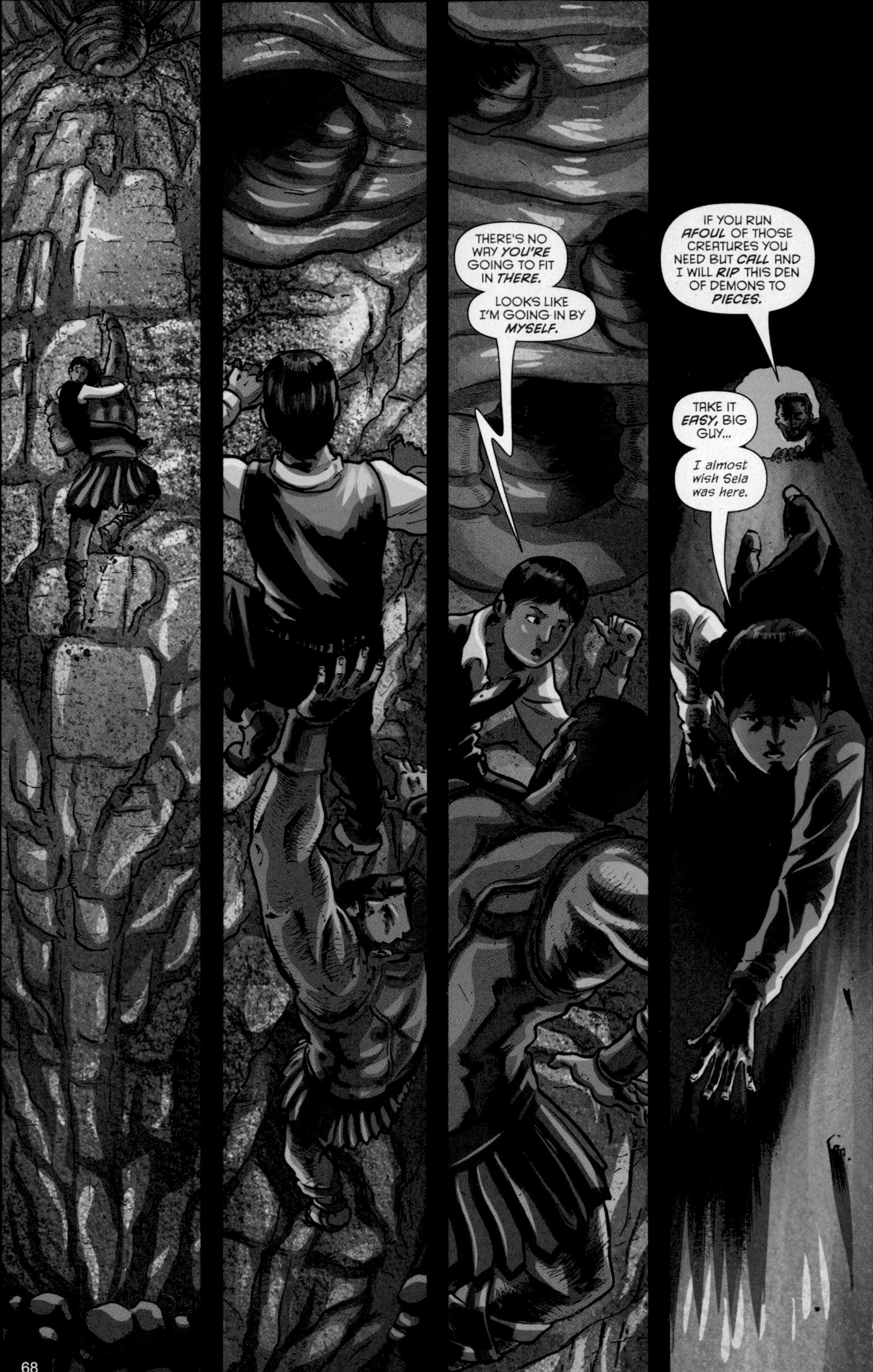
THERE'S NO WAY YOU'RE GOING TO FIT IN THERE.
LOOKS LIKE I'M GOING IN BY MYSELF.
IF YOU RUN AFOUL OF THOSE CREATURES YOU NEED BUT CALL AND I WILL RIP THIS DEN OF DEMONS TO PIECES.
TAKE IT EASY, BIG GUY...
I almost wish Sela was here.

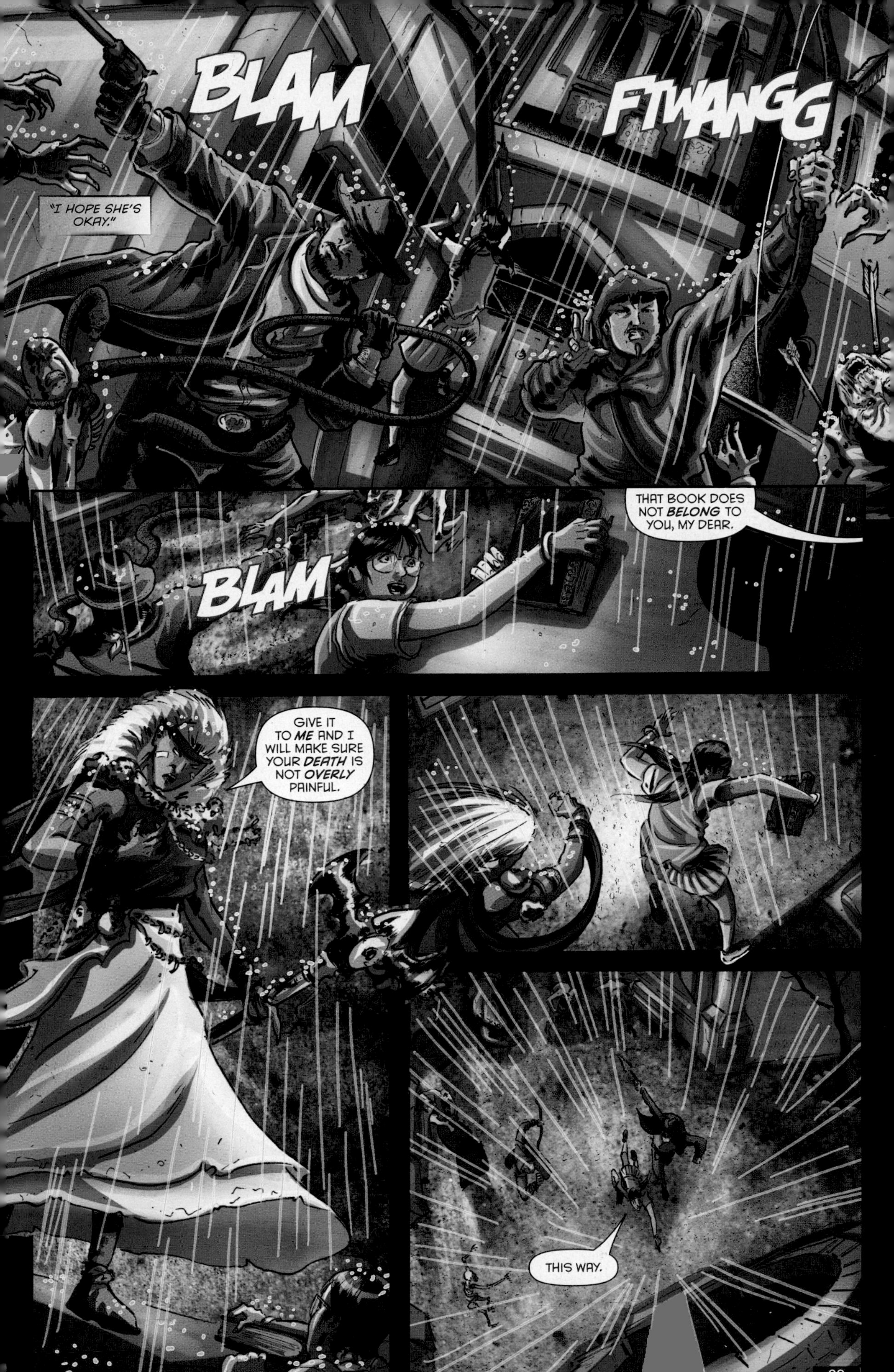

BLAM
FTWANGG
"I HOPE SHE'S OKAY."
THAT BOOK DOES NOT BELONG TO YOU, MY DEAR.
BLAM
GIVE IT TO ME AND I WILL MAKE SURE YOUR DEATH IS NOT OVERLY PAINFUL.
THIS WAY.

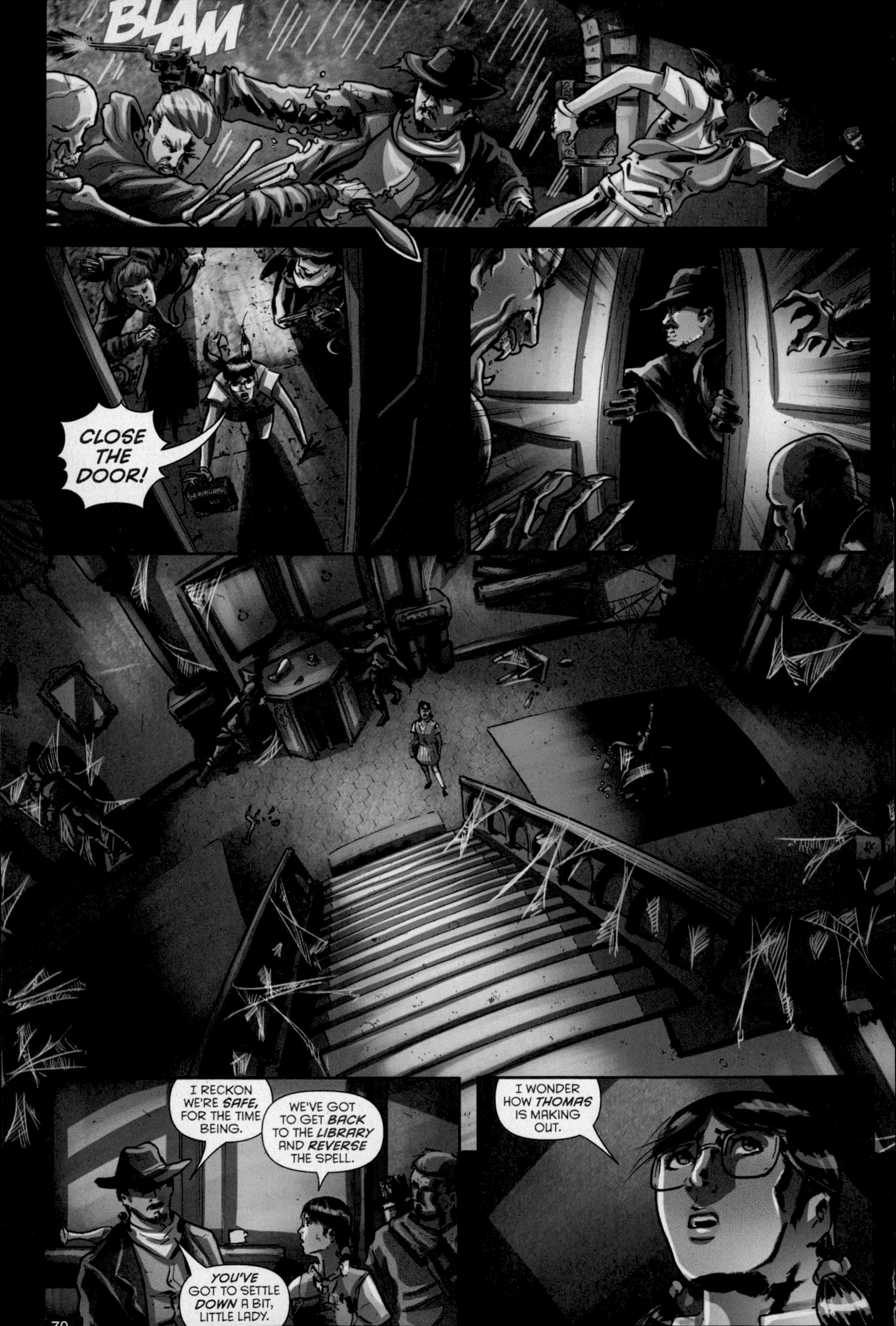
BLAM
CLOSE THE DOOR!
I RECKON WE'RE SAFE, FOR THE TIME BEING.
WE'VE GOT TO GET BACK TO THE LIBRARY AND REVERSE THE SPELL.
YOU'VE GOT TO SETTLE DOWN A BIT, LITTLE LADY.
I WONDER HOW THOMAS IS MAKING OUT.

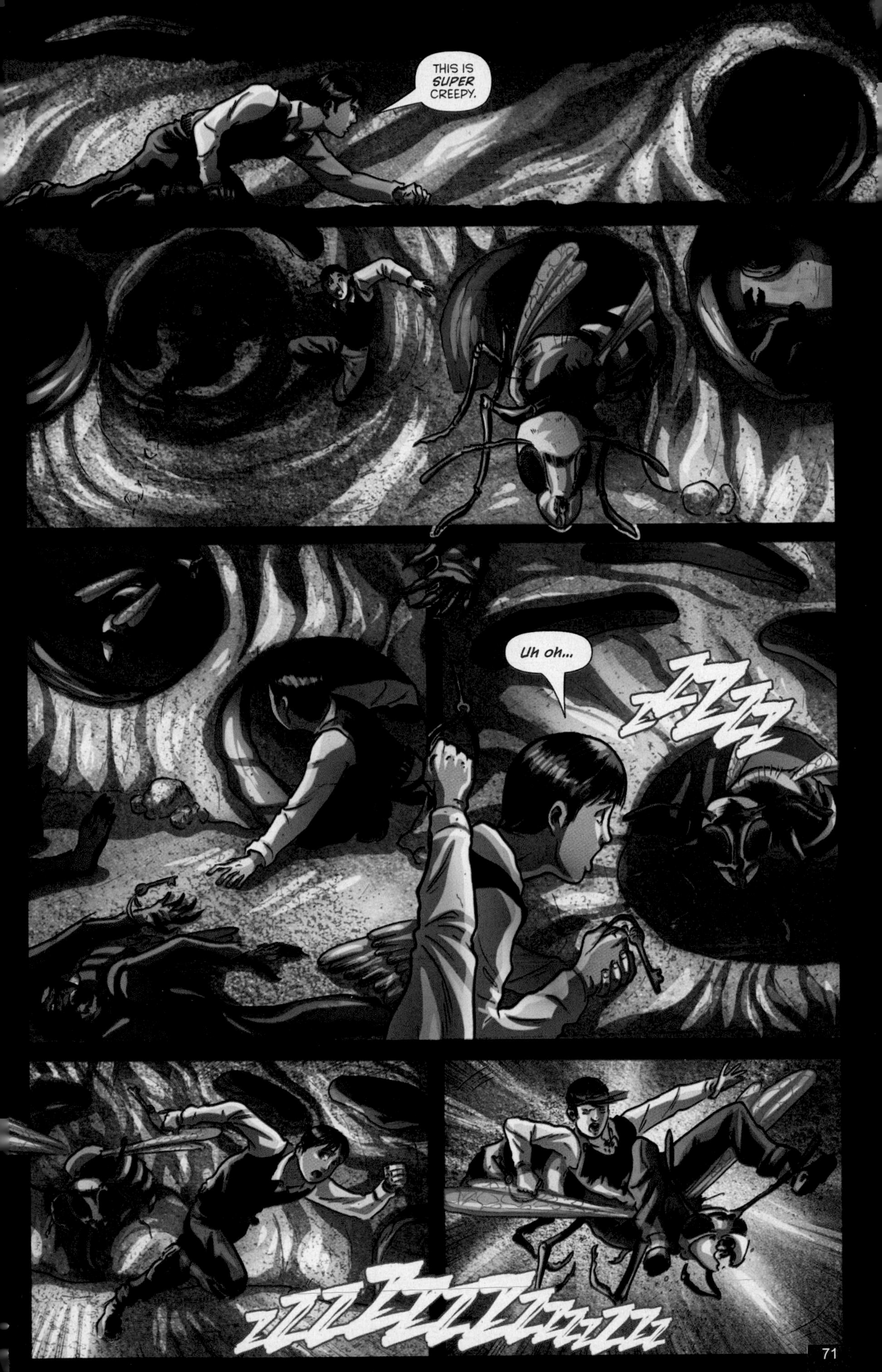
THIS IS SUPER CREEPY.
Uh oh...
ZZZZ
ZZZZZZZZZZZzzzzZZZ

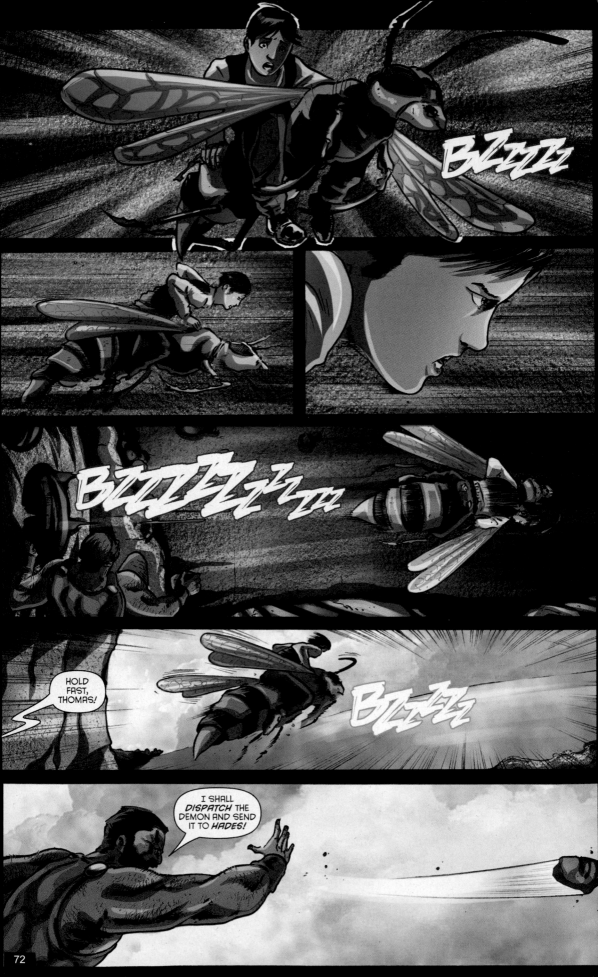

BZzzzz

BZZZZZzzZzZzzz

HOLD FAST, THOMAS!

BZzzz

I SHALL *DISPATCH* THE DEMON AND SEND IT TO *HADES!*

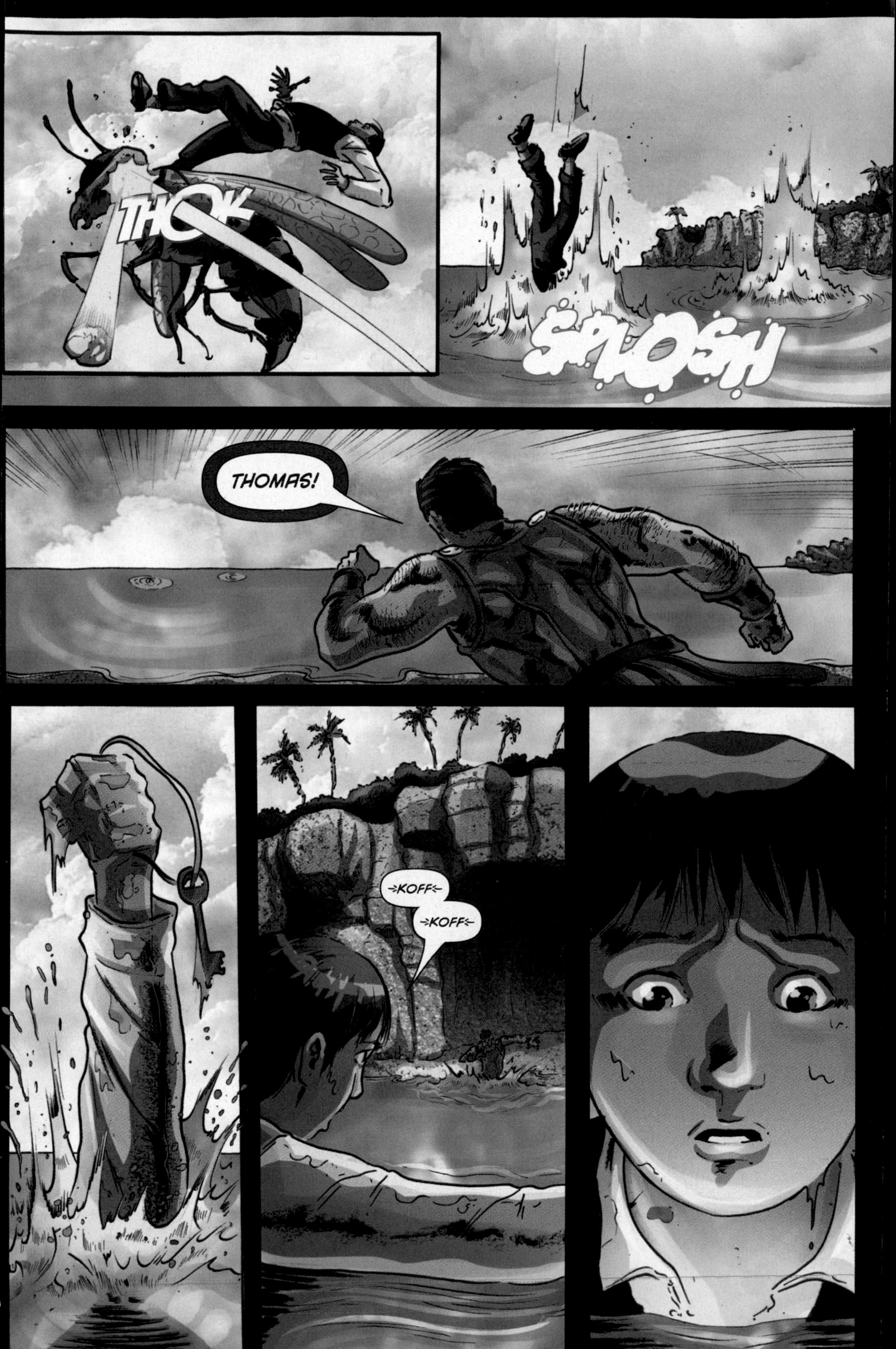
THOK
SPLOSH
THOMAS!
KOFF
KOFF

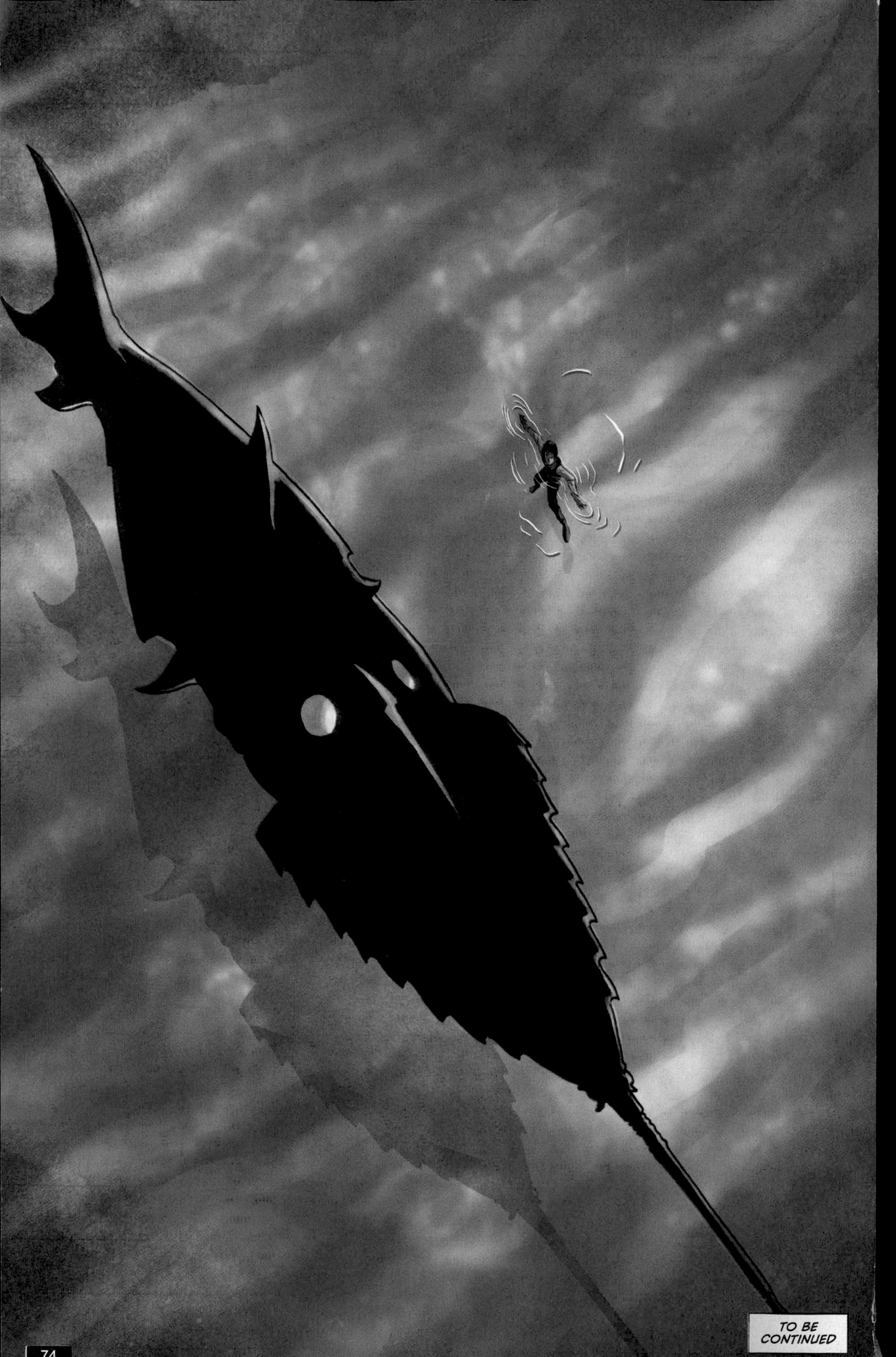
TO BE CONTINUED

Grimm Fairy Tales Presents the Library

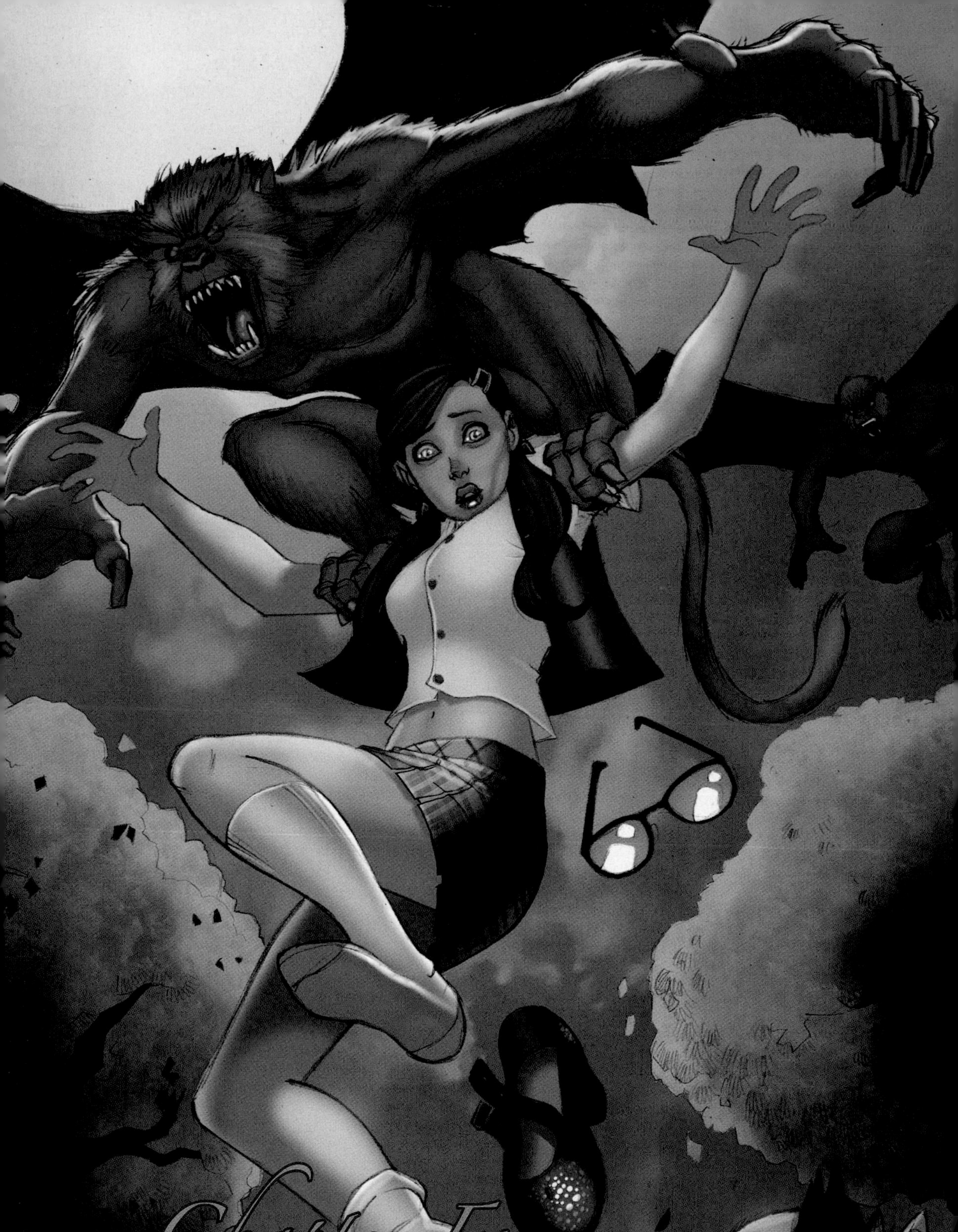

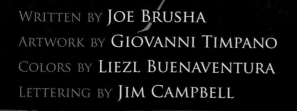

Chapter Four

WRITTEN BY JOE BRUSHA
ARTWORK BY GIOVANNI TIMPANO
COLORS BY LIEZL BUENAVENTURA
LETTERING BY JIM CAMPBELL

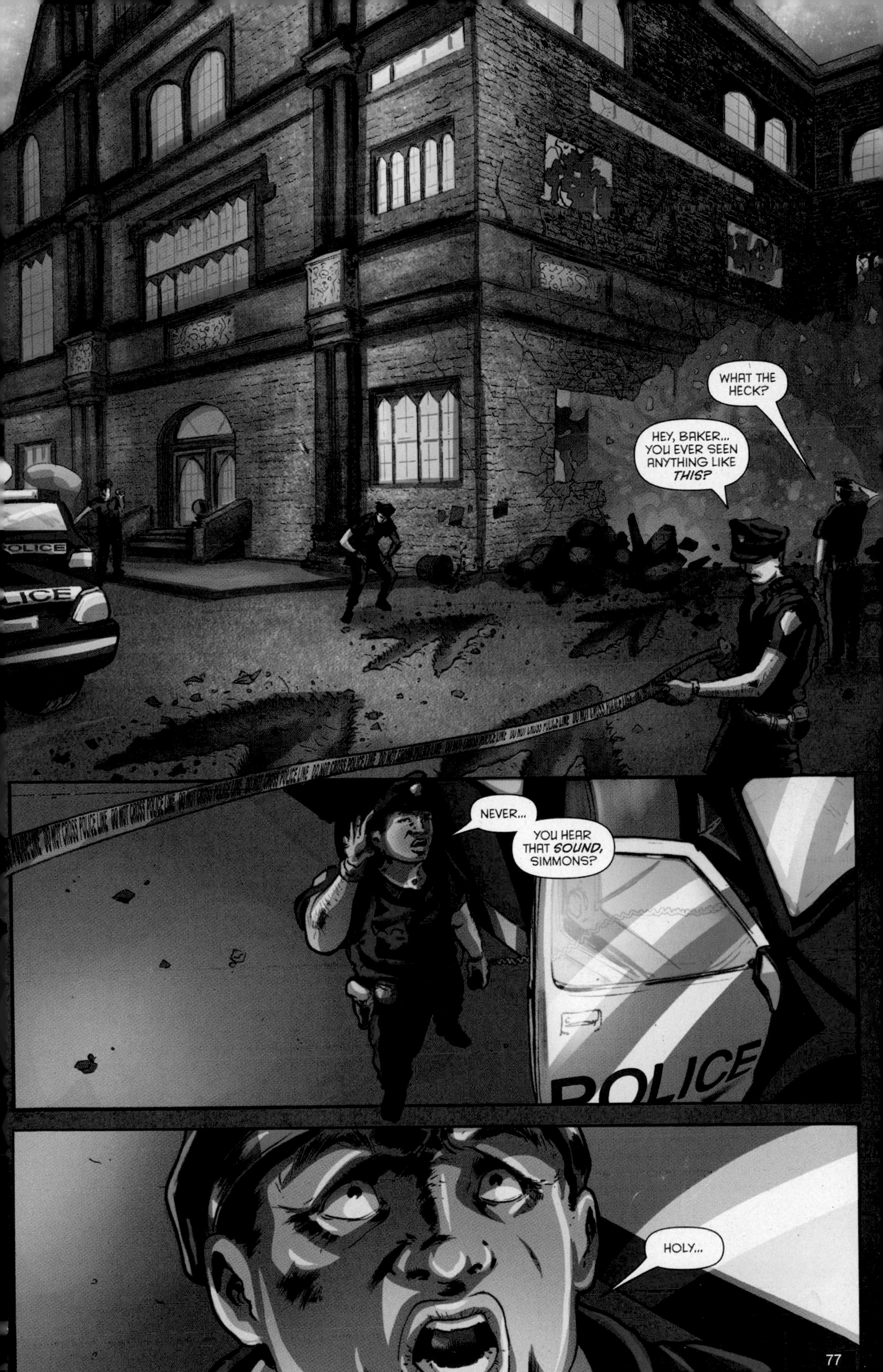

WHAT THE HECK?
HEY, BAKER... YOU EVER SEEN ANYTHING LIKE *THIS?*
DO NOT CROSS POLICE LINE
NEVER...
YOU HEAR THAT *SOUND,* SIMMONS?
POLICE
HOLY...

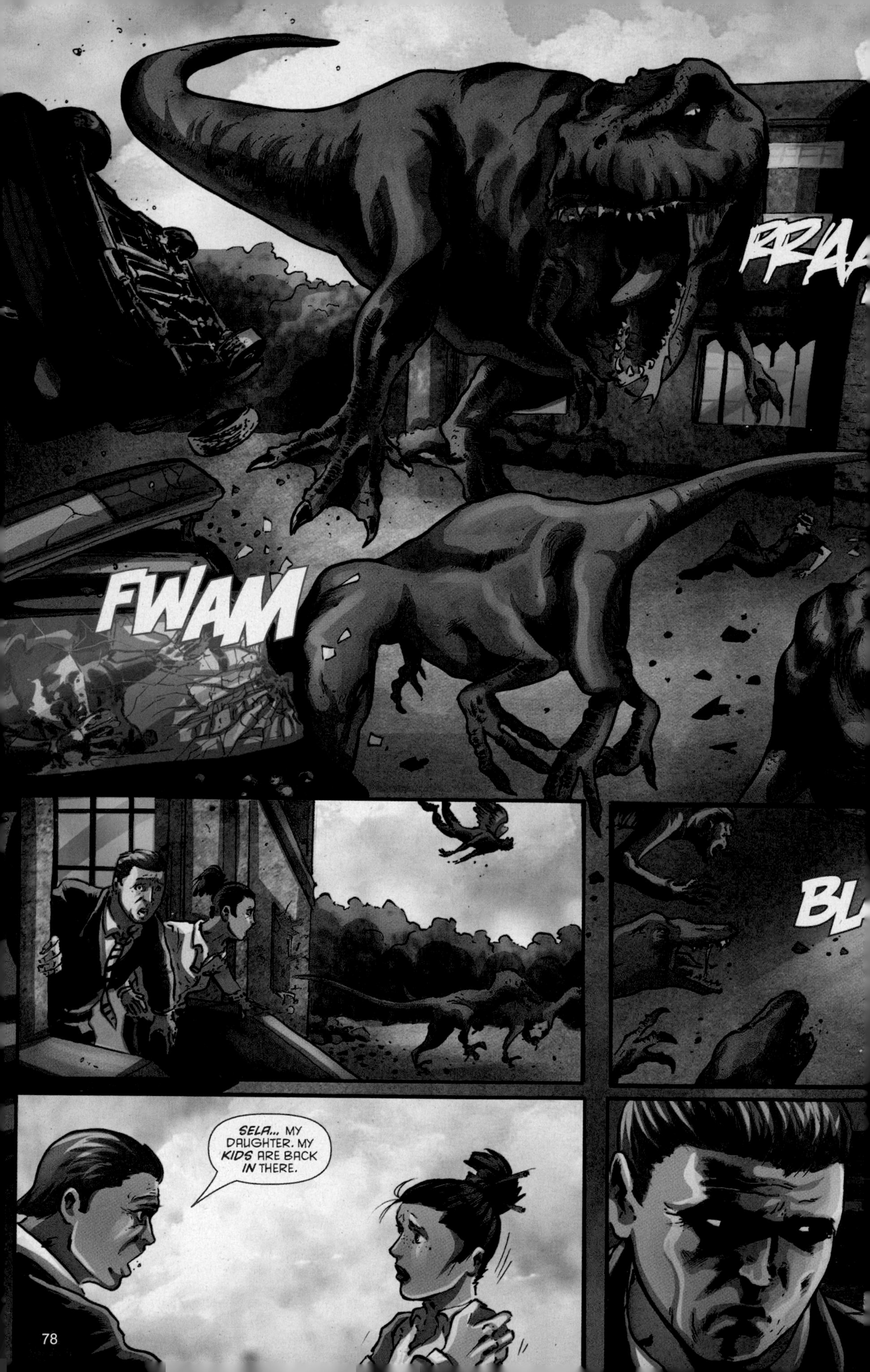

RRAA
FWAM
BL
SELA... MY DAUGHTER. MY KIDS ARE BACK IN THERE.

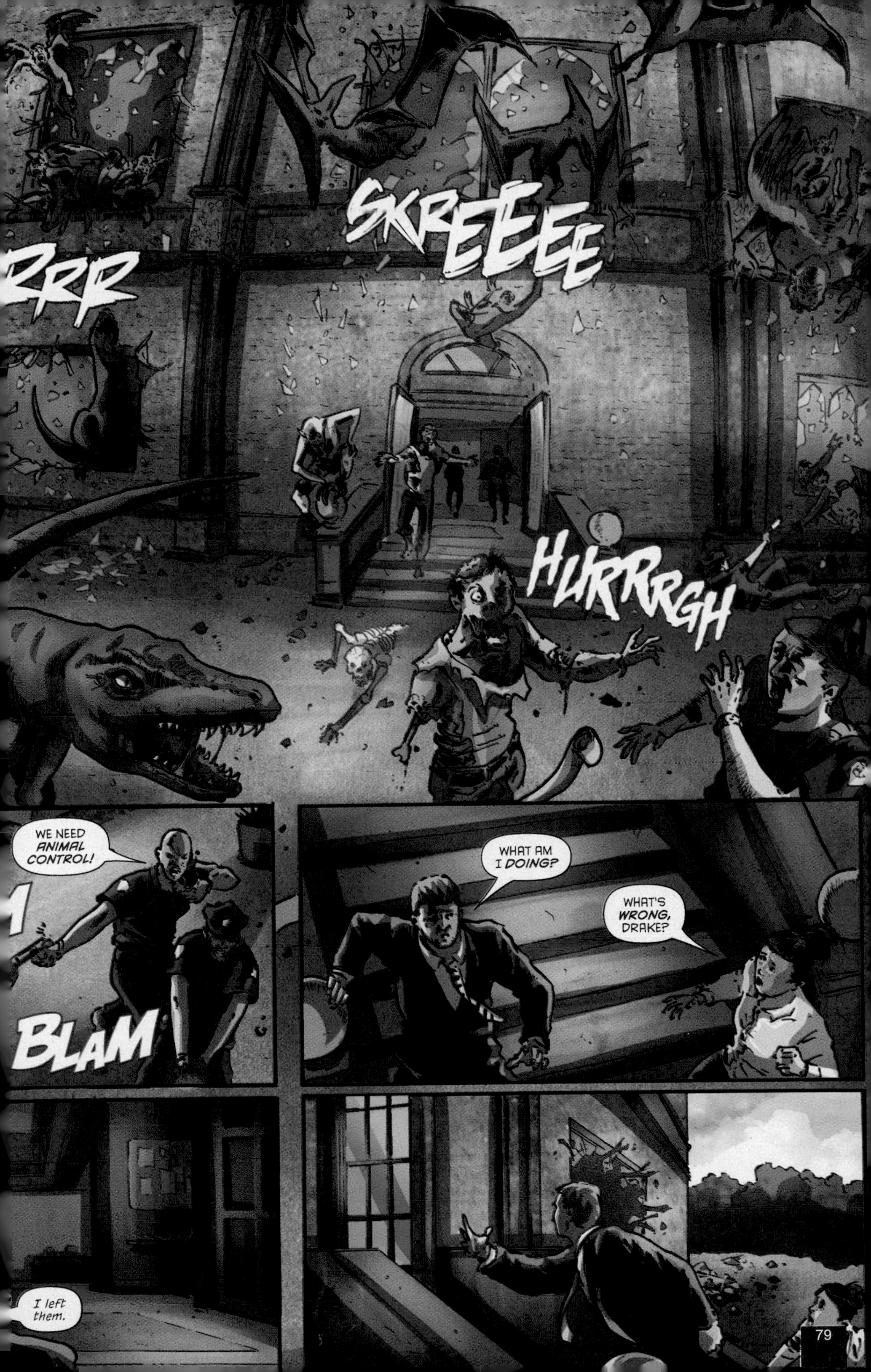
SKREEEEE
RRR
HURRRGH
WE NEED ANIMAL CONTROL!
BLAM
WHAT AM I DOING?
WHAT'S WRONG, DRAKE?
I left them.

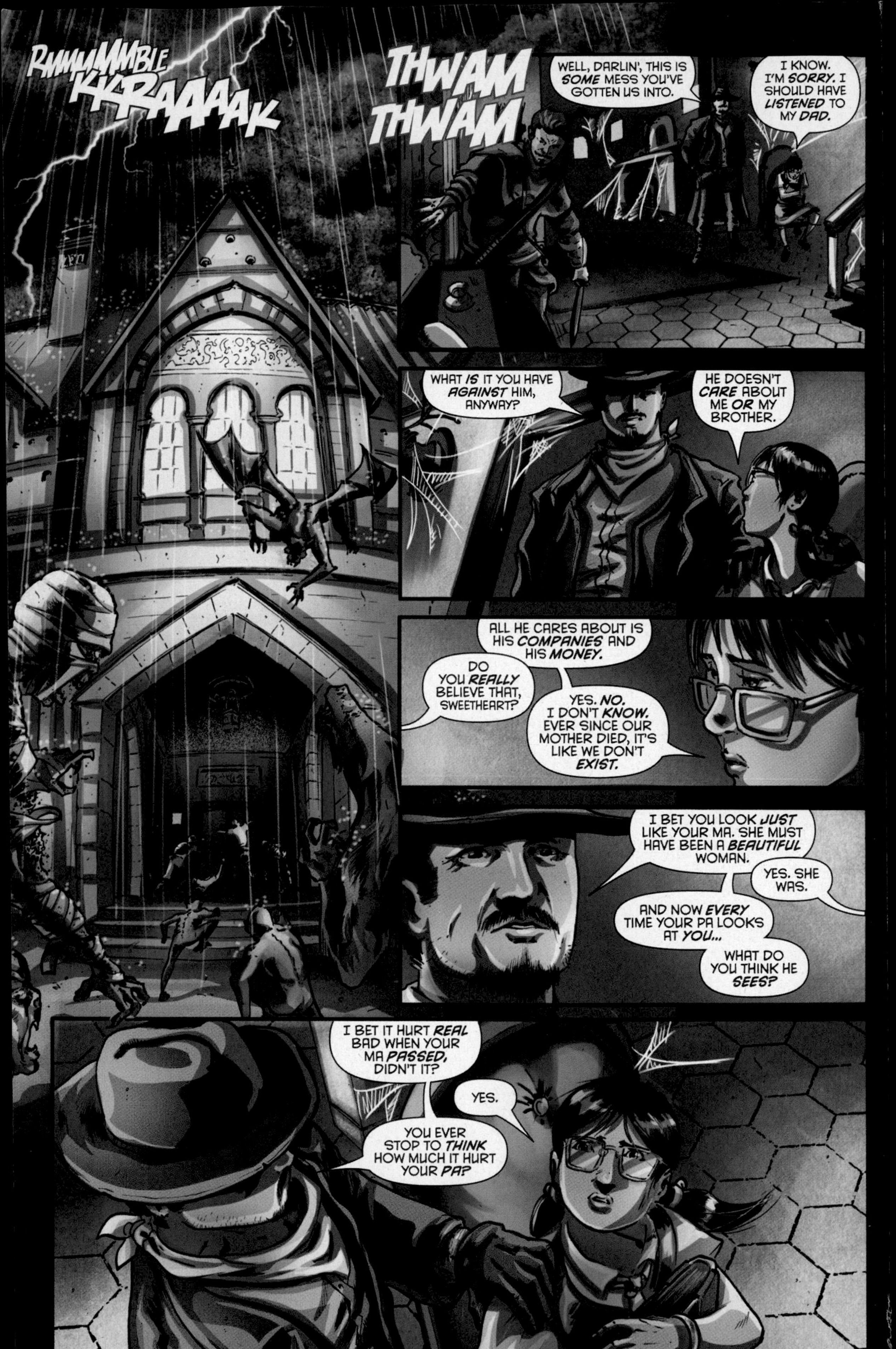
RMMMMMBLE
KKRAAAAK
THWAM
THWAM
WELL, DARLIN', THIS IS SOME MESS YOU'VE GOTTEN US INTO.
I KNOW. I'M SORRY. I SHOULD HAVE LISTENED TO MY DAD.
WHAT IS IT YOU HAVE AGAINST HIM, ANYWAY?
HE DOESN'T CARE ABOUT ME OR MY BROTHER.
ALL HE CARES ABOUT IS HIS COMPANIES AND HIS MONEY.
DO YOU REALLY BELIEVE THAT, SWEETHEART?
YES. NO. I DON'T KNOW. EVER SINCE OUR MOTHER DIED, IT'S LIKE WE DON'T EXIST.
I BET YOU LOOK JUST LIKE YOUR MA. SHE MUST HAVE BEEN A BEAUTIFUL WOMAN.
YES. SHE WAS.
AND NOW EVERY TIME YOUR PA LOOKS AT YOU...
WHAT DO YOU THINK HE SEES?
I BET IT HURT REAL BAD WHEN YOUR MA PASSED, DIDN'T IT?
YES.
YOU EVER STOP TO THINK HOW MUCH IT HURT YOUR PA?

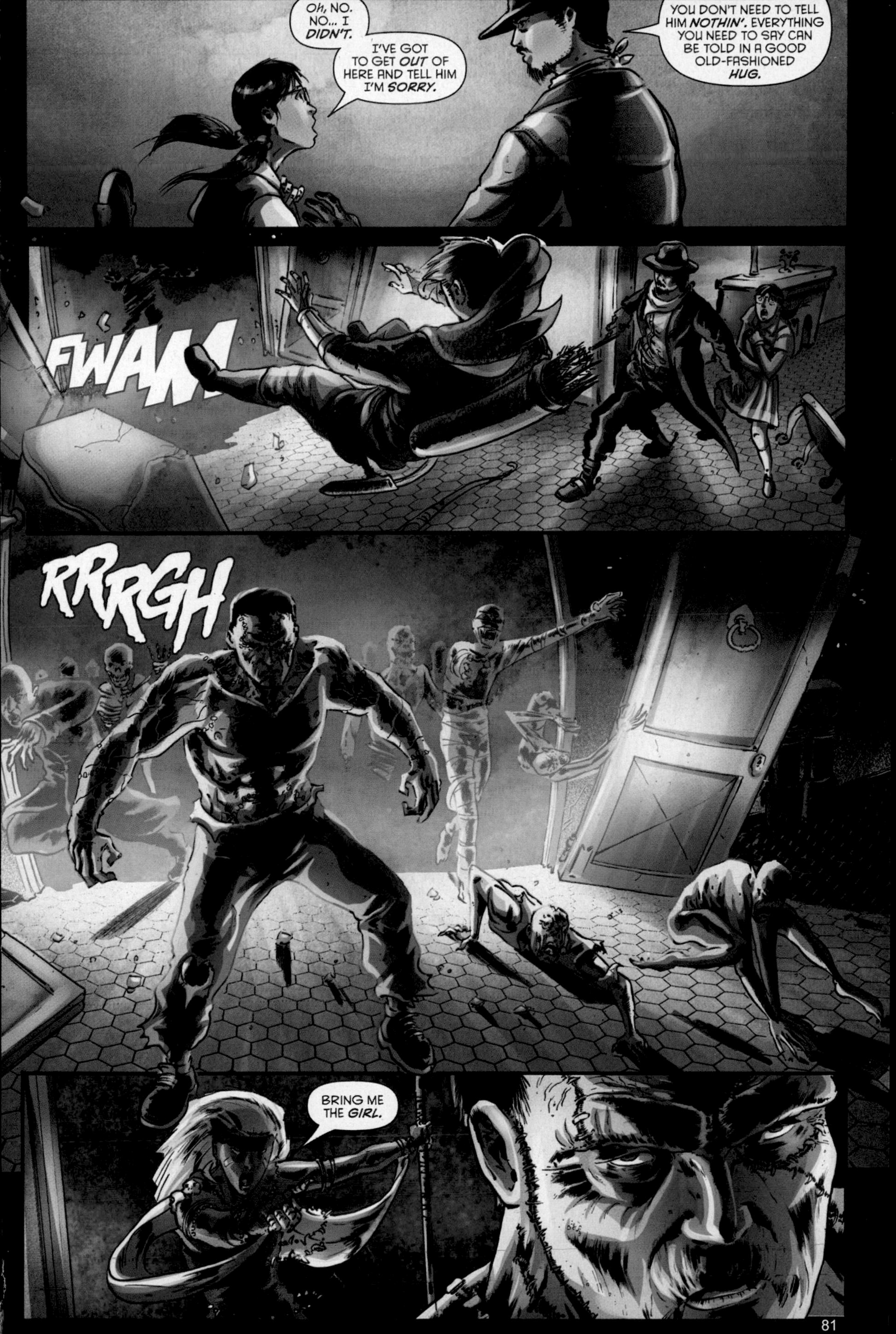

Oh, NO. NO... I DIDN'T.
I'VE GOT TO GET OUT OF HERE AND TELL HIM I'M SORRY.
YOU DON'T NEED TO TELL HIM NOTHIN'. EVERYTHING YOU NEED TO SAY CAN BE TOLD IN A GOOD OLD-FASHIONED HUG.
FWAM
RRRGH
BRING ME THE GIRL.

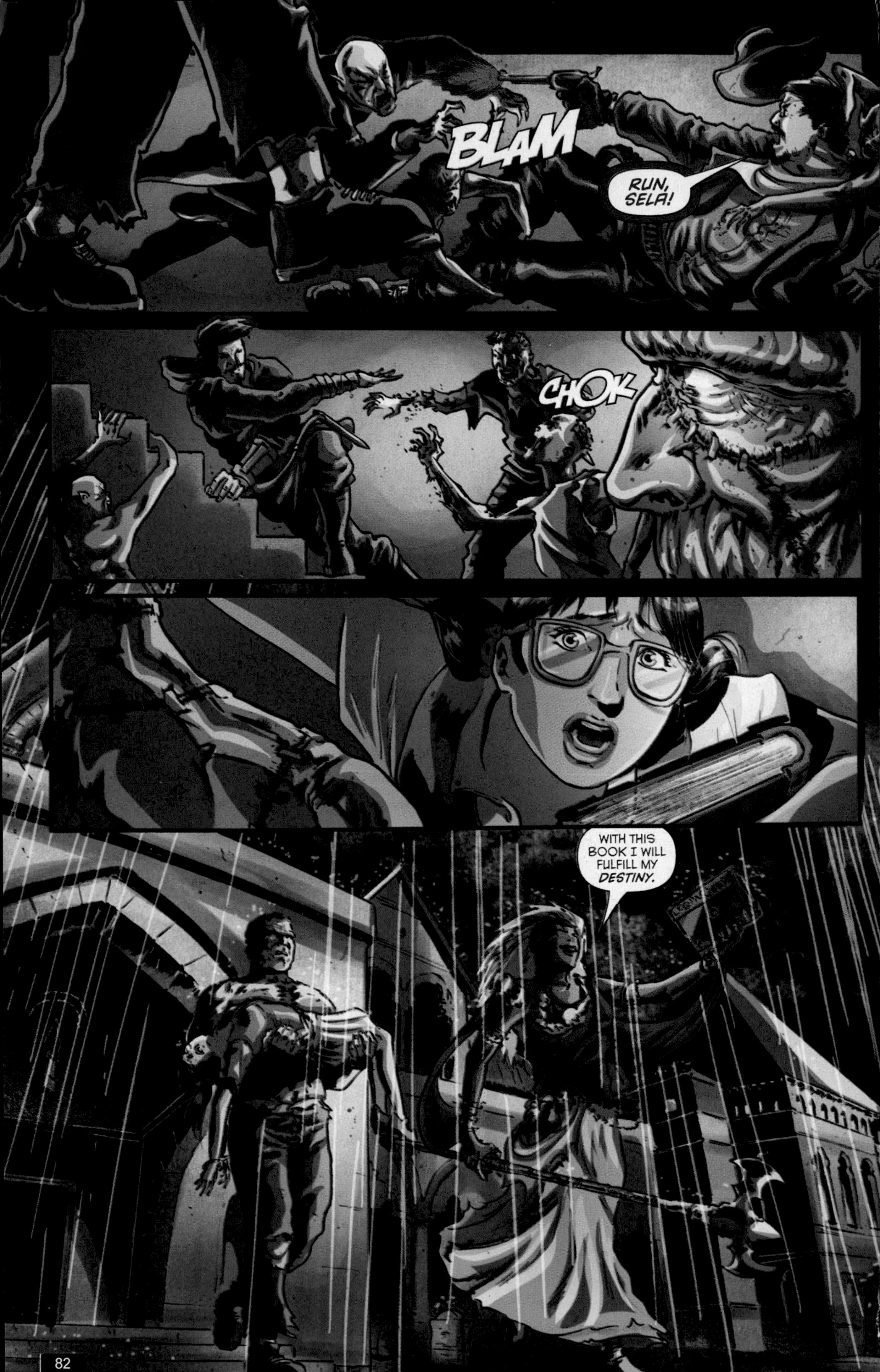
BLAM
RUN, SELA!
CHOK
WITH THIS BOOK I WILL FULFILL MY *DESTINY*.

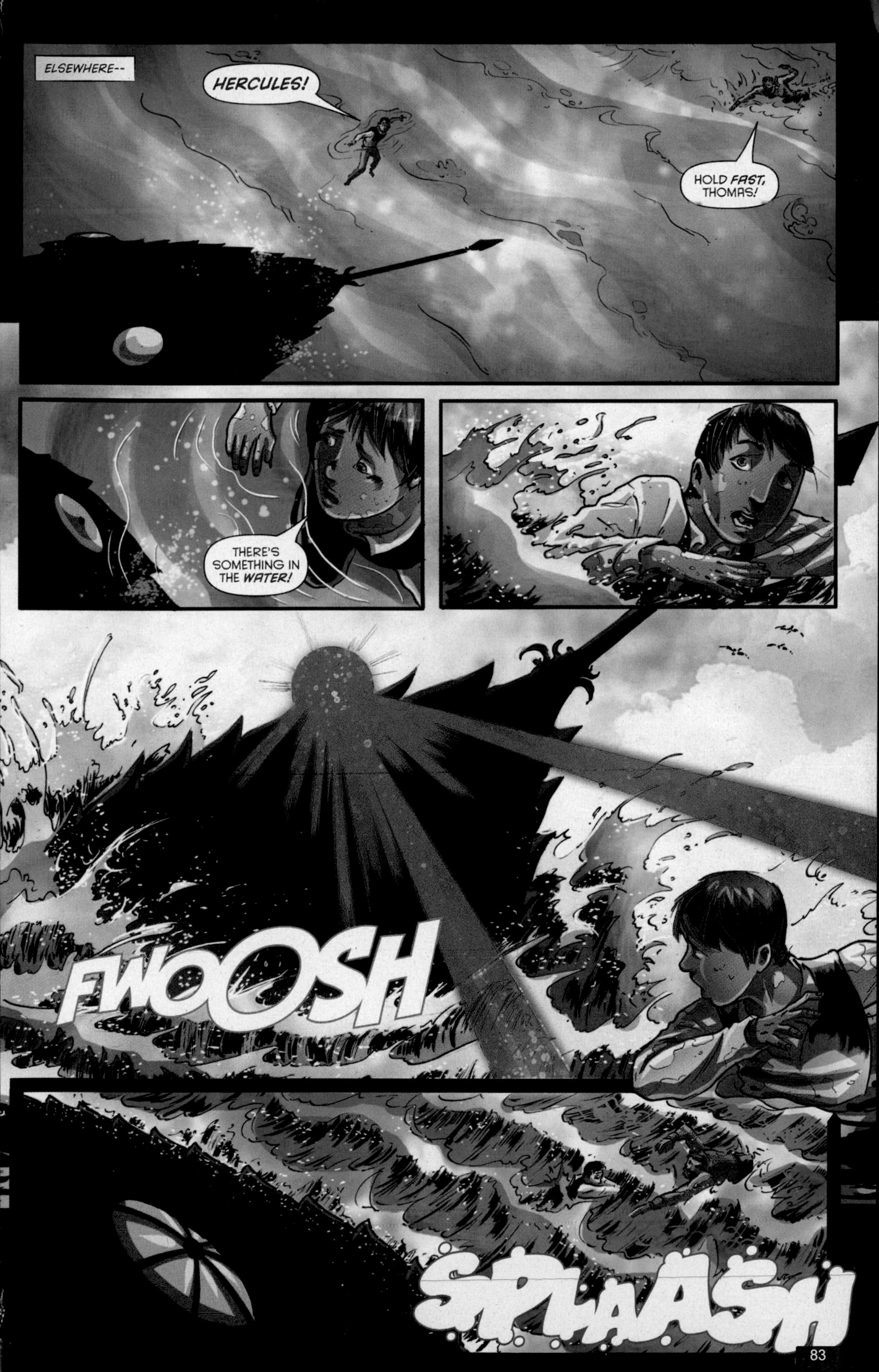
ELSEWHERE--
HERCULES!
HOLD FAST, THOMAS!
THERE'S SOMETHING IN THE WATER!
FWOOSH
SPLAASH

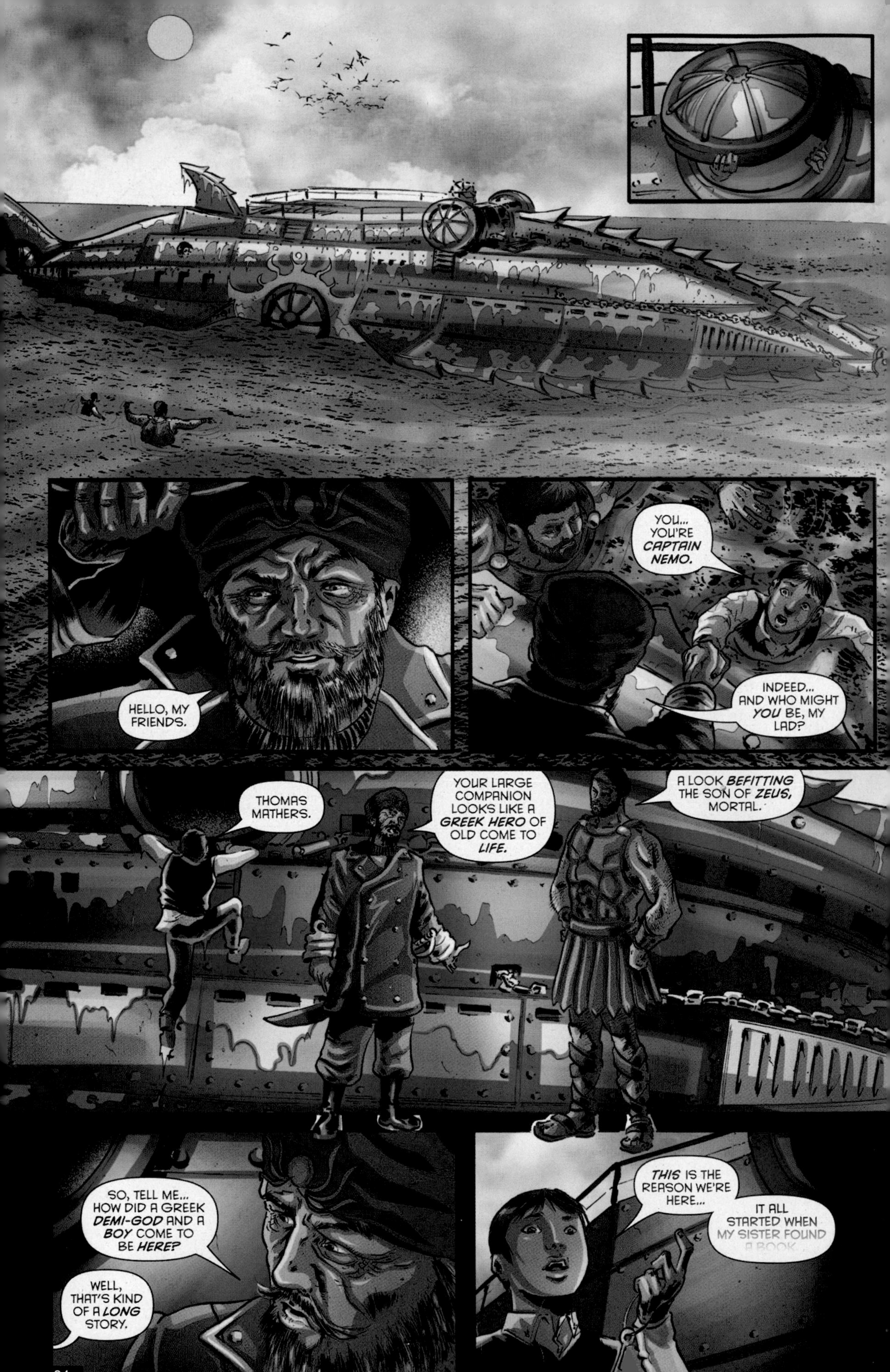
HELLO, MY FRIENDS.
YOU... YOU'RE *CAPTAIN NEMO.*
INDEED... AND WHO MIGHT *YOU* BE, MY LAD?
THOMAS MATHERS.
YOUR LARGE COMPANION LOOKS LIKE A *GREEK HERO* OF OLD COME TO *LIFE.*
A LOOK *BEFITTING* THE SON OF *ZEUS,* MORTAL.
SO, TELL ME... HOW DID A GREEK *DEMI-GOD* AND A *BOY* COME TO BE *HERE?*
WELL, THAT'S KIND OF A *LONG* STORY.
THIS IS THE REASON WE'RE HERE...
IT ALL STARTED WHEN MY SISTER FOUND

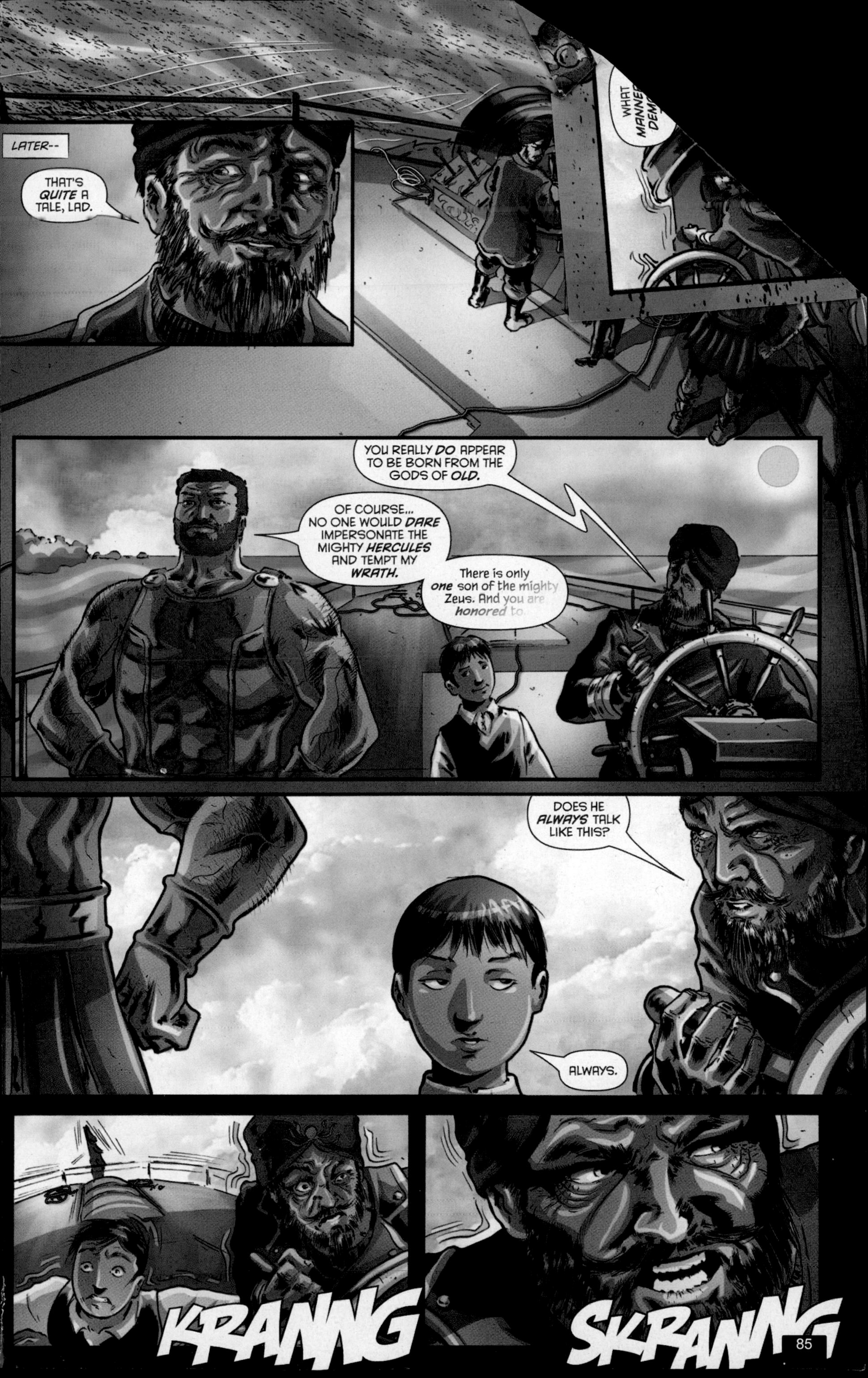

LATER--
THAT'S QUITE A TALE, LAD.
YOU REALLY DO APPEAR TO BE BORN FROM THE GODS OF OLD.
OF COURSE... NO ONE WOULD DARE IMPERSONATE THE MIGHTY HERCULES AND TEMPT MY WRATH.
There is only one son of the mighty Zeus. And you are honored to...
DOES HE ALWAYS TALK LIKE THIS?
ALWAYS.
KRANNG
SKRANNG

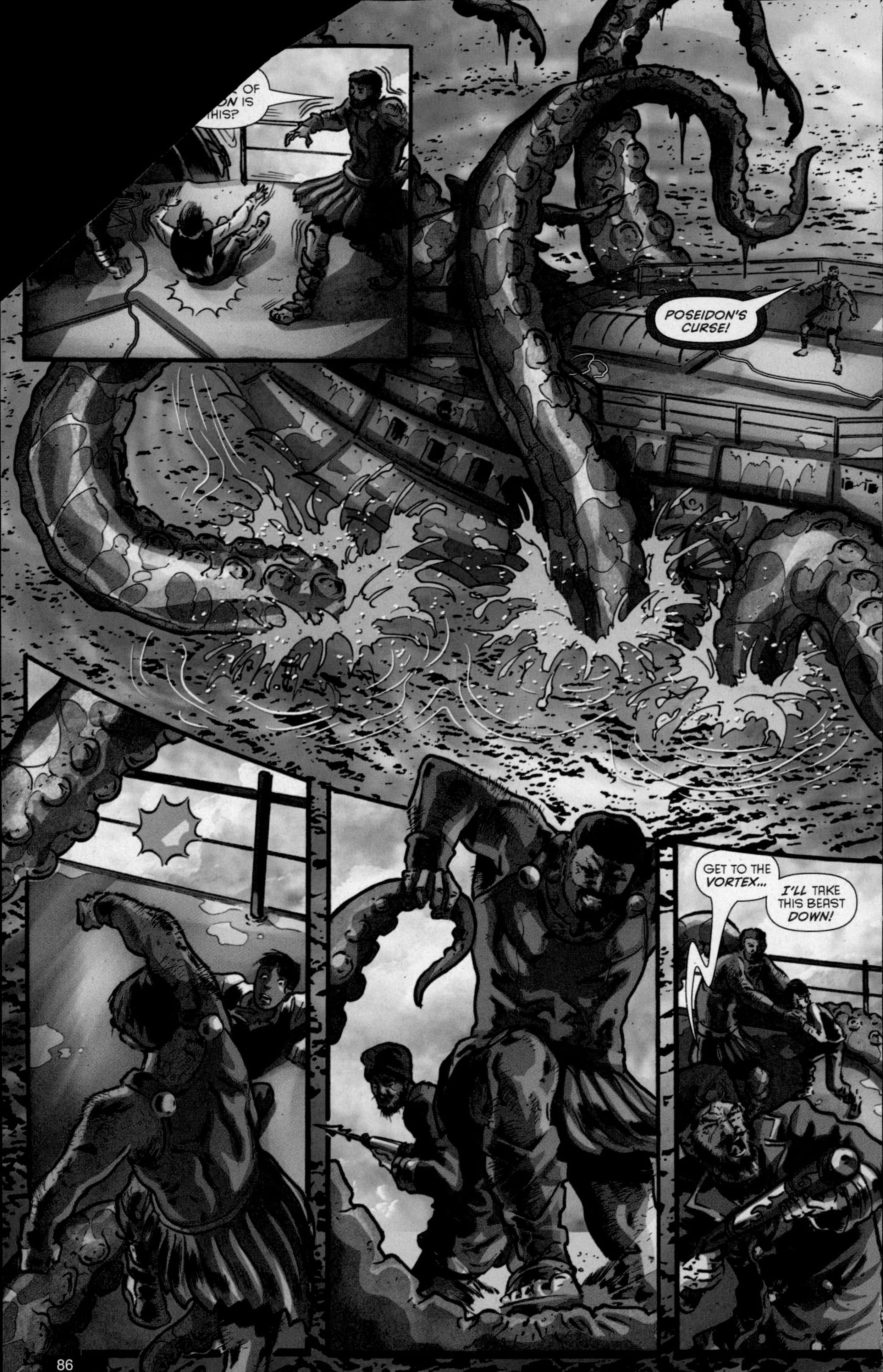
POSEIDON'S CURSE!
GET TO THE VORTEX...
I'LL TAKE THIS BEAST DOWN!

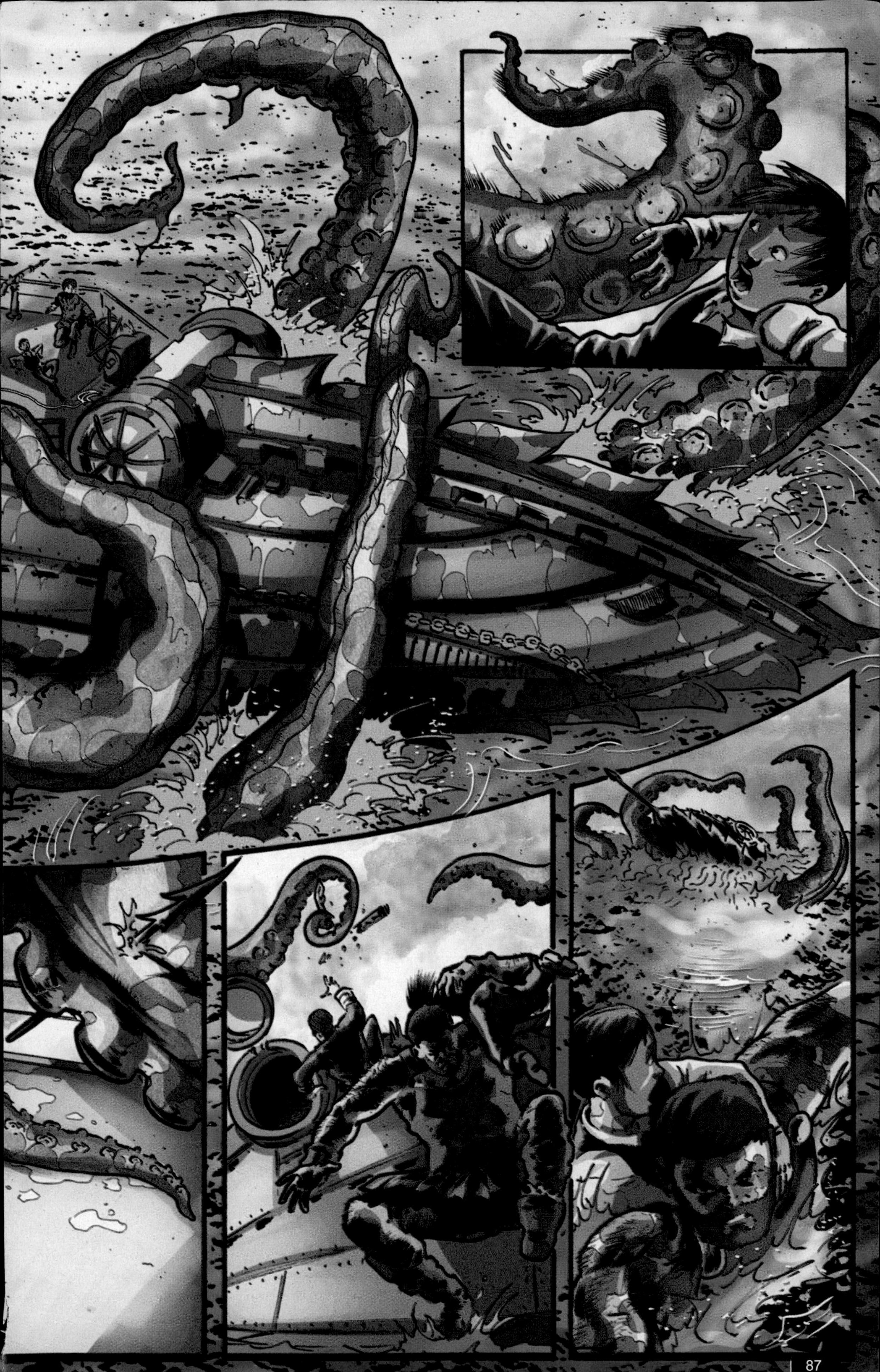

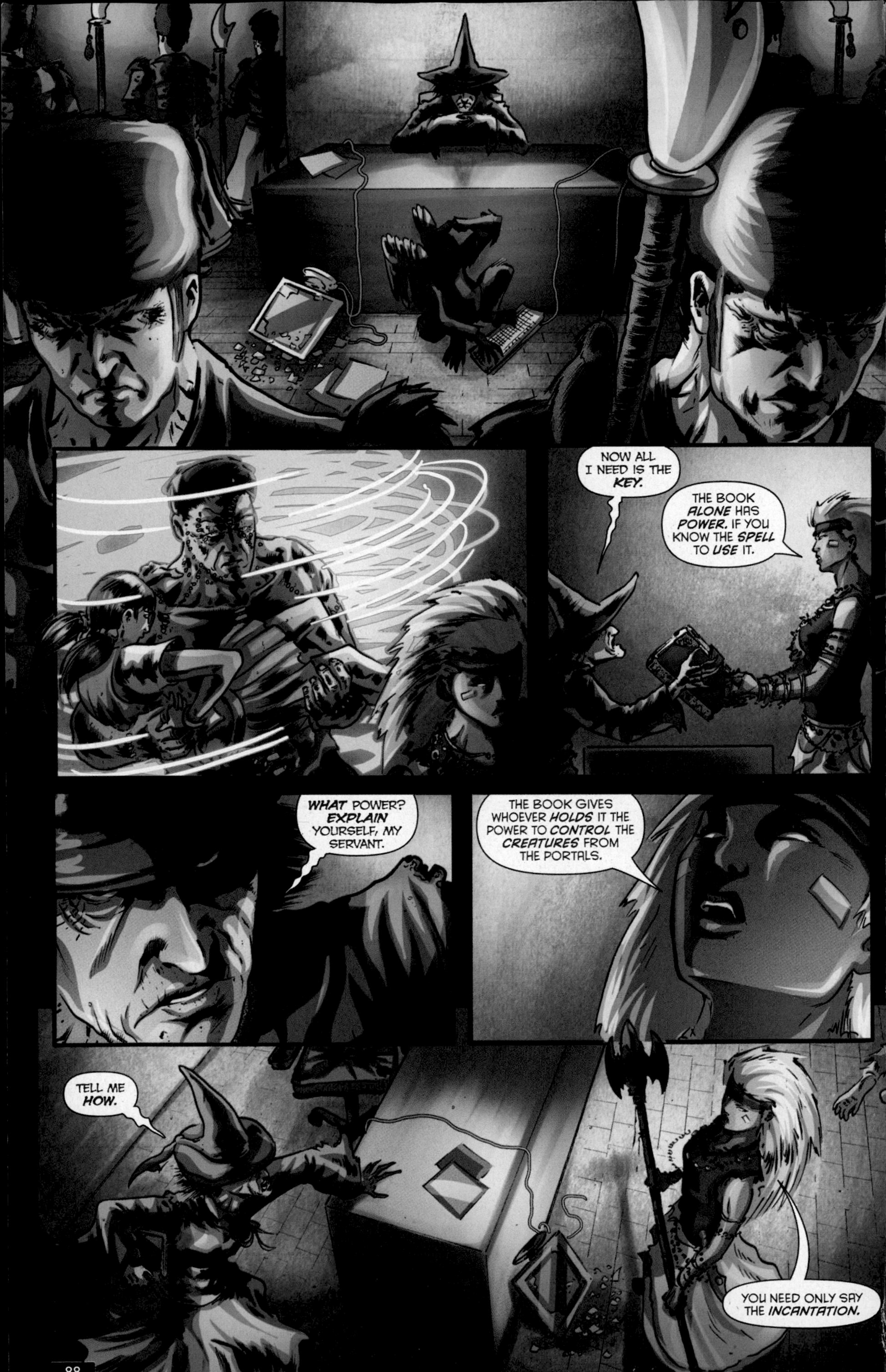
NOW ALL
I NEED IS THE
KEY.
THE BOOK
ALONE HAS
POWER. IF YOU
KNOW THE SPELL
TO USE IT.
WHAT POWER?
EXPLAIN
YOURSELF, MY
SERVANT.
THE BOOK GIVES
WHOEVER HOLDS IT THE
POWER TO CONTROL THE
CREATURES FROM
THE PORTALS.
TELL ME
HOW.
YOU NEED ONLY SAY
THE INCANTATION.

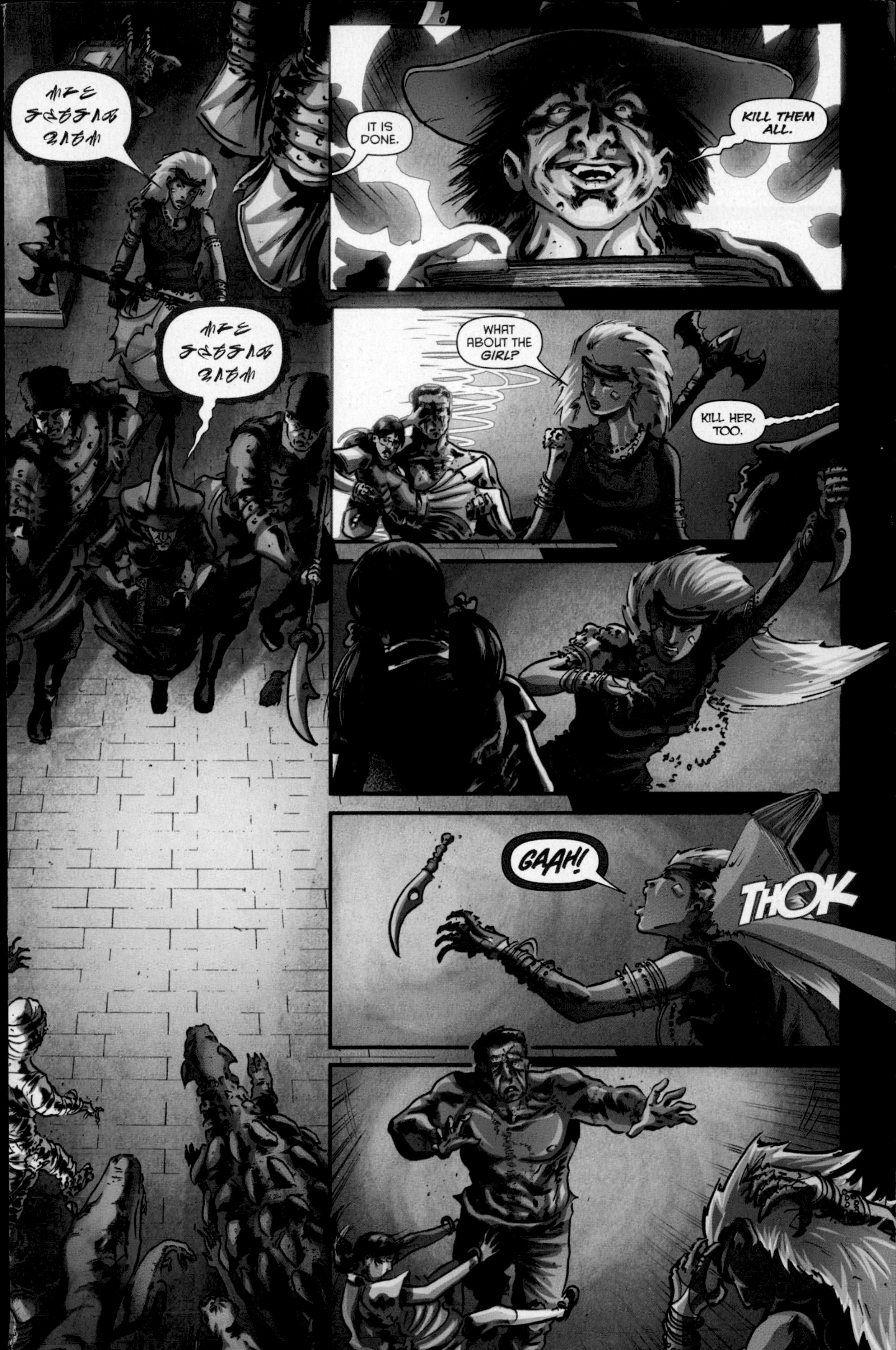

IT IS DONE.
KILL THEM ALL.
WHAT ABOUT THE GIRL?
KILL HER, TOO.
GAAH!
THOK

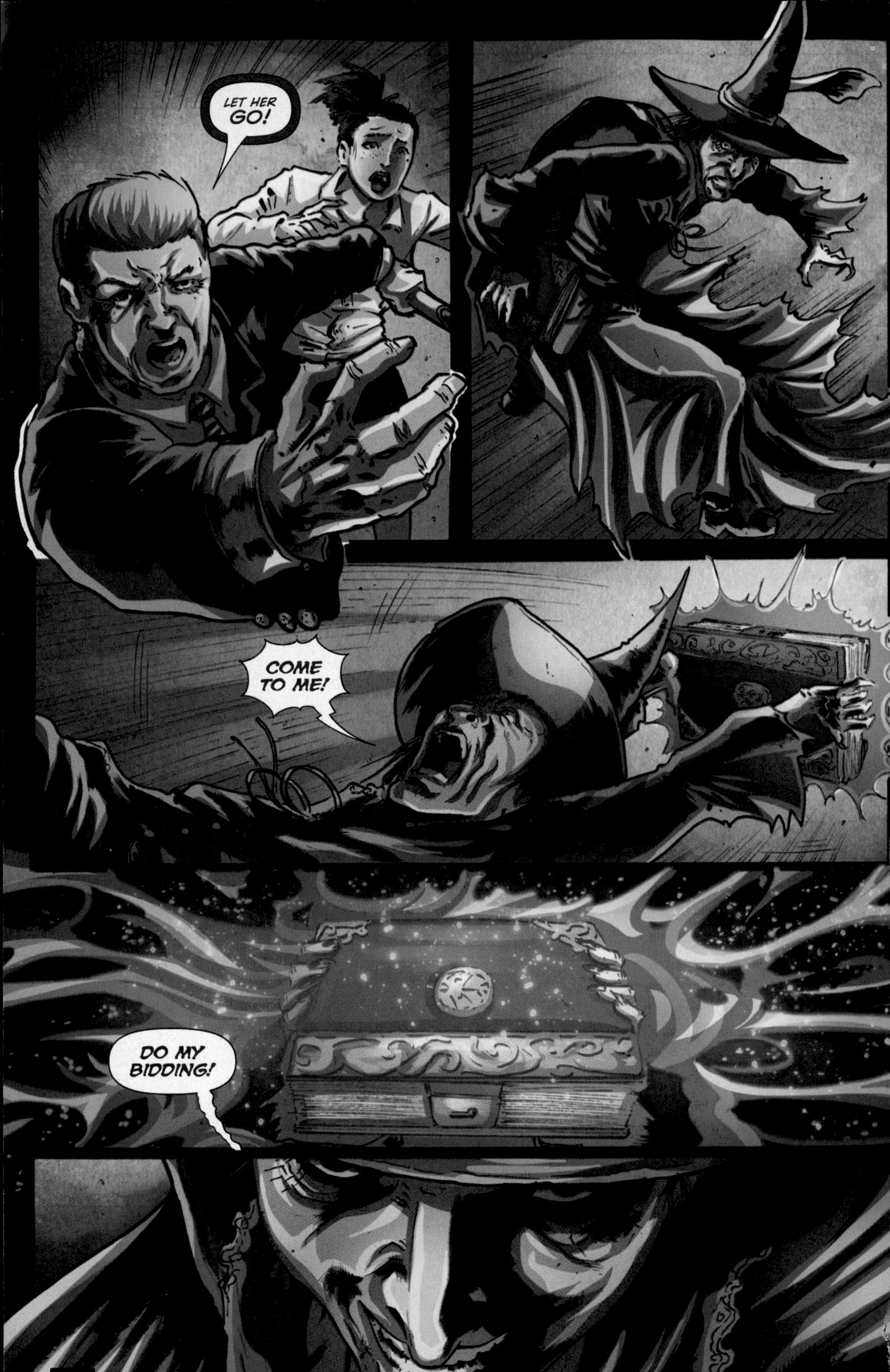
LET HER GO!
COME TO ME!
DO MY BIDDING!

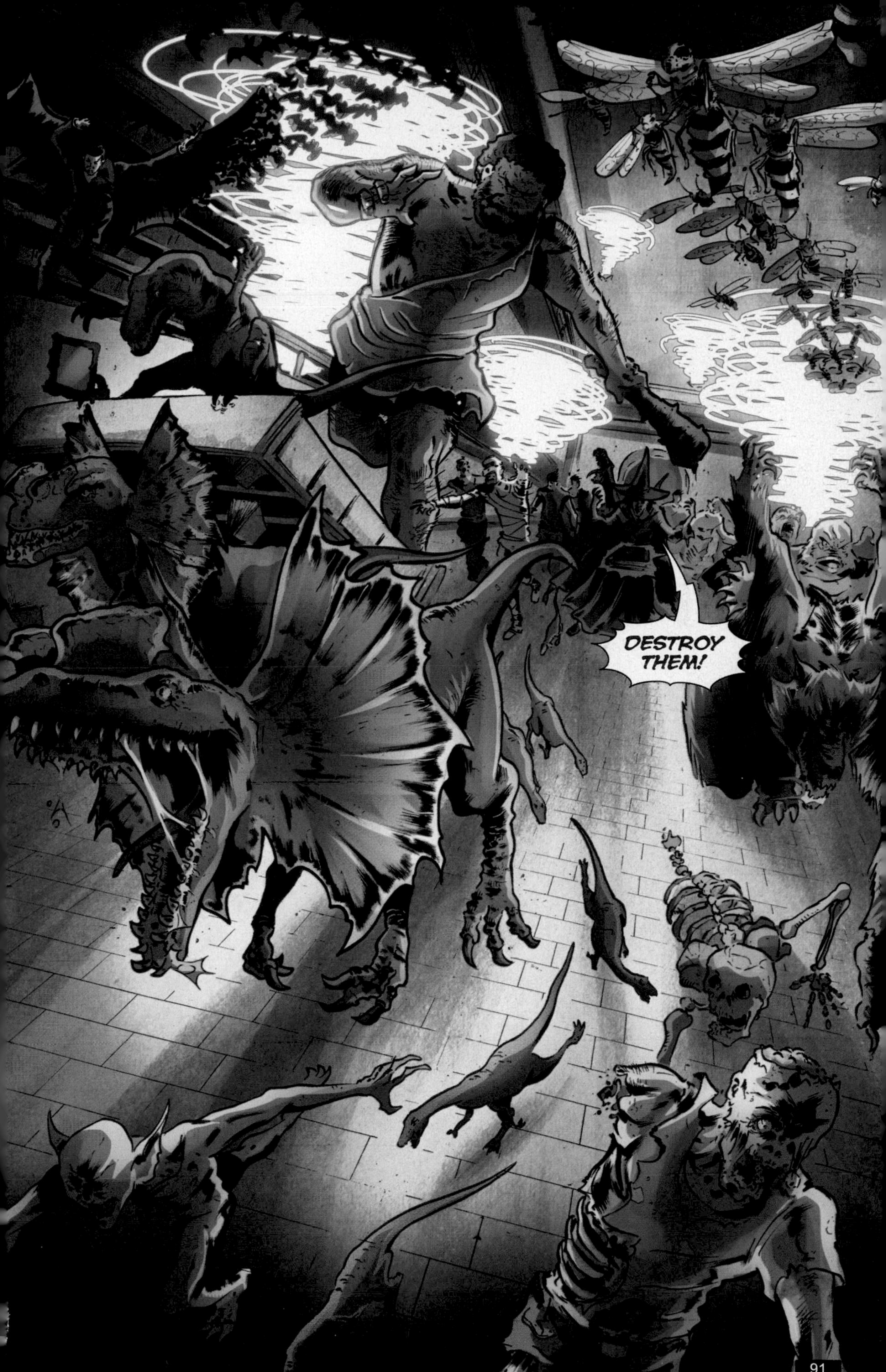
DESTROY THEM!

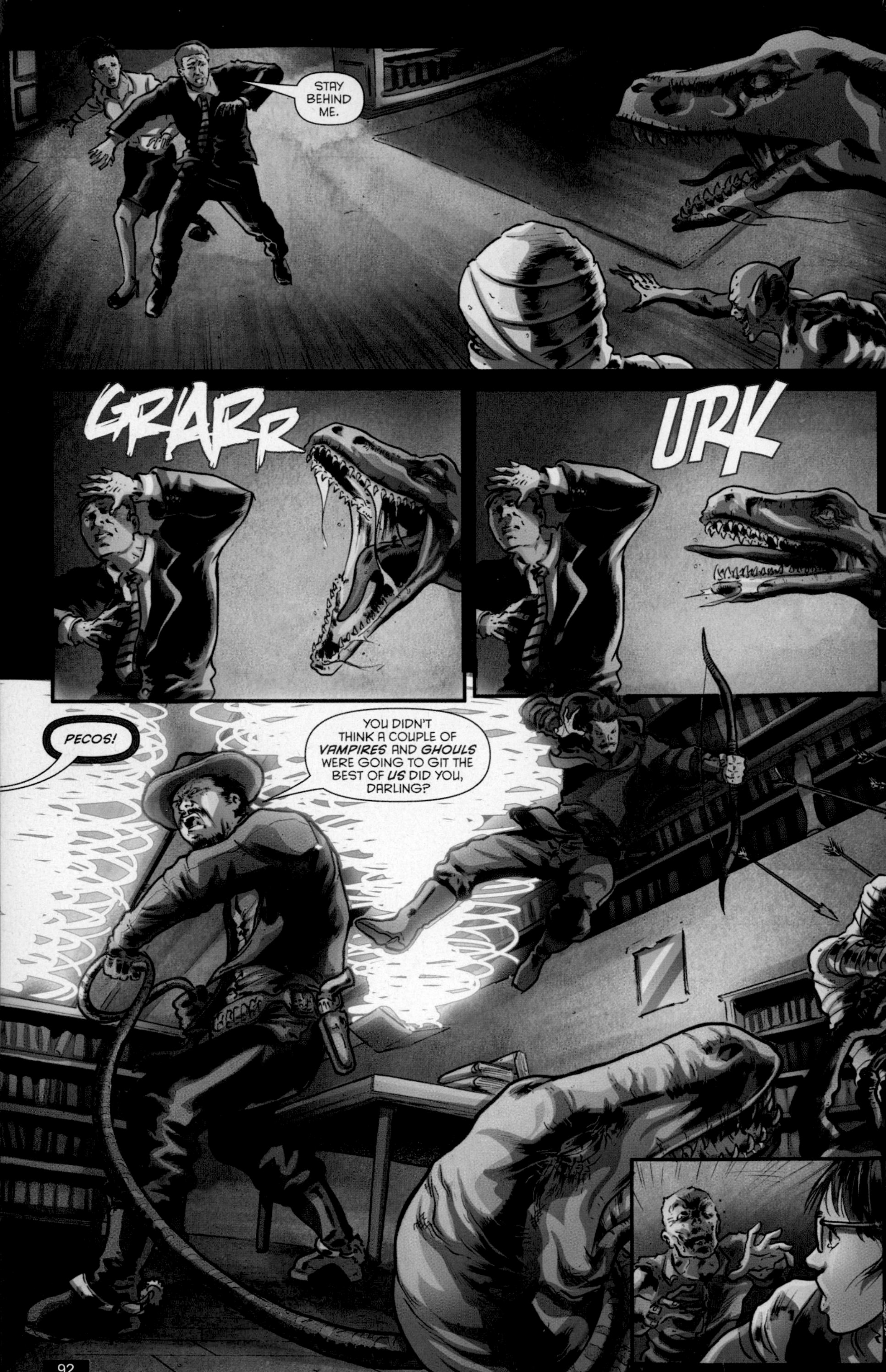
STAY BEHIND ME.
GRARR
URK
PECOS!
YOU DIDN'T THINK A COUPLE OF VAMPIRES AND GHOULS WERE GOING TO GIT THE BEST OF US DID YOU, DARLING?

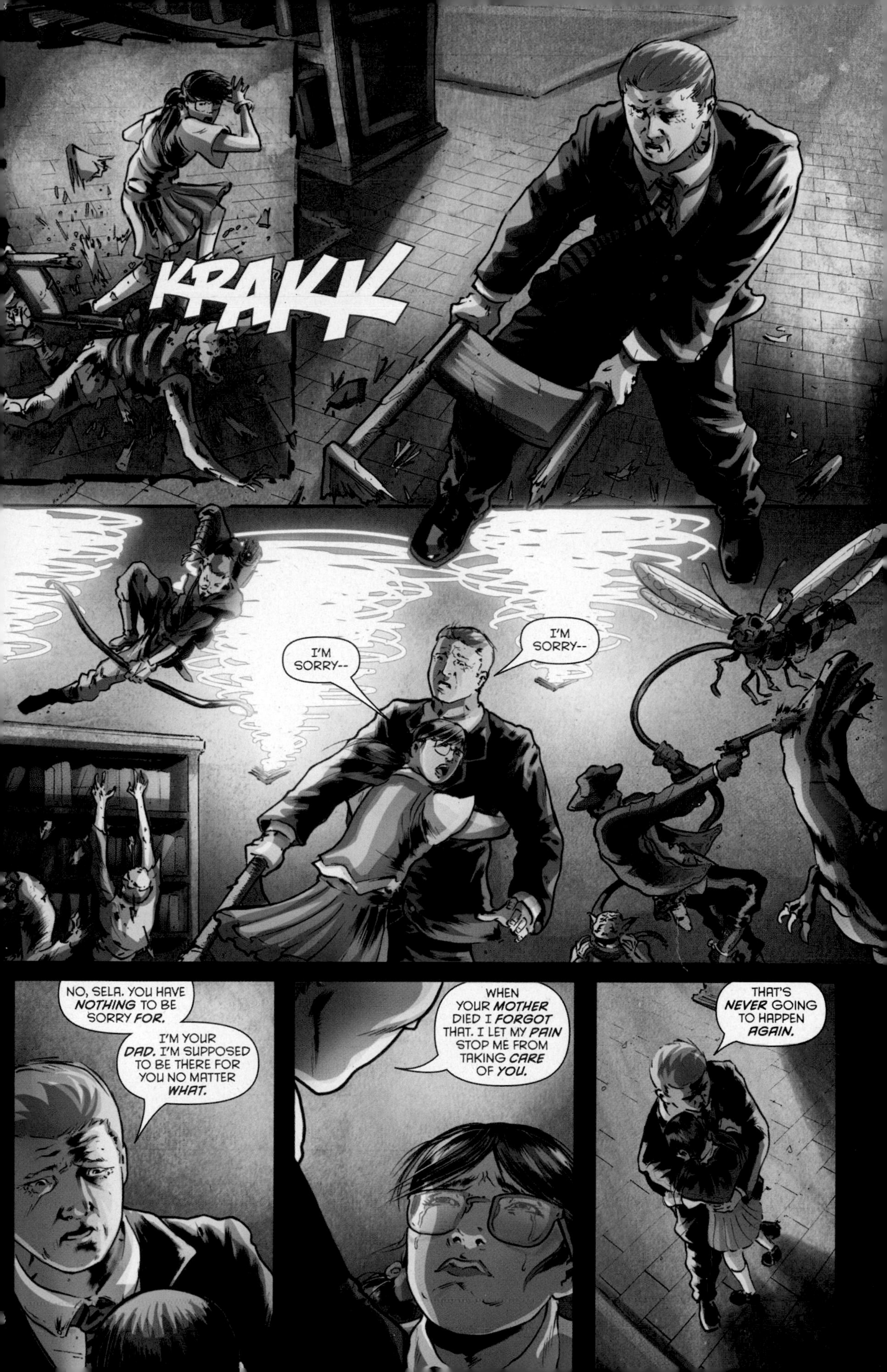
KRAKK
I'M SORRY--
I'M SORRY--
NO, SELA. YOU HAVE NOTHING TO BE SORRY FOR.
I'M YOUR DAD. I'M SUPPOSED TO BE THERE FOR YOU NO MATTER WHAT.
WHEN YOUR MOTHER DIED I FORGOT THAT. I LET MY PAIN STOP ME FROM TAKING CARE OF YOU.
THAT'S NEVER GOING TO HAPPEN AGAIN.

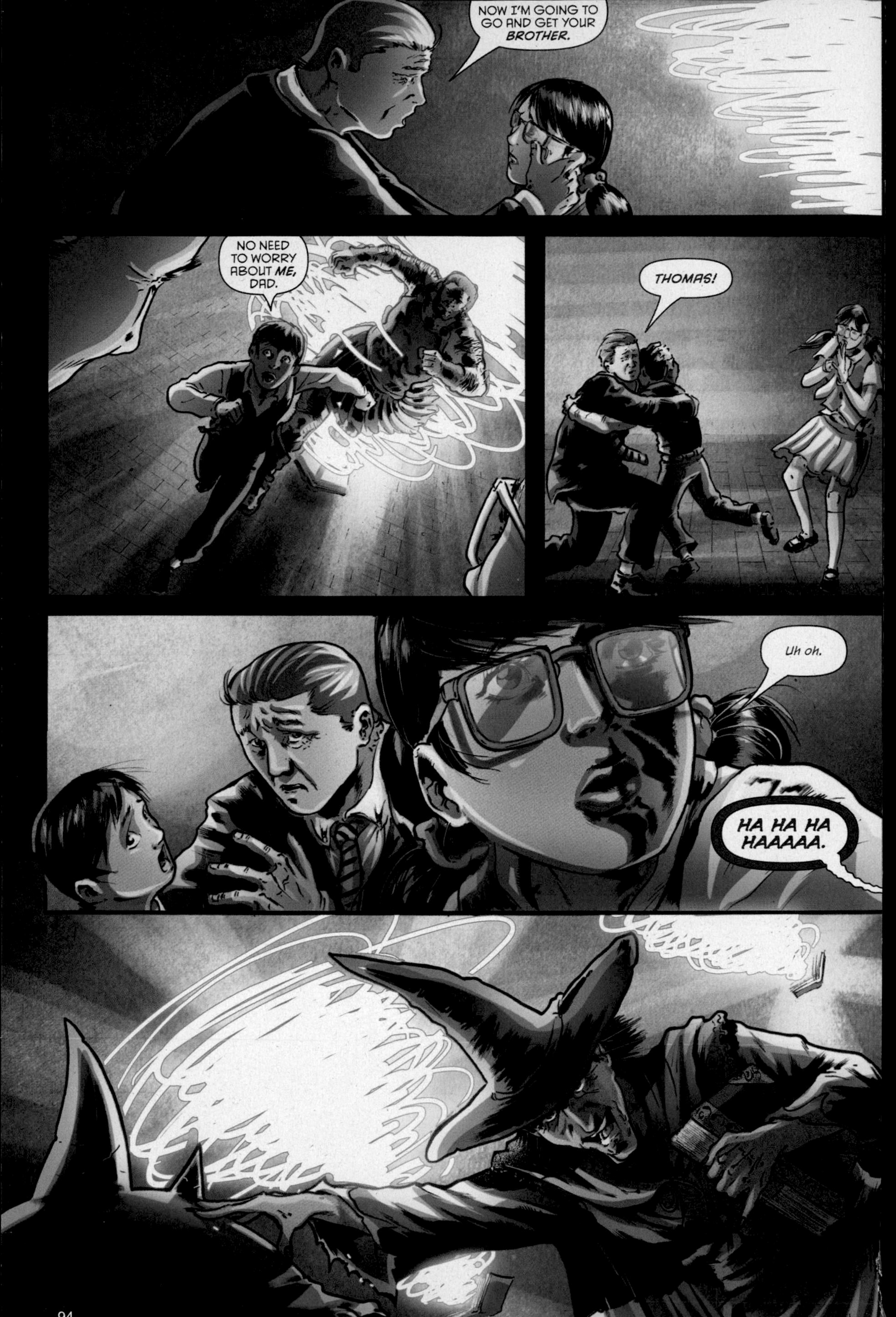
NOW I'M GOING TO GO AND GET YOUR *BROTHER.*
NO NEED TO WORRY ABOUT *ME,* DAD.
THOMAS!
Uh oh.
HA HA HA HAAAAA.

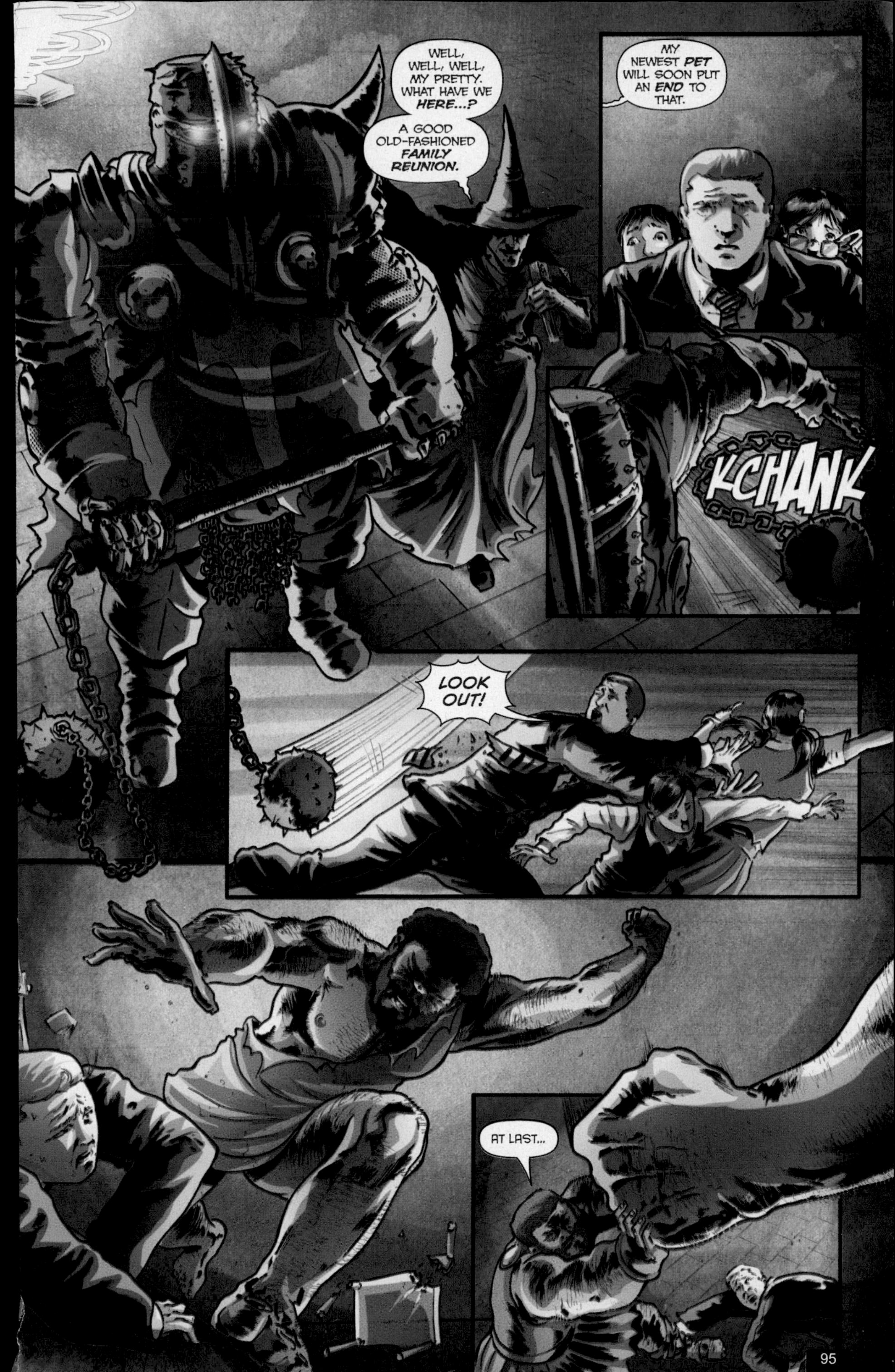

WELL, WELL, WELL, MY PRETTY. WHAT HAVE WE HERE...?
A GOOD OLD-FASHIONED FAMILY REUNION.
MY NEWEST PET WILL SOON PUT AN END TO THAT.
KCHANK
LOOK OUT!
AT LAST...

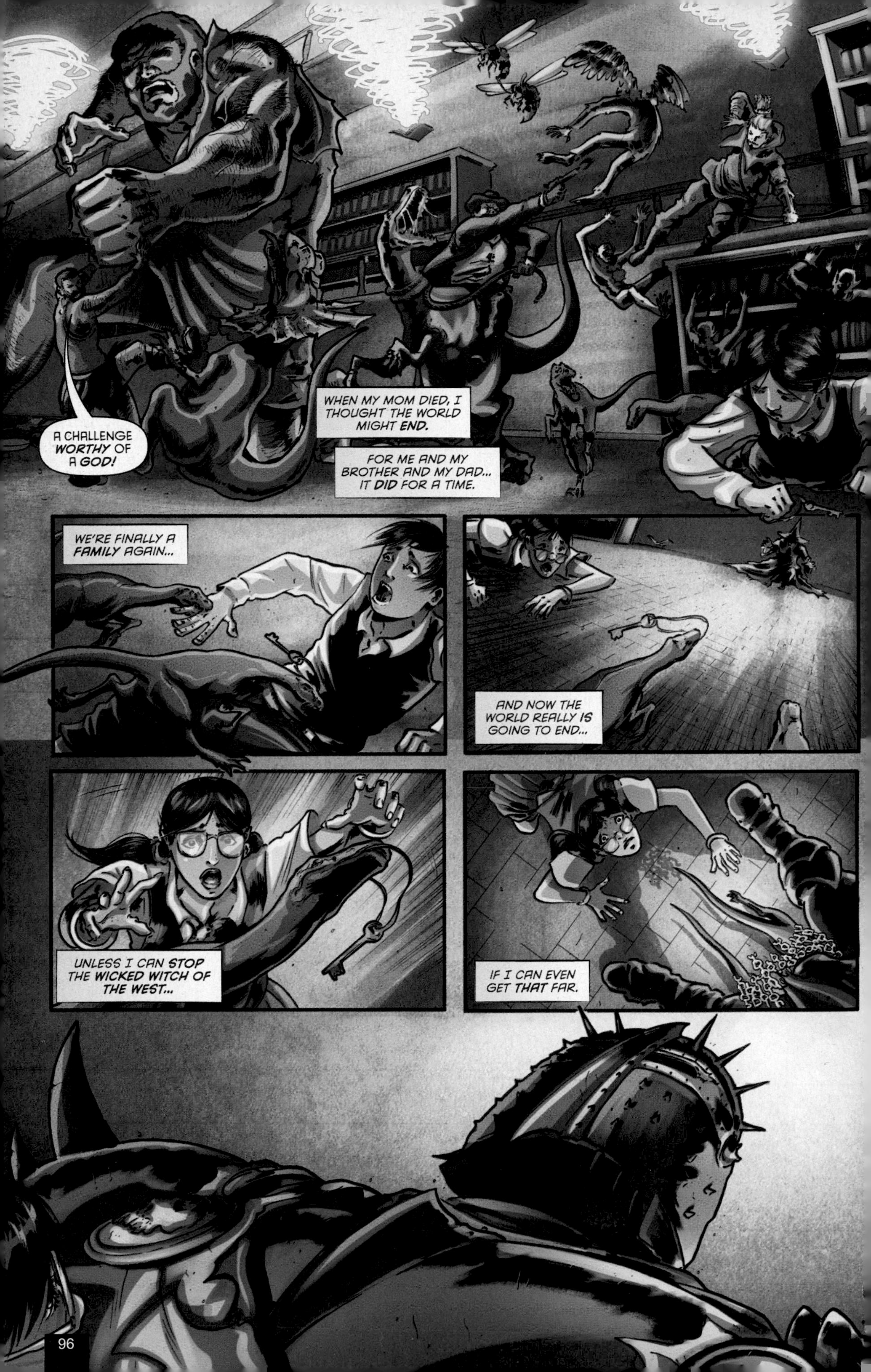
A CHALLENGE WORTHY OF A GOD!
WHEN MY MOM DIED, I THOUGHT THE WORLD MIGHT END.
FOR ME AND MY BROTHER AND MY DAD... IT DID FOR A TIME.
WE'RE FINALLY A FAMILY AGAIN...
AND NOW THE WORLD REALLY IS GOING TO END...
UNLESS I CAN STOP THE WICKED WITCH OF THE WEST...
IF I CAN EVEN GET THAT FAR.

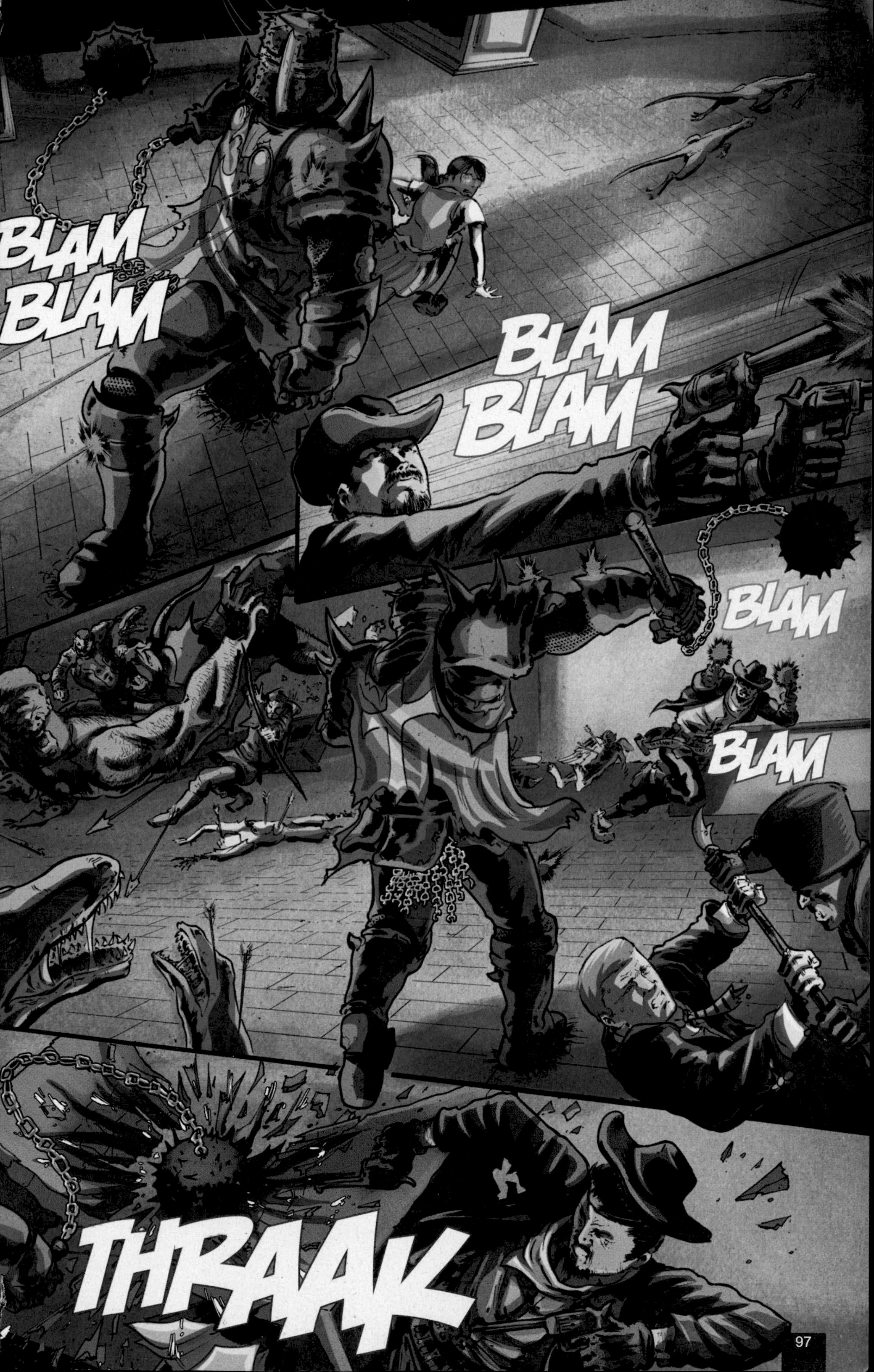
BLAM
BLAM
BLAM
BLAM
BLAM
BLAM
THRAAK

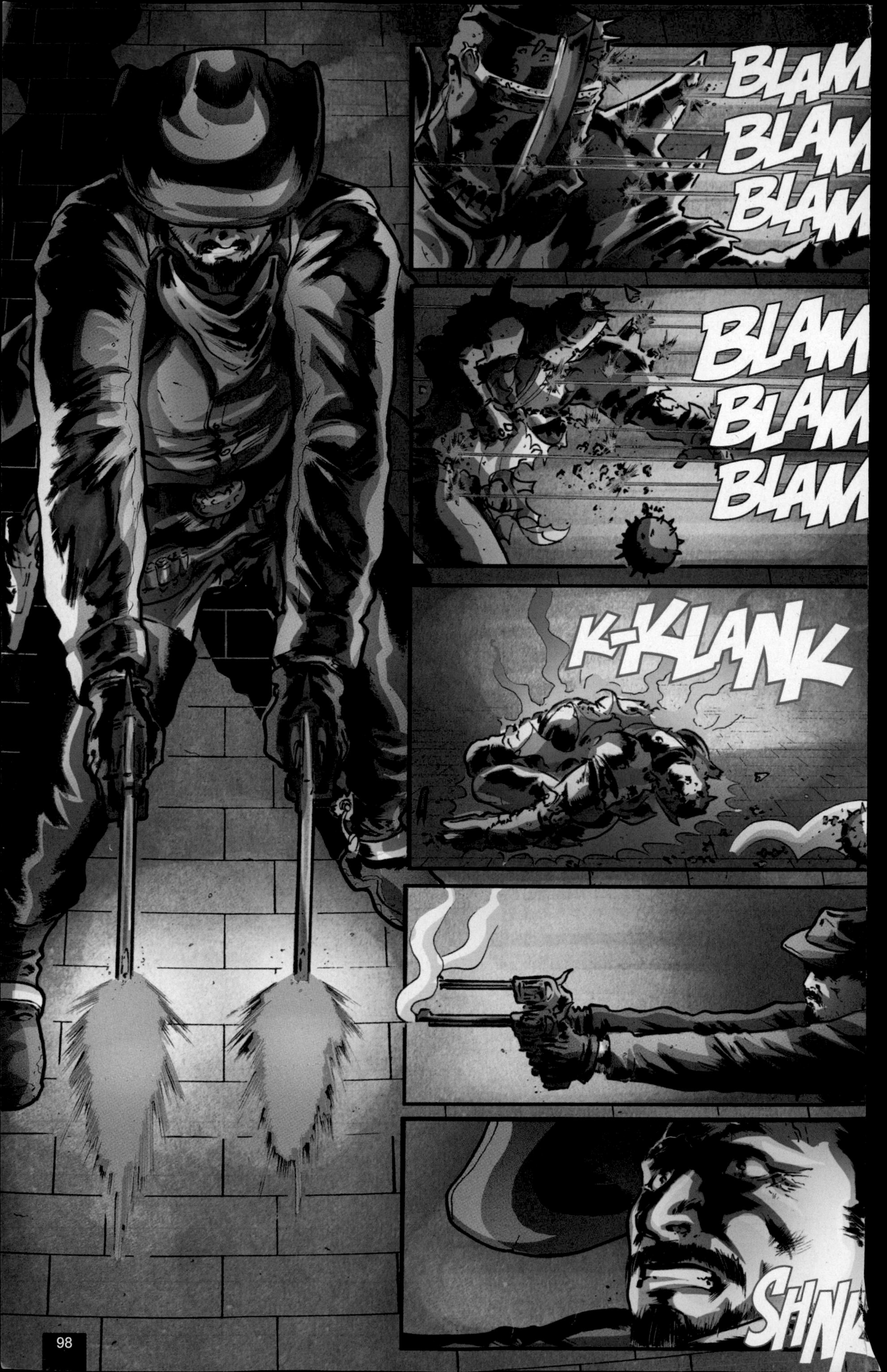
BLAM
BLAM
BLAM
BLAM
BLAM
BLAM
K-KLANK
SHNK

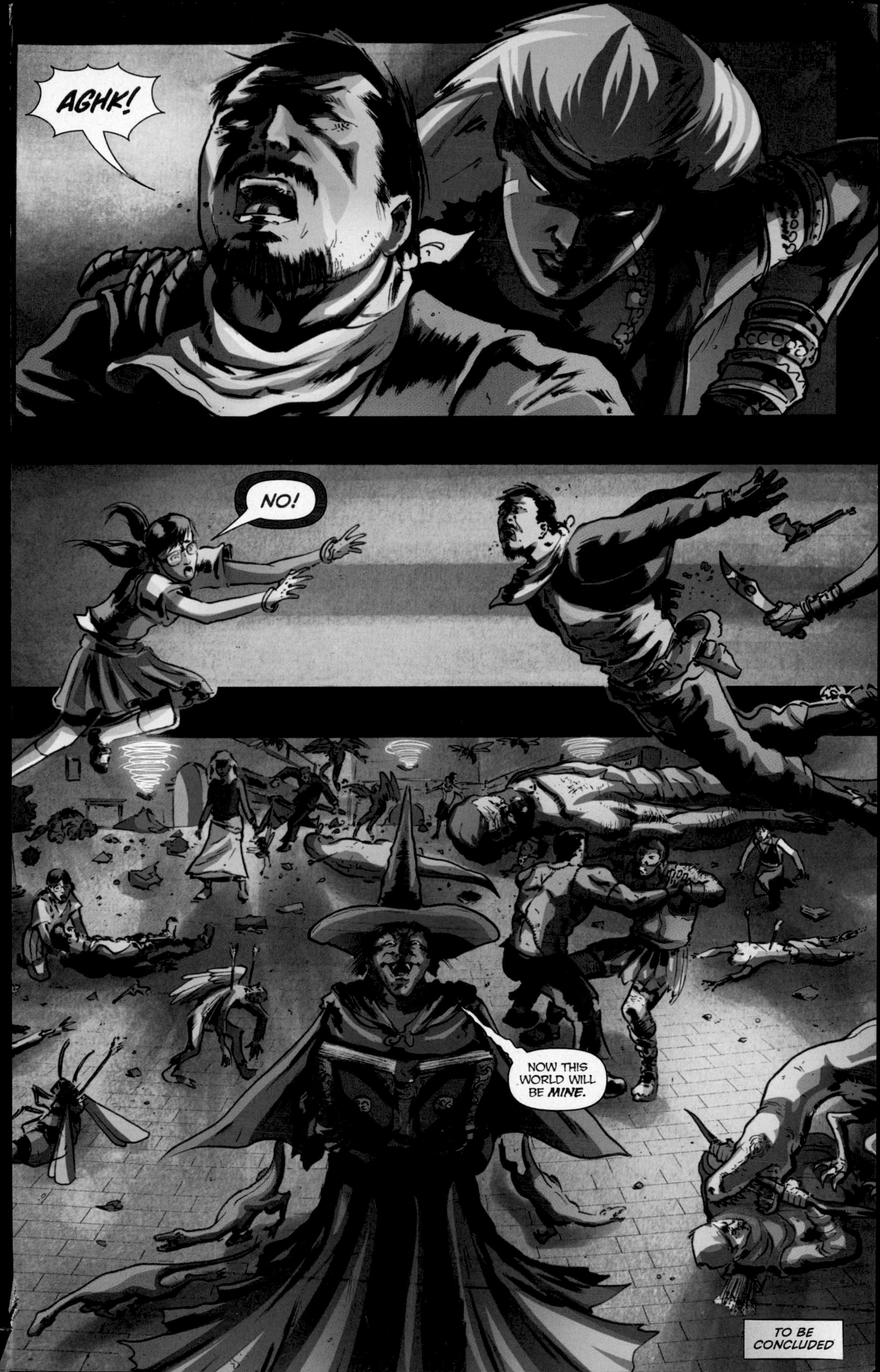
AGHK!
NO!
NOW THIS WORLD WILL BE *MINE.*
TO BE CONCLUDED

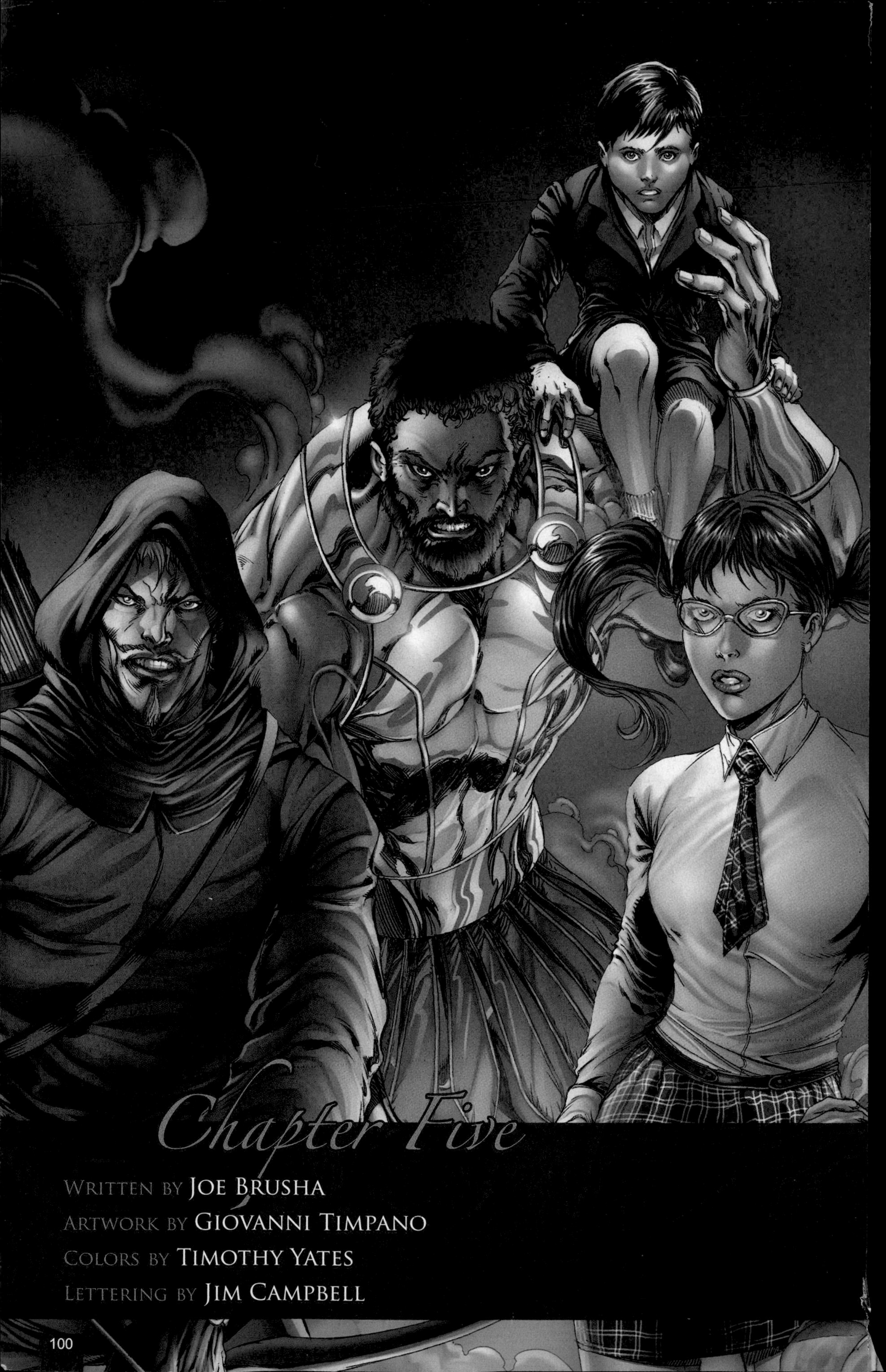

Chapter Five

WRITTEN BY JOE BRUSHA
ARTWORK BY GIOVANNI TIMPANO
COLORS BY TIMOTHY YATES
LETTERING BY JIM CAMPBELL

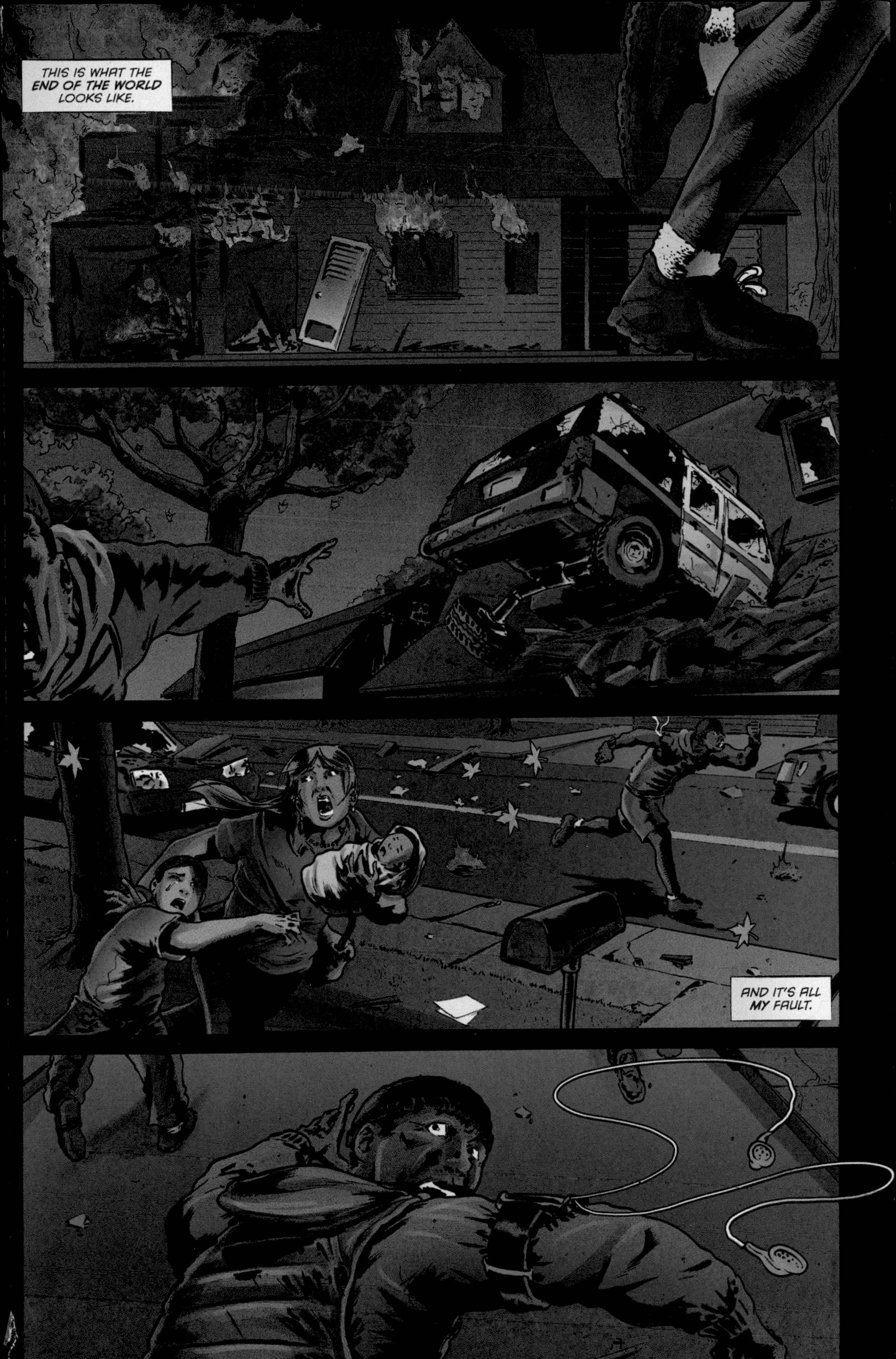
THIS IS WHAT THE END OF THE WORLD LOOKS LIKE.
AND IT'S ALL MY FAULT.

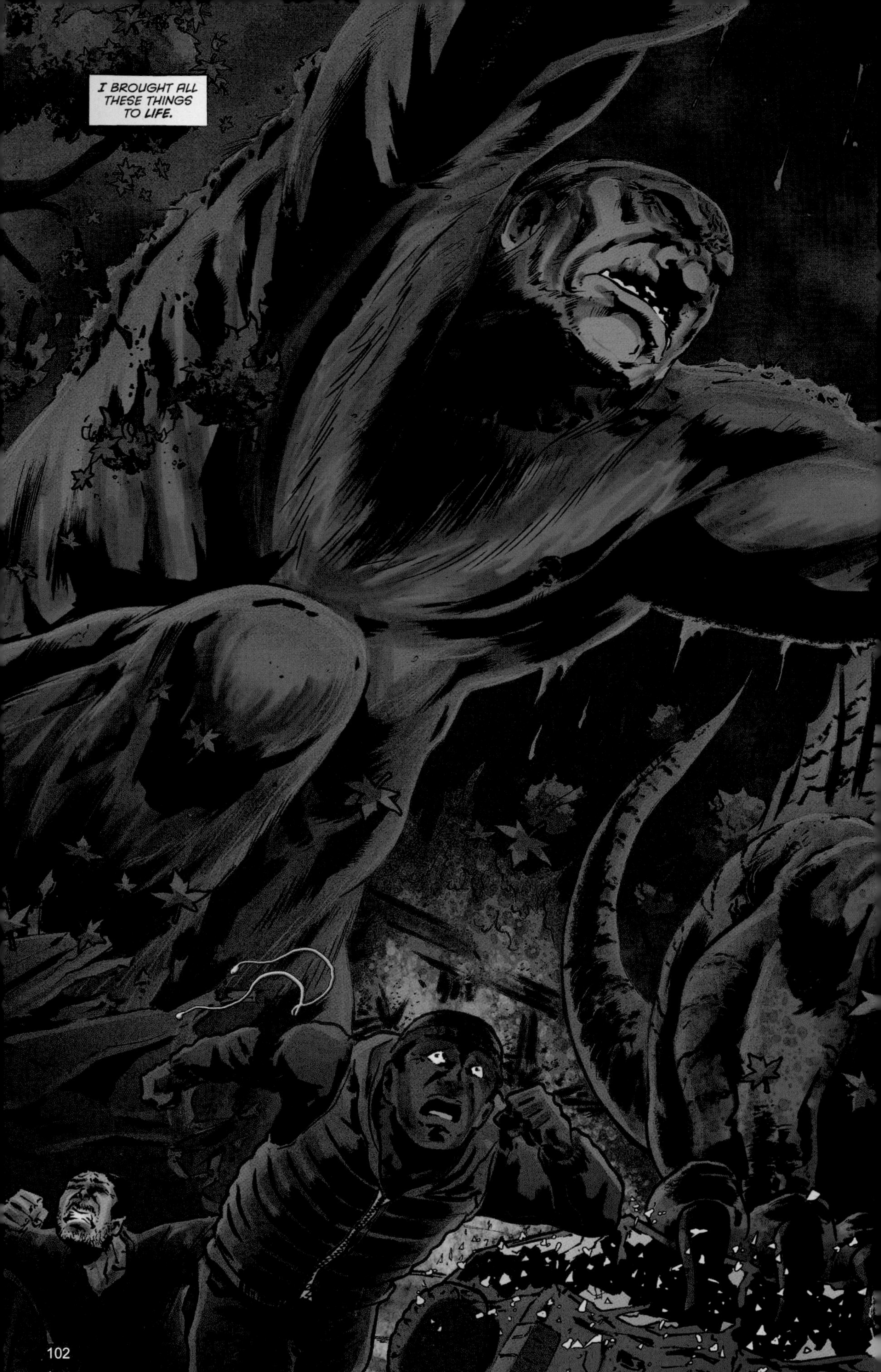
I BROUGHT ALL THESE THINGS TO LIFE.

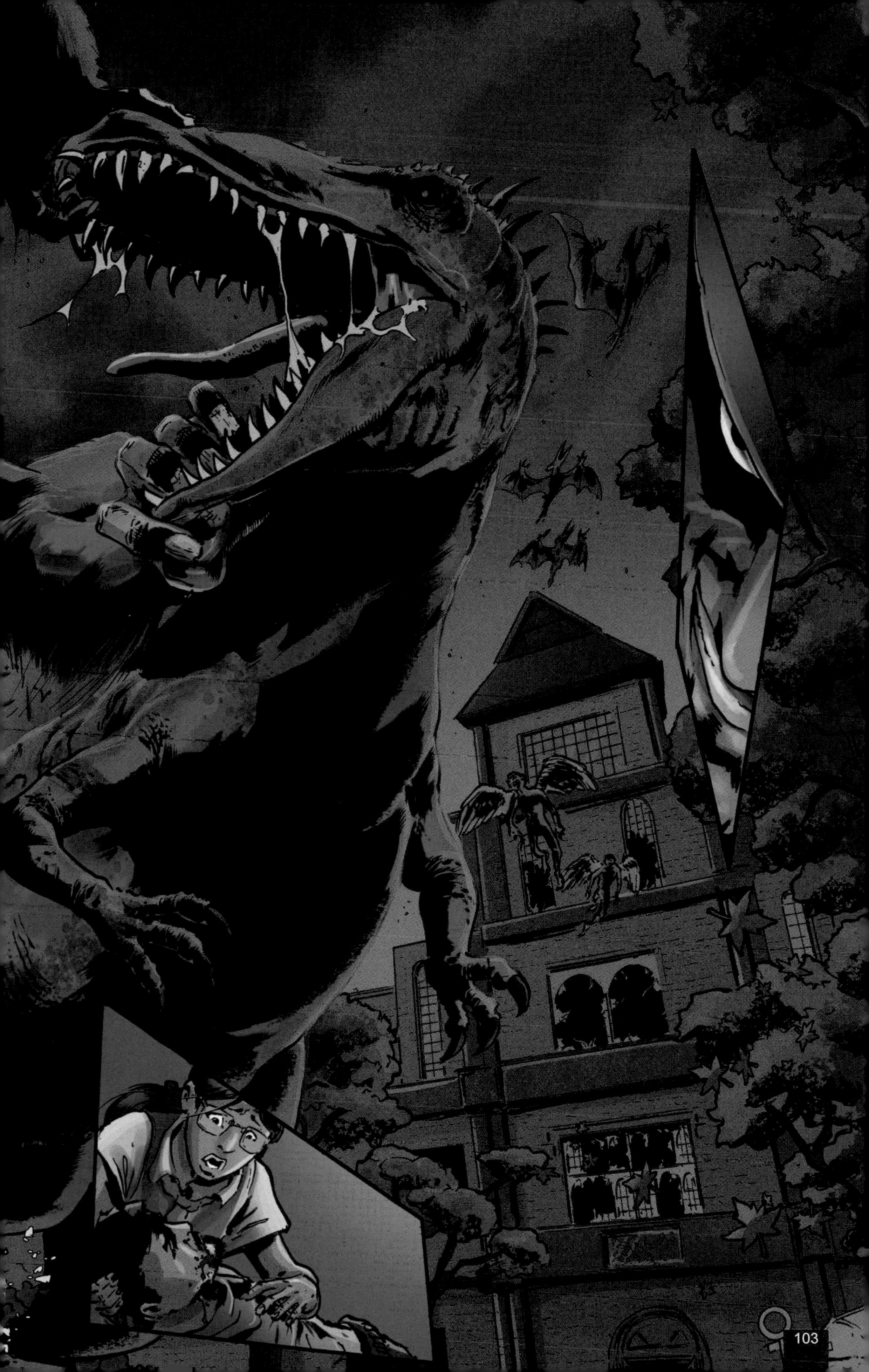

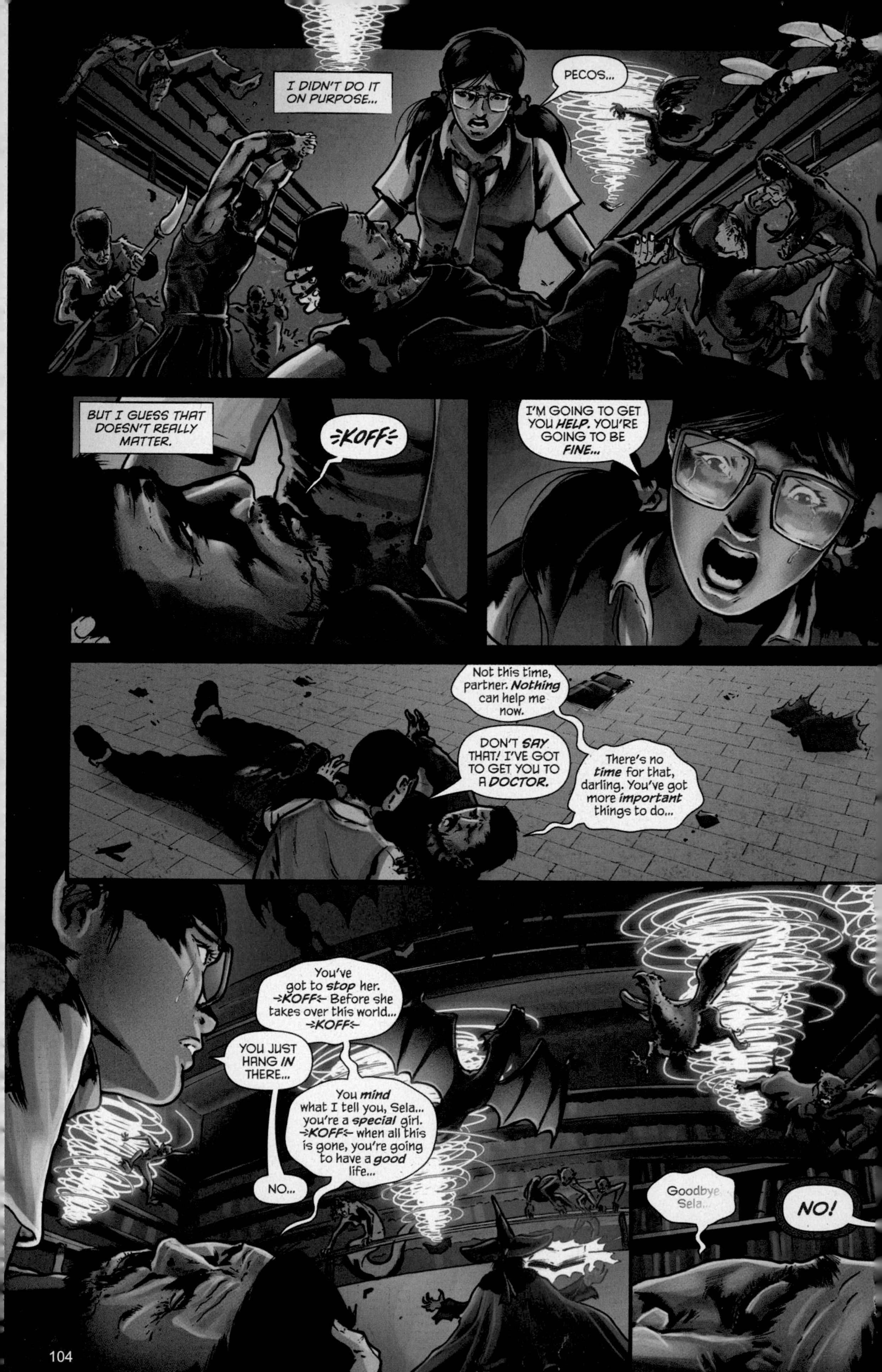
I DIDN'T DO IT ON PURPOSE...
PECOS...
BUT I GUESS THAT DOESN'T REALLY MATTER.
KOFF
I'M GOING TO GET YOU HELP. YOU'RE GOING TO BE FINE...
Not this time, partner. Nothing can help me now.
DON'T SAY THAT! I'VE GOT TO GET YOU TO A DOCTOR.
There's no time for that, darling. You've got more important things to do...
You've got to stop her. KOFF Before she takes over this world... KOFF
YOU JUST HANG IN THERE...
You mind what I tell you, Sela... you're a special girl. KOFF when all this is gone, you're going to have a good life...
NO...
Goodbye, Sela...
NO!

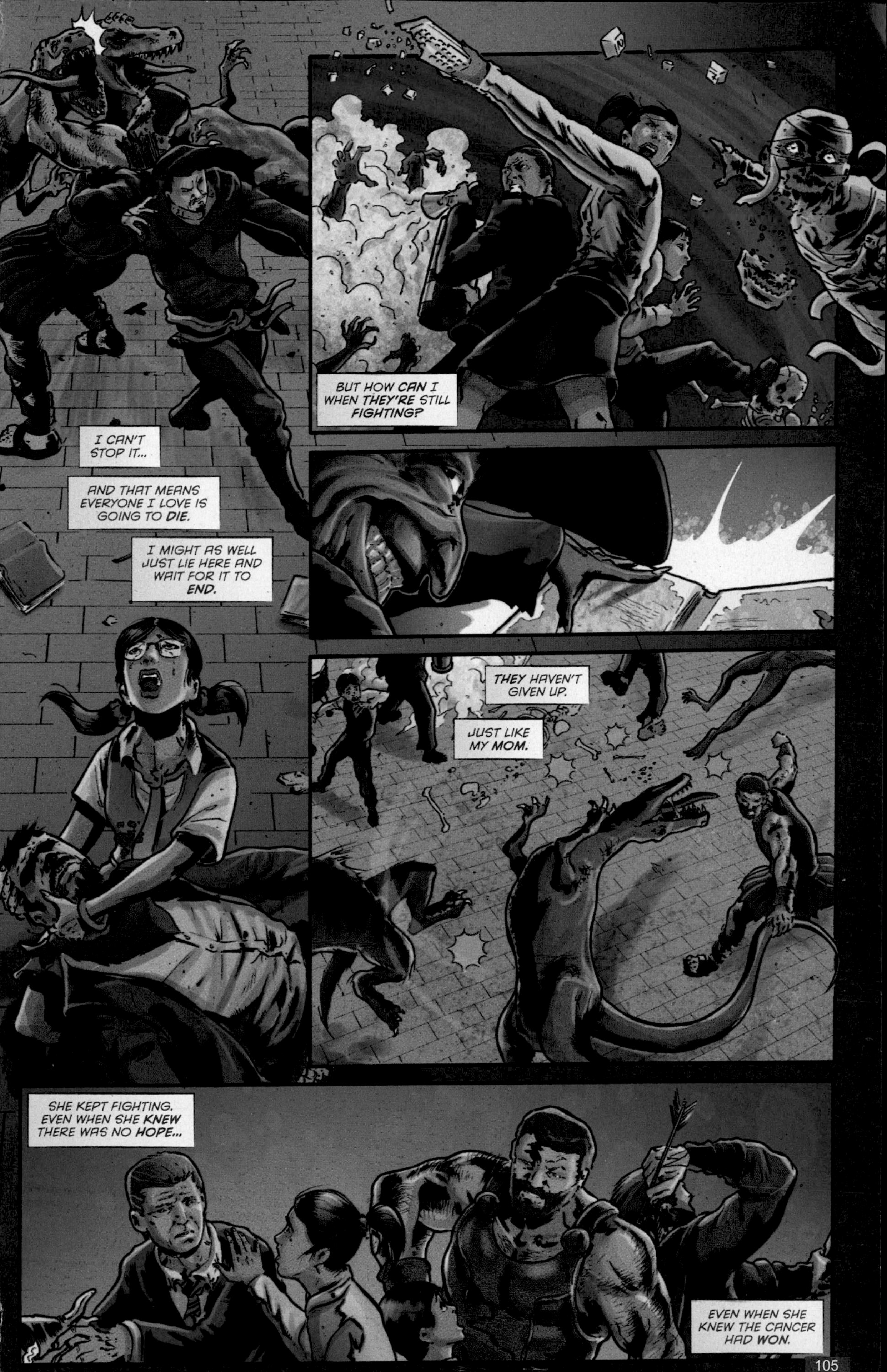
BUT HOW CAN I WHEN THEY'RE STILL FIGHTING?
I CAN'T STOP IT...
AND THAT MEANS EVERYONE I LOVE IS GOING TO DIE.
I MIGHT AS WELL JUST LIE HERE AND WAIT FOR IT TO END.
THEY HAVEN'T GIVEN UP.
JUST LIKE MY MOM.
SHE KEPT FIGHTING. EVEN WHEN SHE KNEW THERE WAS NO HOPE...
EVEN WHEN SHE KNEW THE CANCER HAD WON.

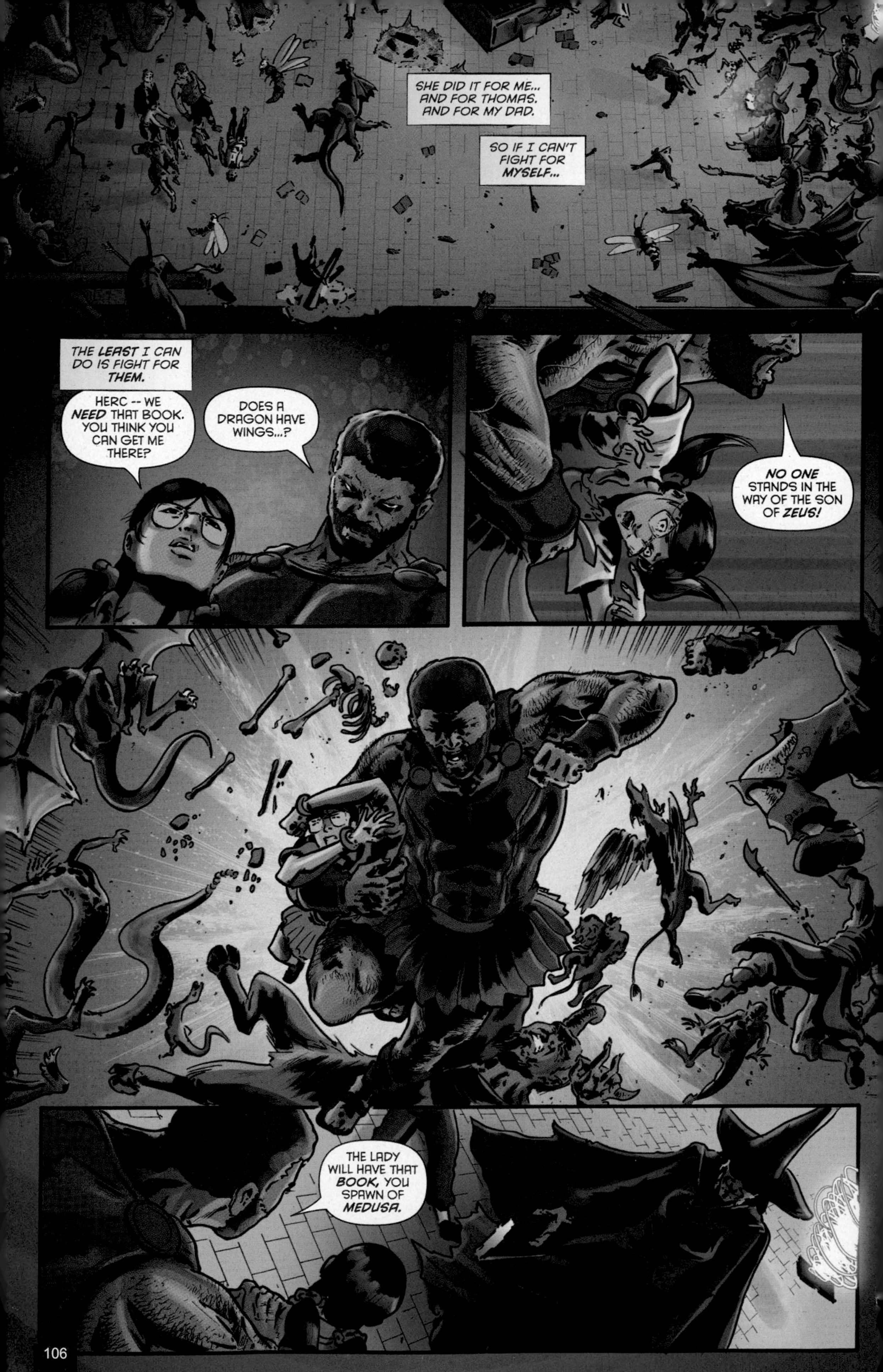

SHE DID IT FOR ME... AND FOR THOMAS. AND FOR MY DAD.
SO IF I CAN'T FIGHT FOR MYSELF...
THE LEAST I CAN DO IS FIGHT FOR THEM.
HERC -- WE NEED THAT BOOK. YOU THINK YOU CAN GET ME THERE?
DOES A DRAGON HAVE WINGS...?
NO ONE STANDS IN THE WAY OF THE SON OF ZEUS!
THE LADY WILL HAVE THAT BOOK, YOU SPAWN OF MEDUSA.

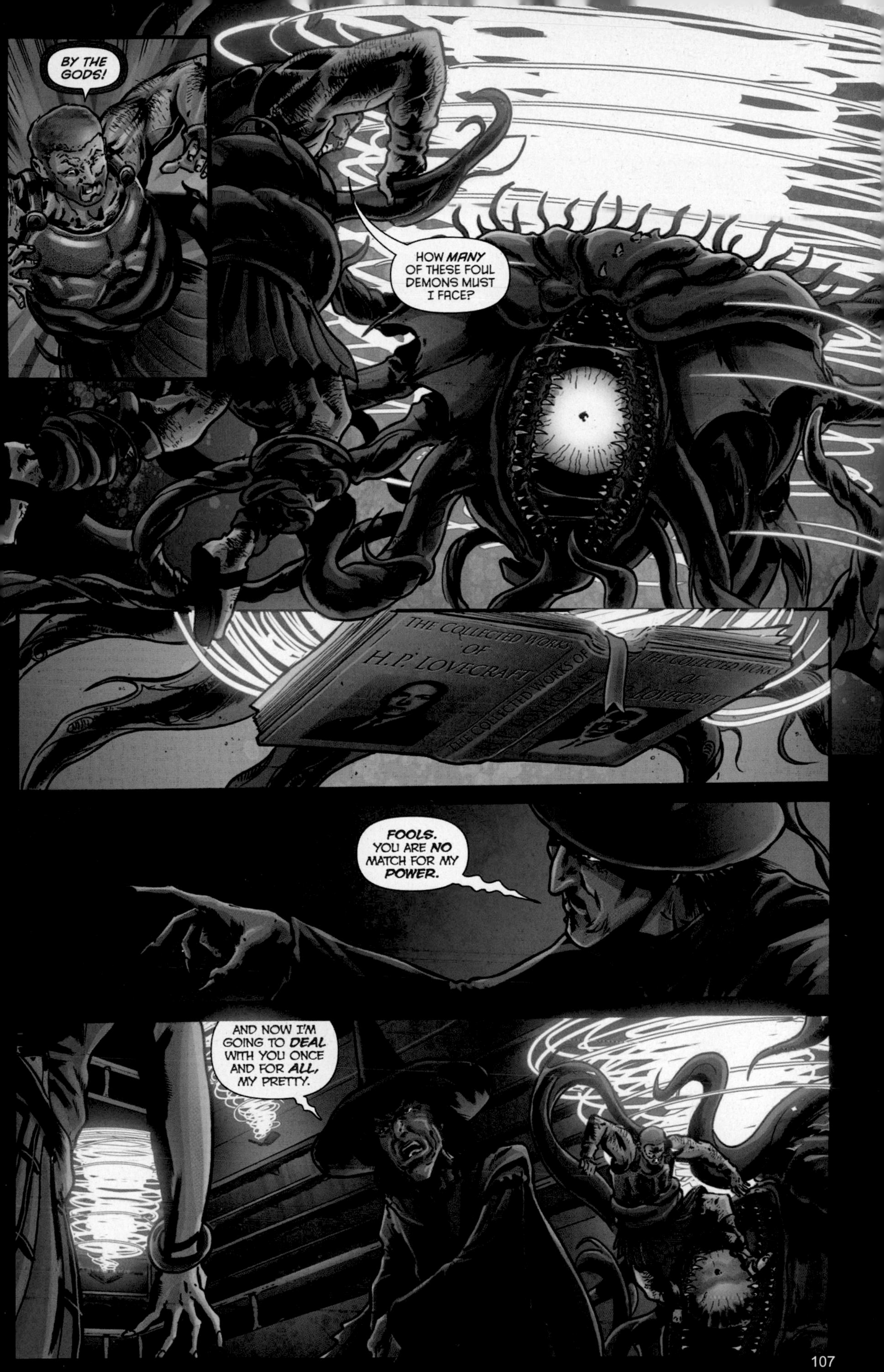
BY THE GODS!
HOW MANY OF THESE FOUL DEMONS MUST I FACE?
THE COLLECTED WORKS OF H.P. LOVECRAFT
FOOLS. YOU ARE NO MATCH FOR MY POWER.
AND NOW I'M GOING TO DEAL WITH YOU ONCE AND FOR ALL, MY PRETTY.

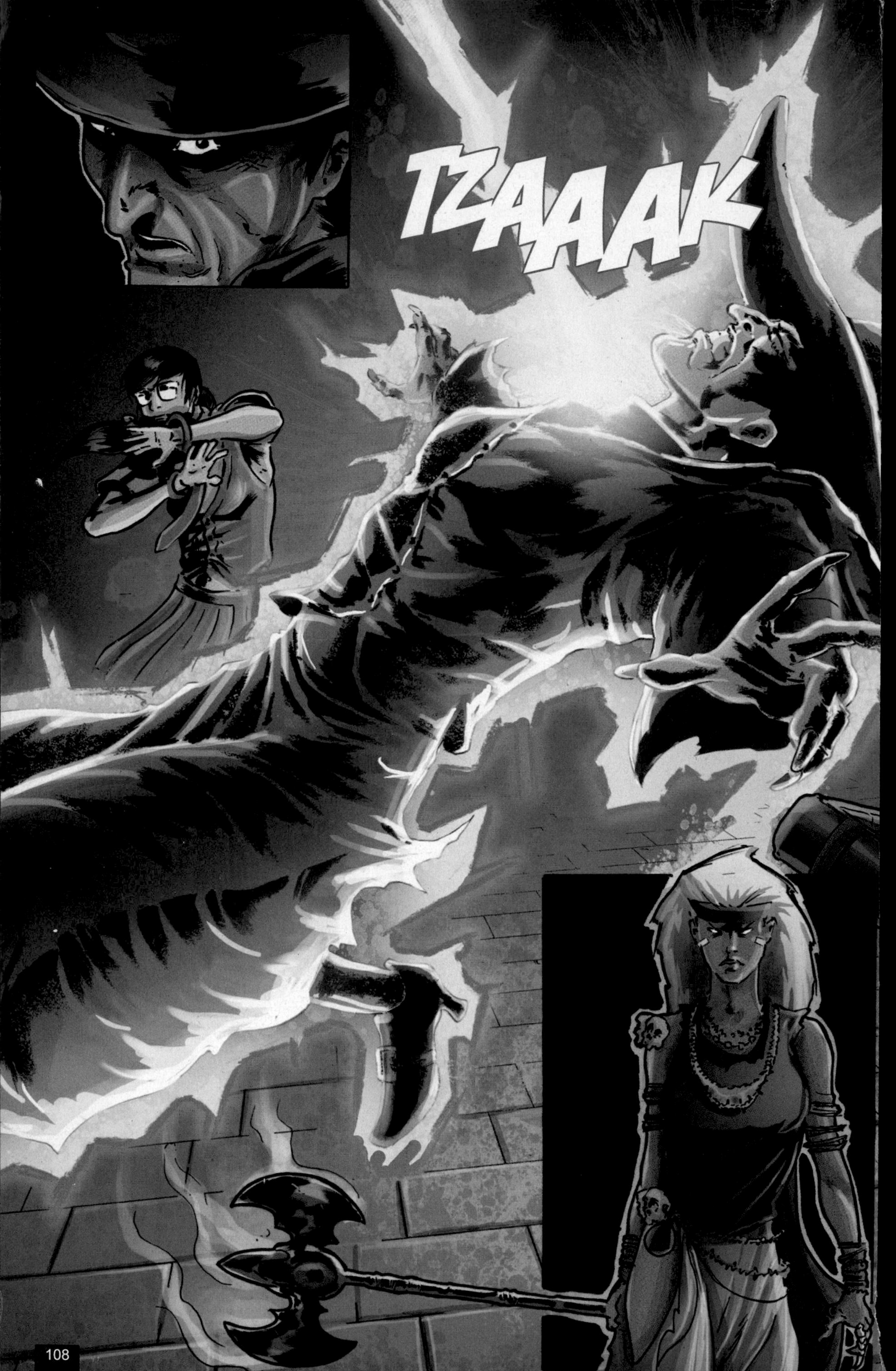
TZAAAK

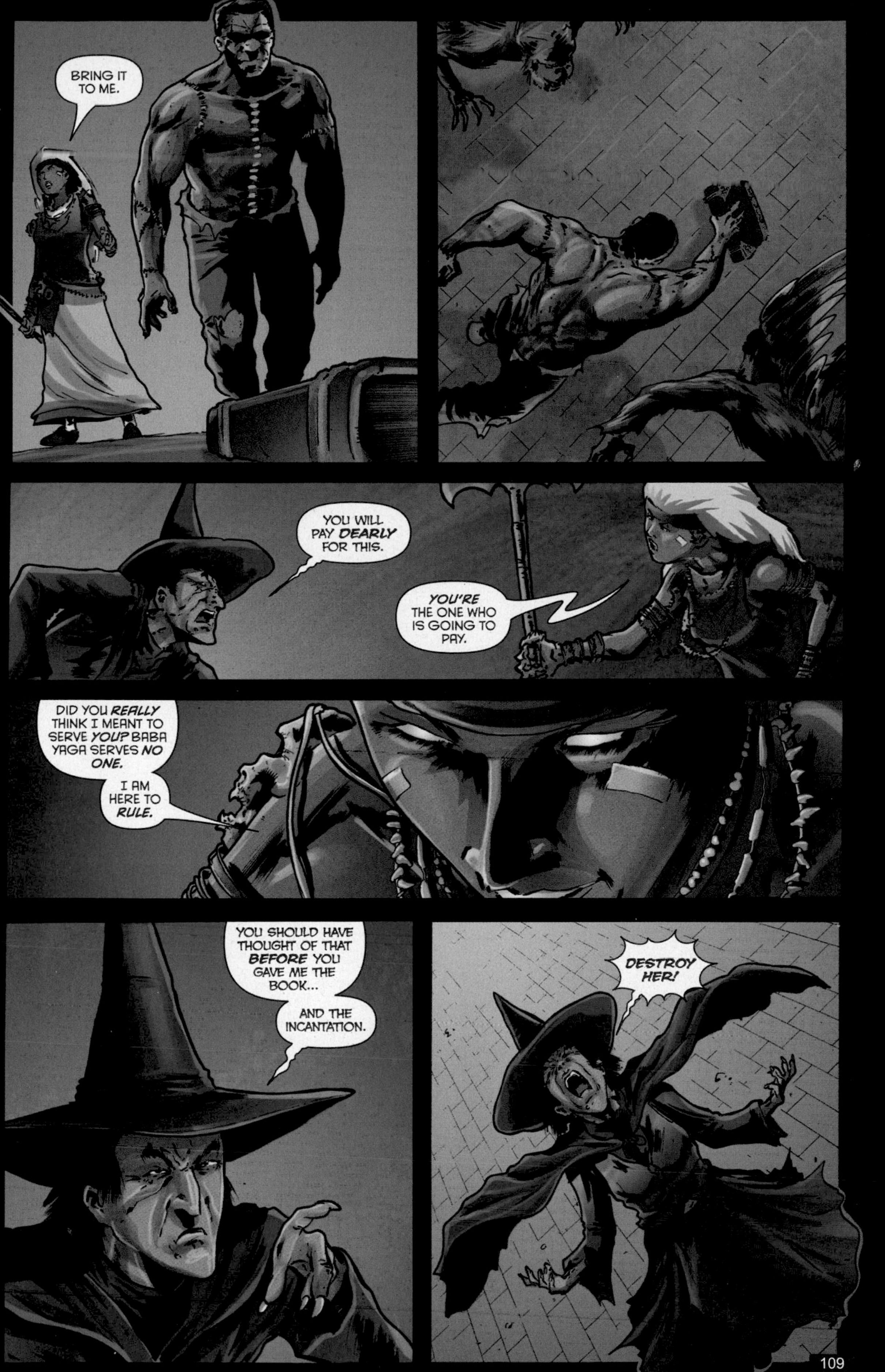
BRING IT TO ME.
YOU WILL PAY DEARLY FOR THIS.
YOU'RE THE ONE WHO IS GOING TO PAY.
DID YOU REALLY THINK I MEANT TO SERVE YOU? BABA YAGA SERVES NO ONE.
I AM HERE TO RULE.
YOU SHOULD HAVE THOUGHT OF THAT BEFORE YOU GAVE ME THE BOOK...
AND THE INCANTATION.
DESTROY HER!

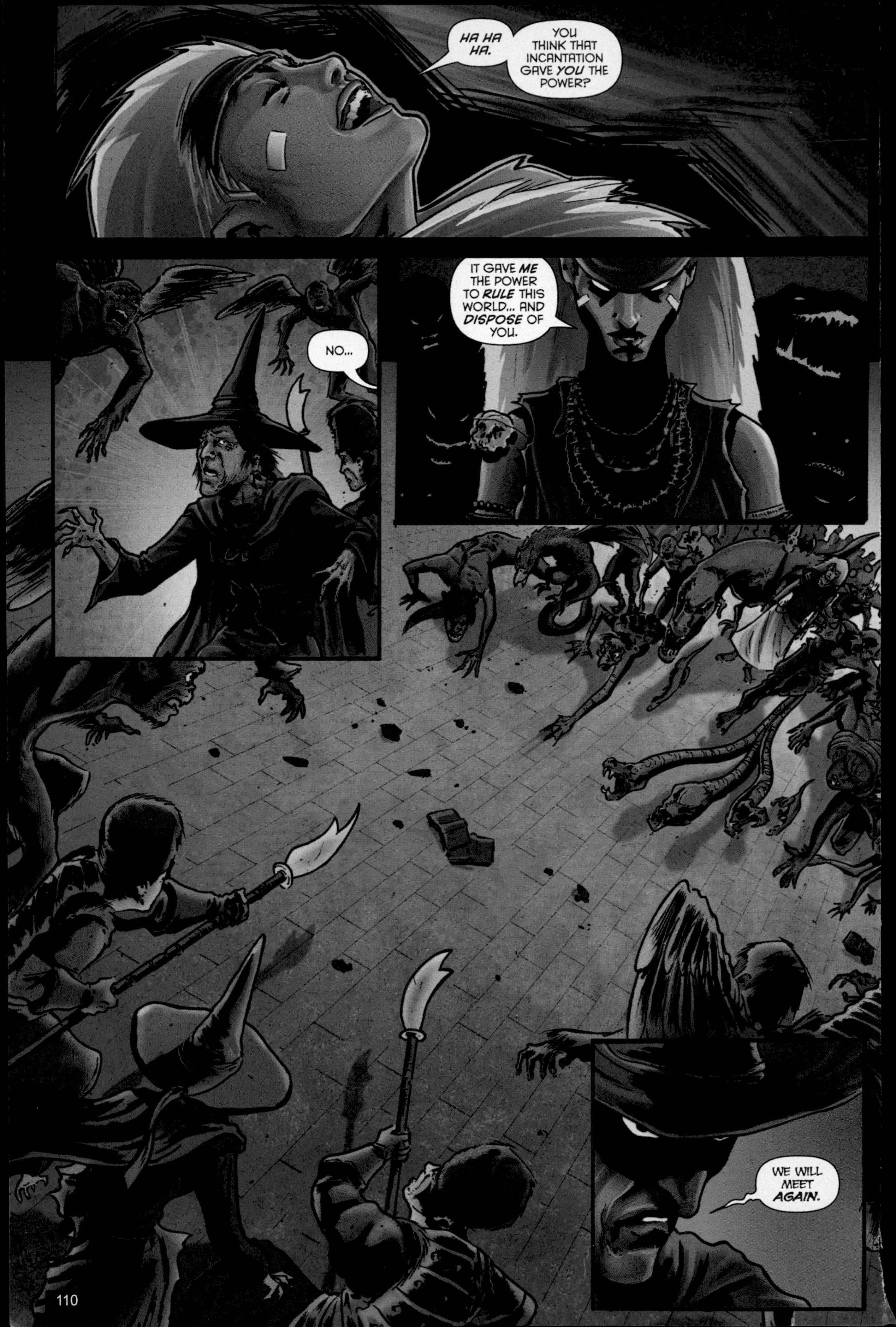
HA HA HA.
YOU THINK THAT INCANTATION GAVE YOU THE POWER?
NO...
IT GAVE ME THE POWER TO RULE THIS WORLD... AND DISPOSE OF YOU.
WE WILL MEET AGAIN.

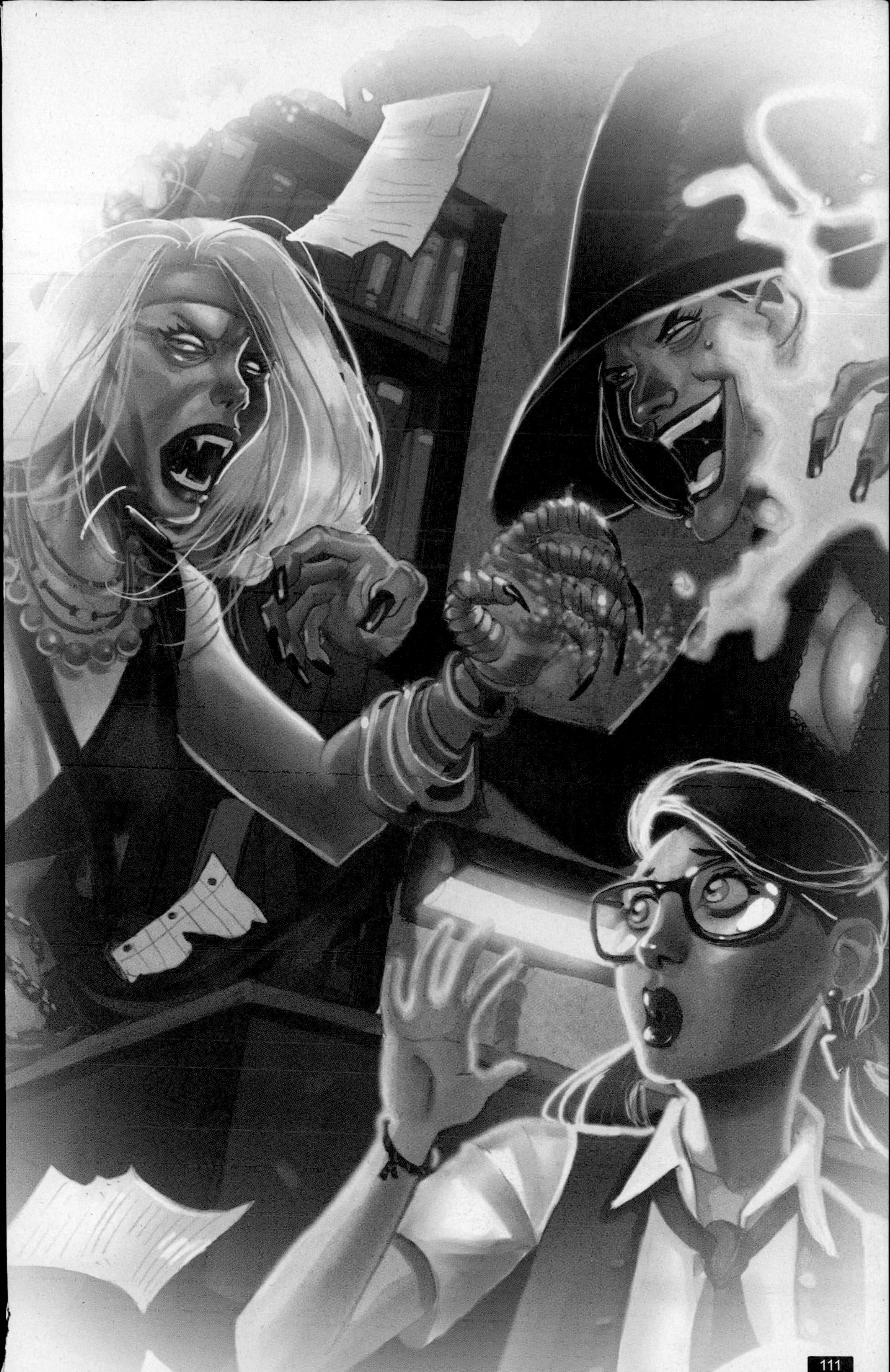

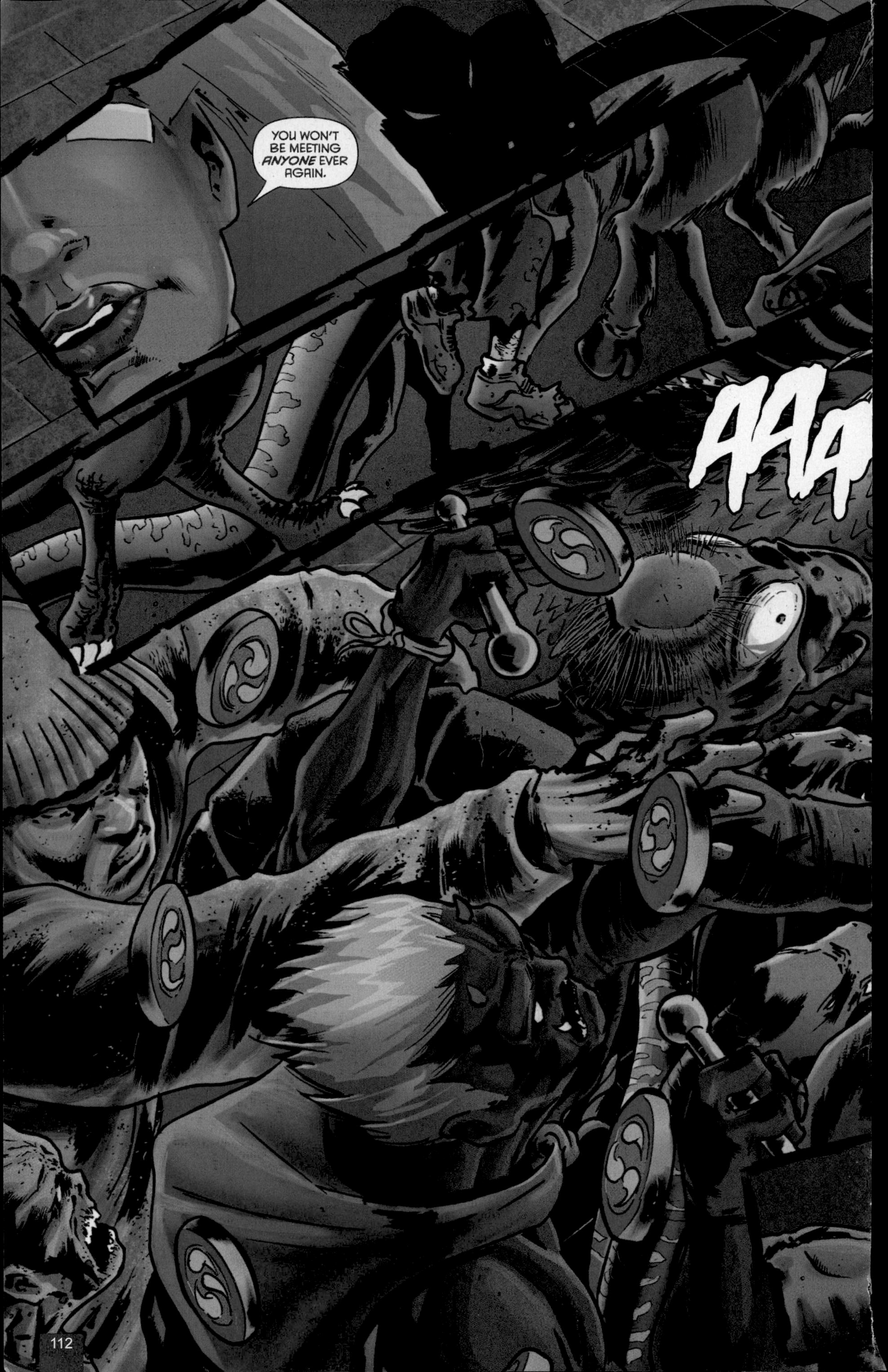
YOU WON'T BE MEETING ANYONE EVER AGAIN.
AAA

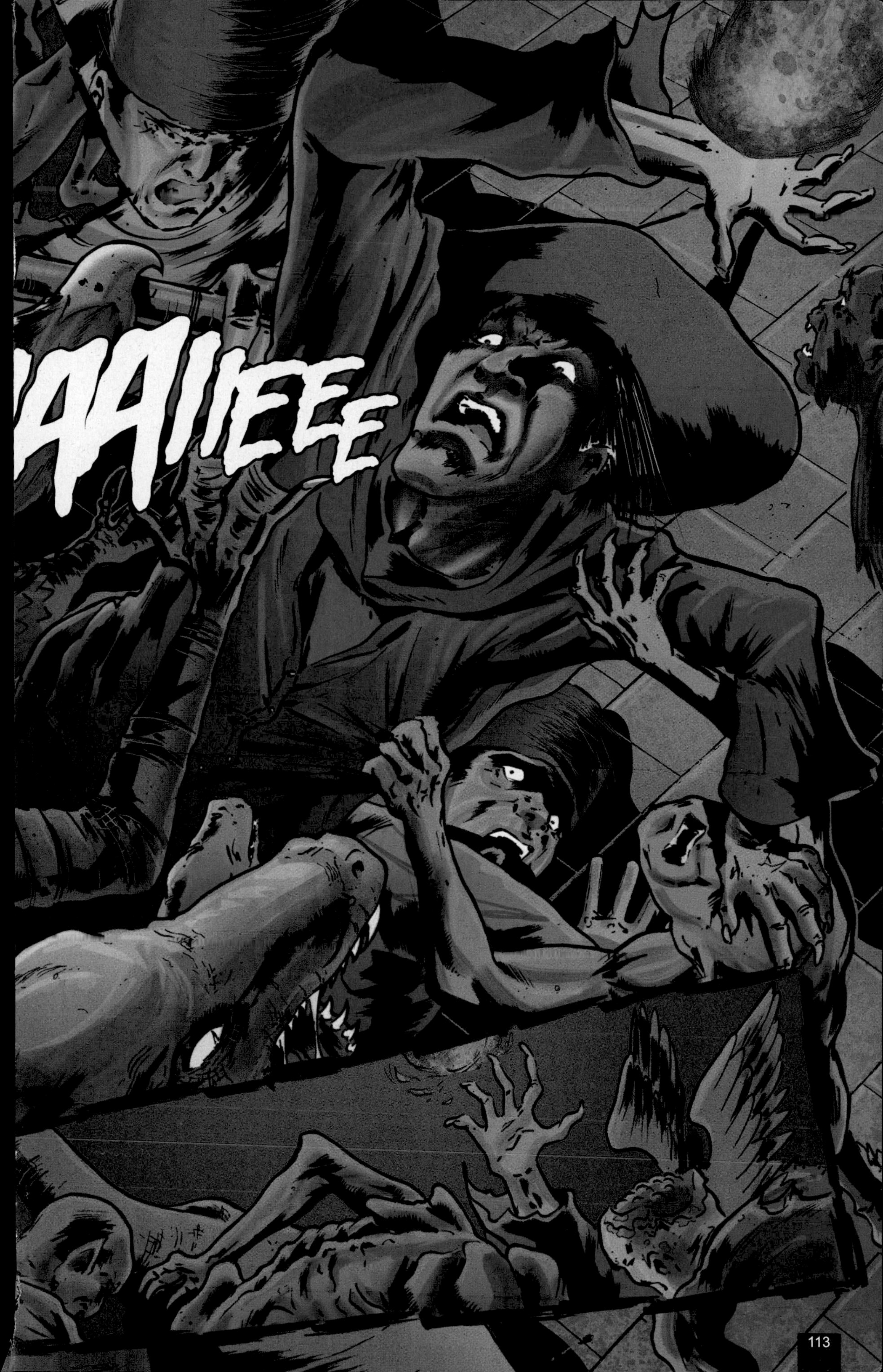
AAAIIEEE

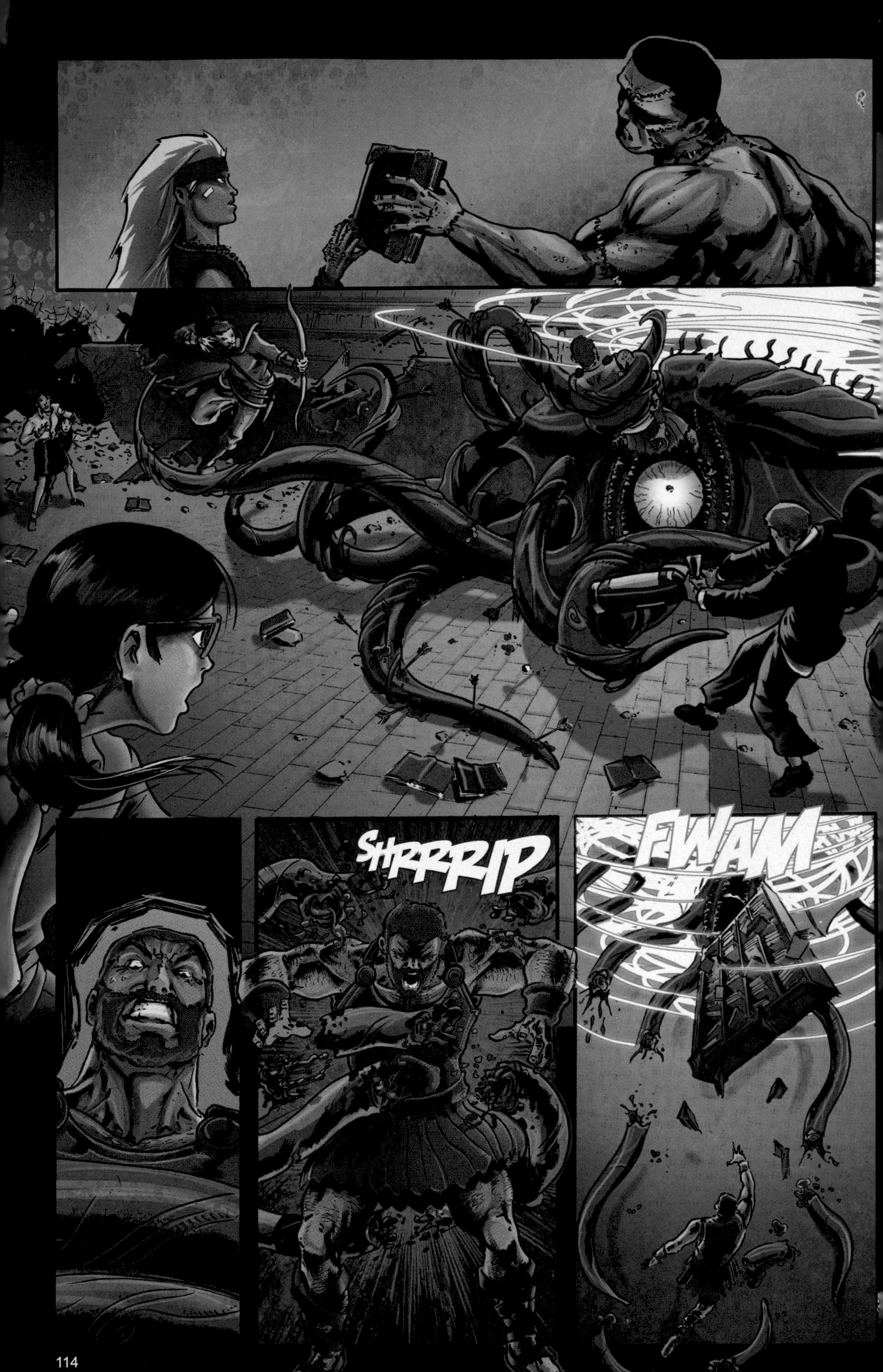
SHRRRIP
FWAM

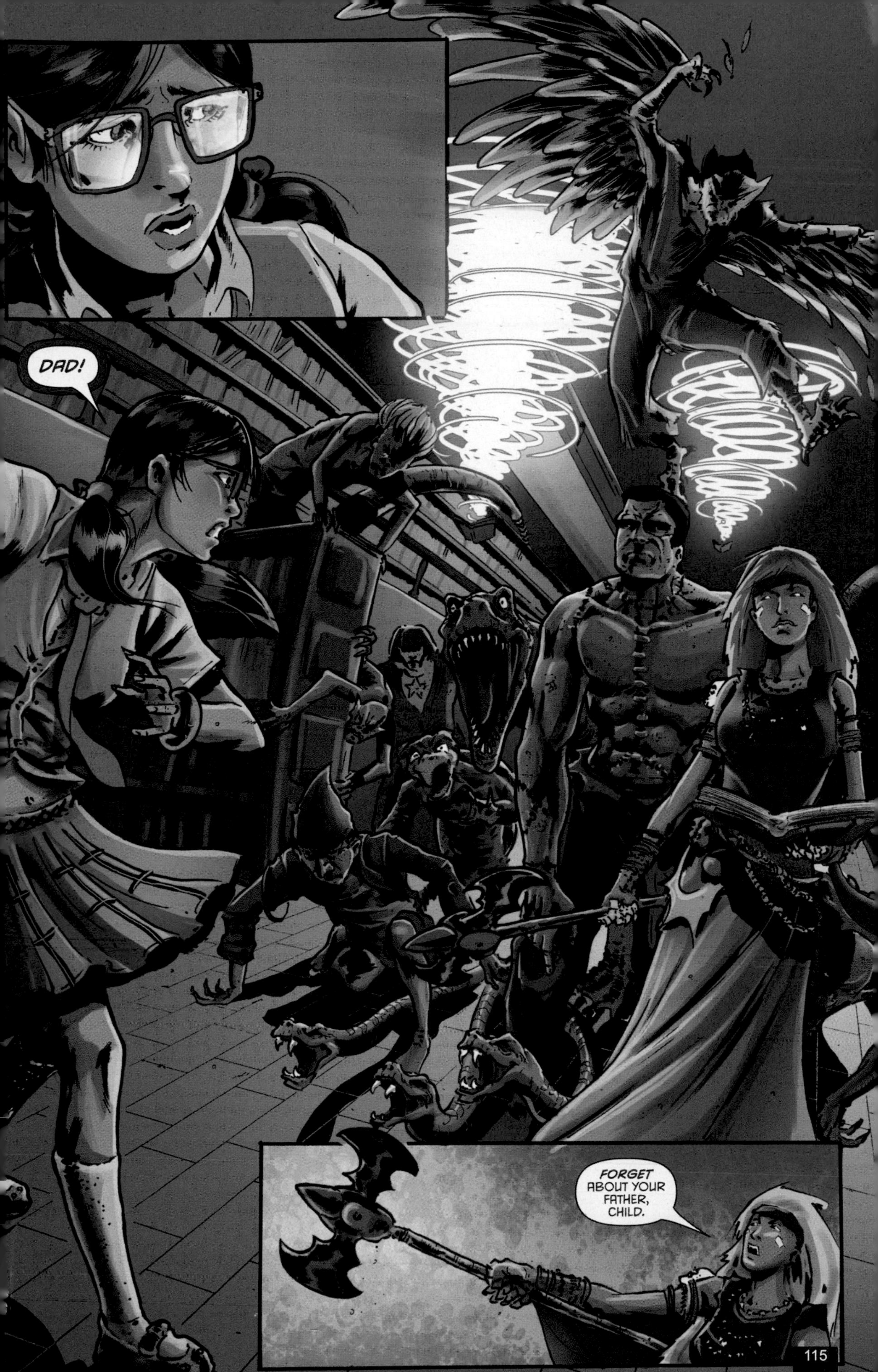
DAD!
FORGET ABOUT YOUR FATHER, CHILD.

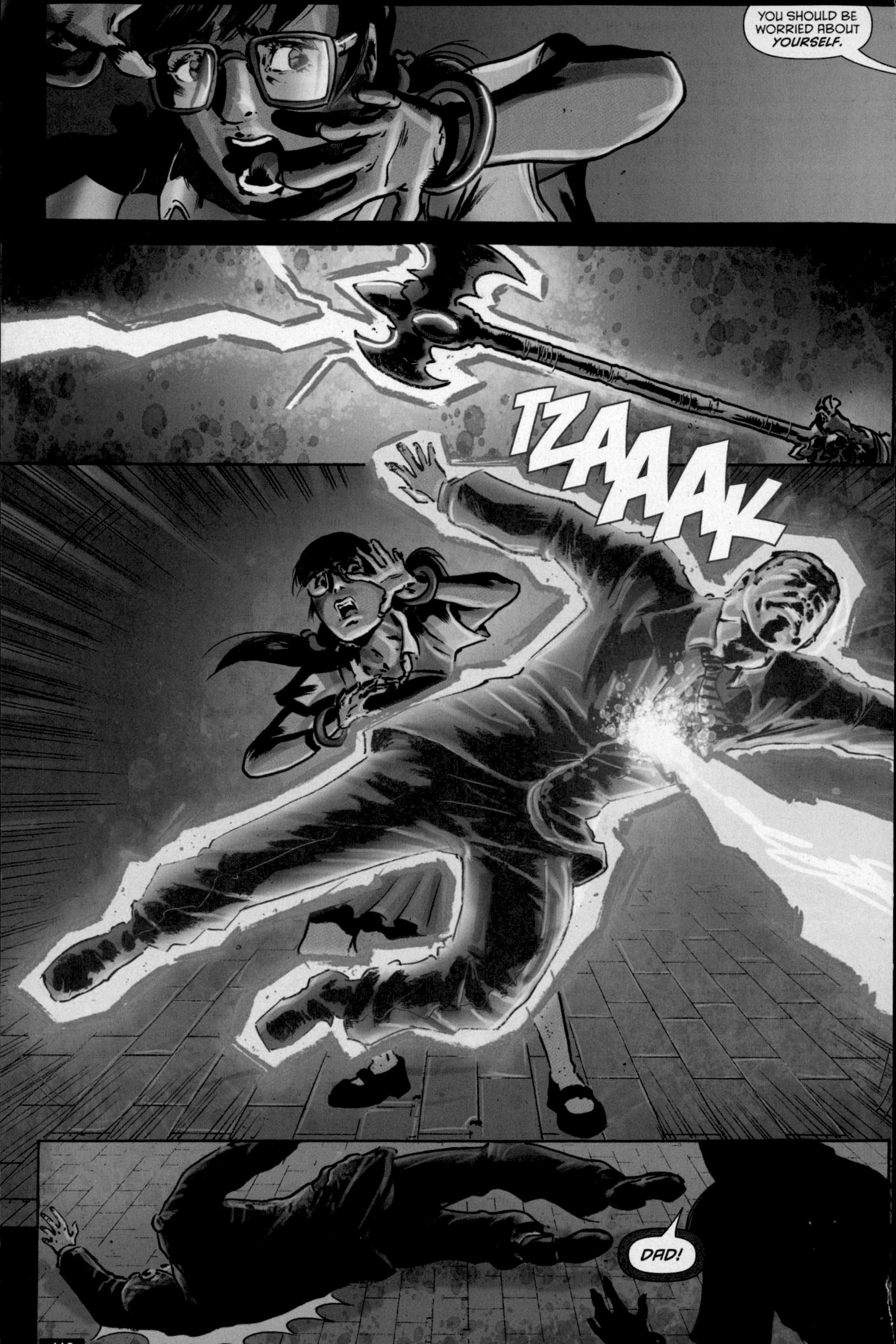
YOU SHOULD BE WORRIED ABOUT *YOURSELF.*
TZAAAAK
DAD!

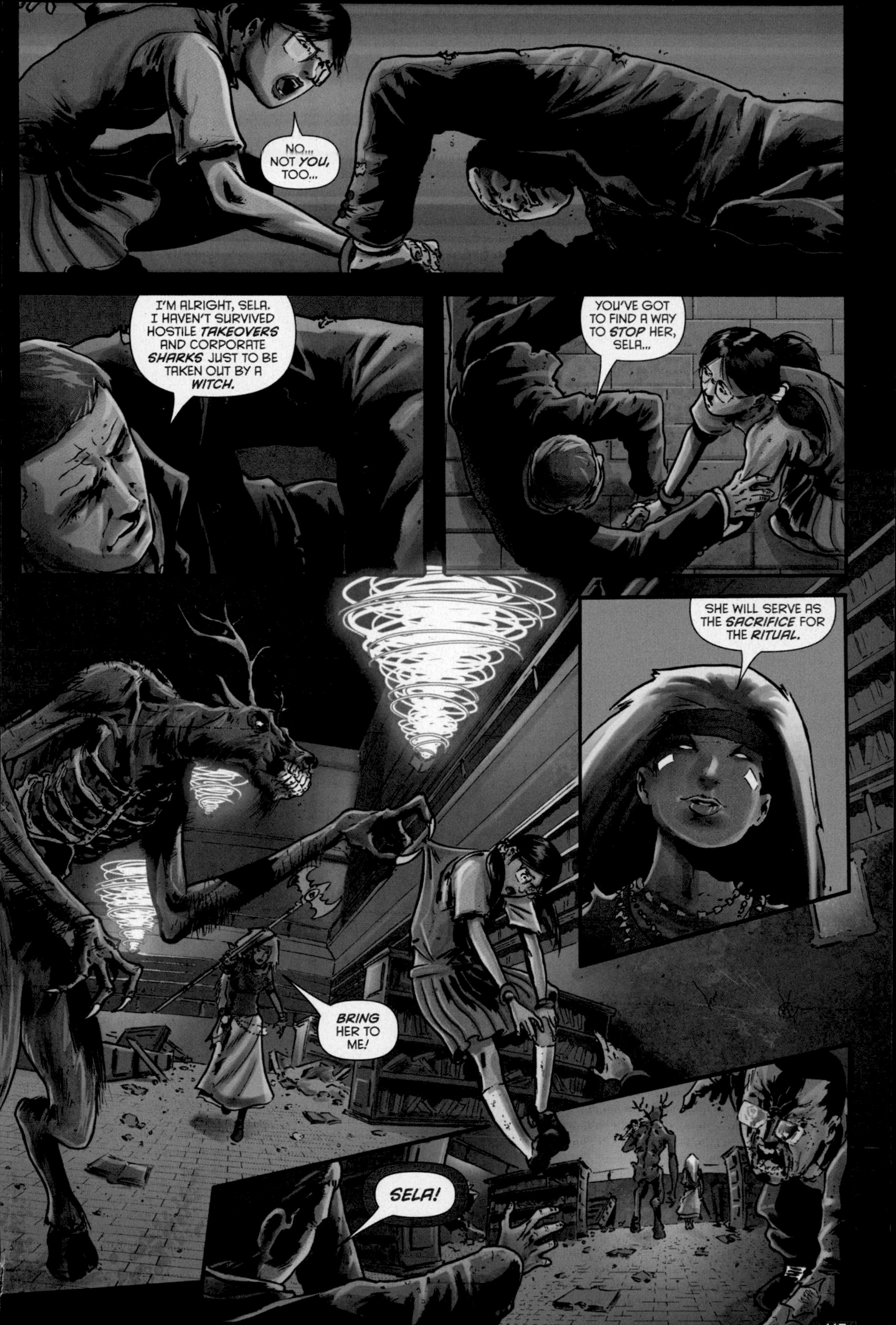
NO... NOT *YOU,* TOO...
I'M ALRIGHT, SELA. I HAVEN'T SURVIVED HOSTILE *TAKEOVERS* AND CORPORATE *SHARKS* JUST TO BE TAKEN OUT BY A *WITCH.*
YOU'VE GOT TO FIND A WAY TO *STOP* HER, SELA...
SHE WILL SERVE AS THE *SACRIFICE* FOR THE *RITUAL.*
BRING HER TO ME!
SELA!

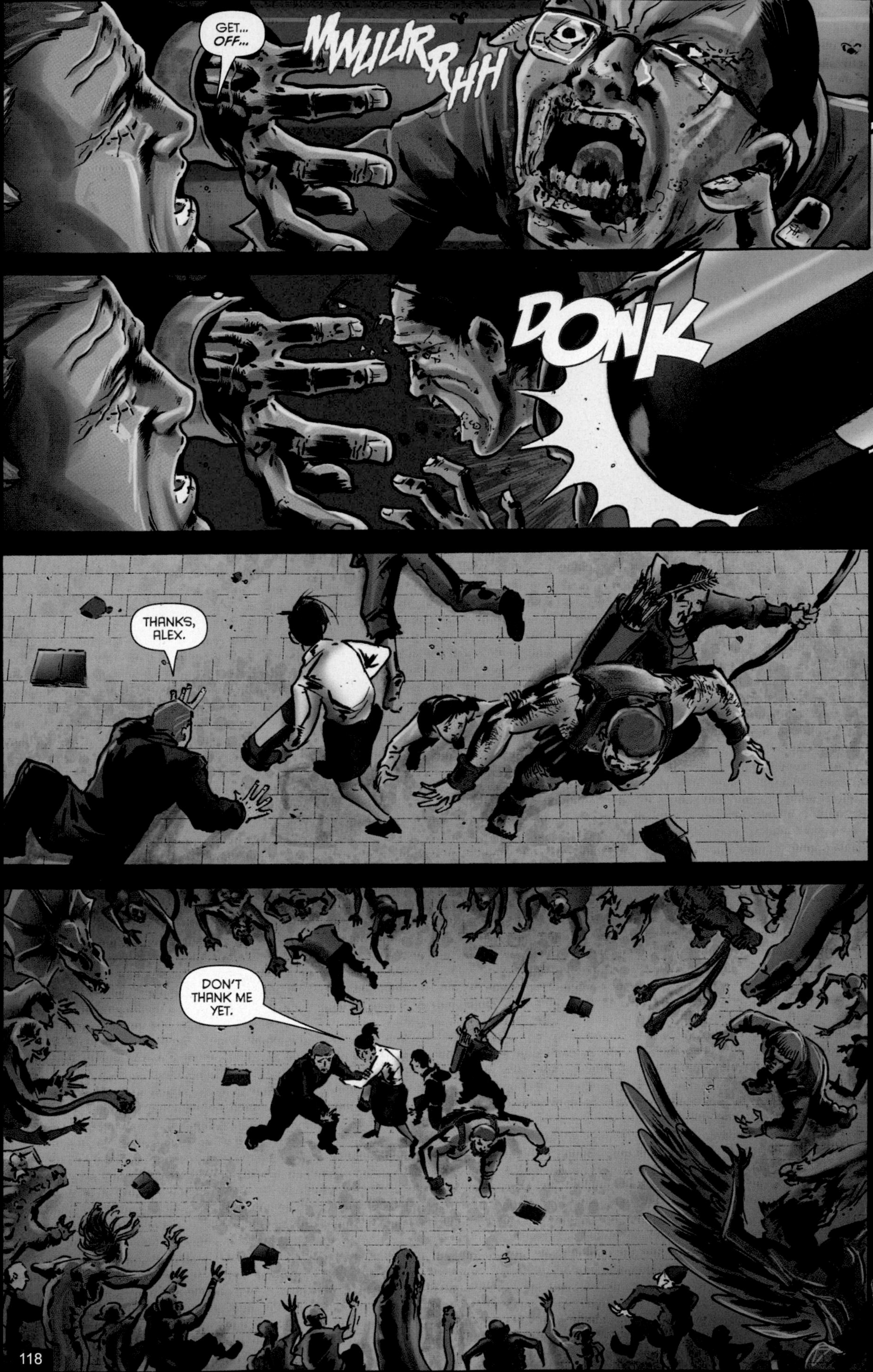
GET... OFF...
MWUURRHH
DONK
THANKS, ALEX.
DON'T THANK ME YET.

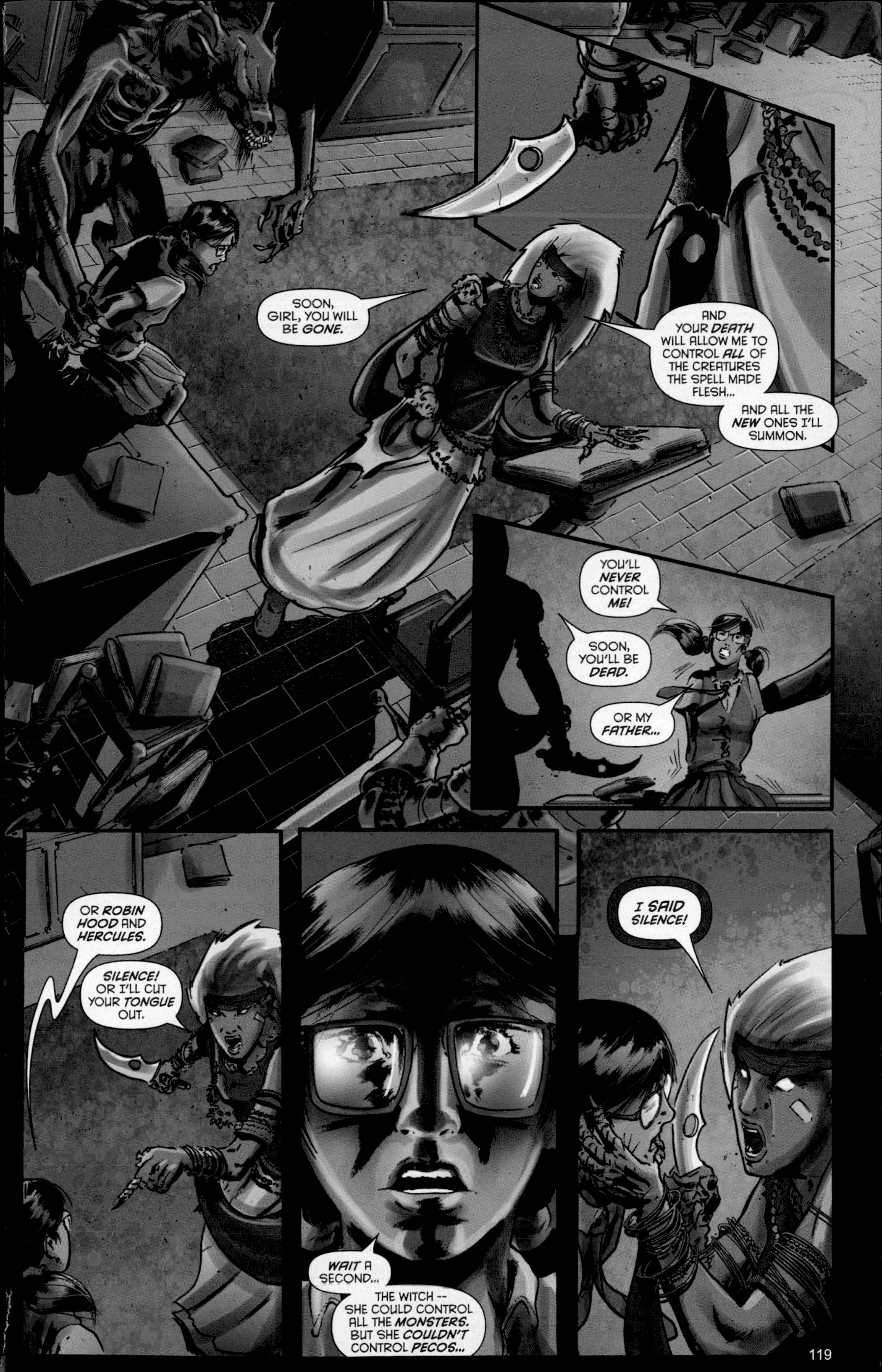
SOON, GIRL, YOU WILL BE GONE.
AND YOUR DEATH WILL ALLOW ME TO CONTROL ALL OF THE CREATURES THE SPELL MADE FLESH...
AND ALL THE NEW ONES I'LL SUMMON.
YOU'LL NEVER CONTROL ME!
SOON, YOU'LL BE DEAD.
OR MY FATHER...
OR ROBIN HOOD AND HERCULES.
SILENCE! OR I'LL CUT YOUR TONGUE OUT.
WAIT A SECOND...
THE WITCH -- SHE COULD CONTROL ALL THE MONSTERS. BUT SHE COULDN'T CONTROL PECOS...
I SAID SILENCE!

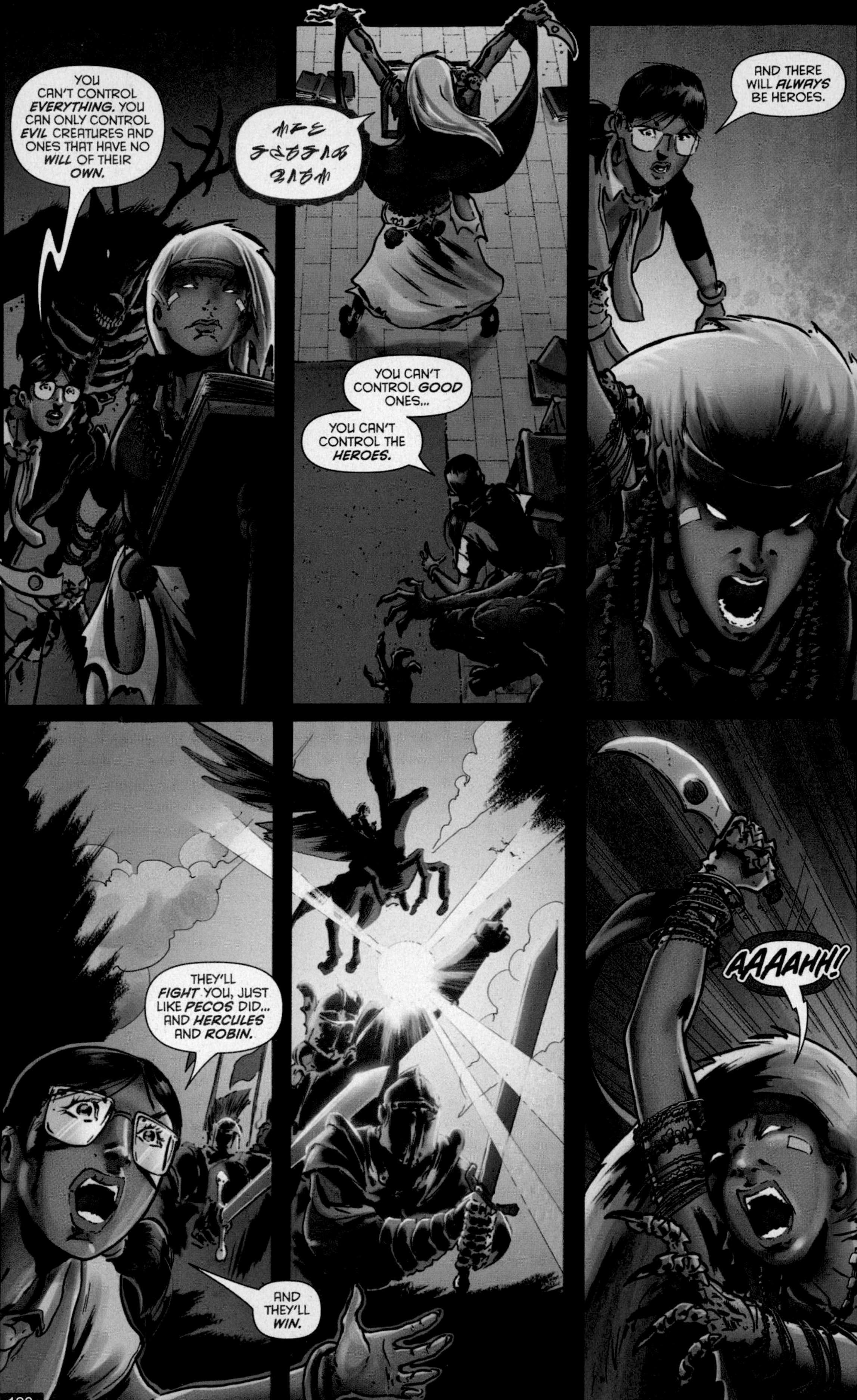

YOU CAN'T CONTROL *EVERYTHING.* YOU CAN ONLY CONTROL *EVIL* CREATURES AND ONES THAT HAVE NO *WILL* OF THEIR *OWN.*
YOU CAN'T CONTROL *GOOD* ONES...
YOU CAN'T CONTROL THE *HEROES.*
AND THERE WILL *ALWAYS* BE HEROES.
THEY'LL *FIGHT* YOU, JUST LIKE *PECOS* DID... AND *HERCULES* AND *ROBIN.*
AND THEY'LL *WIN.*
AAAAHH!

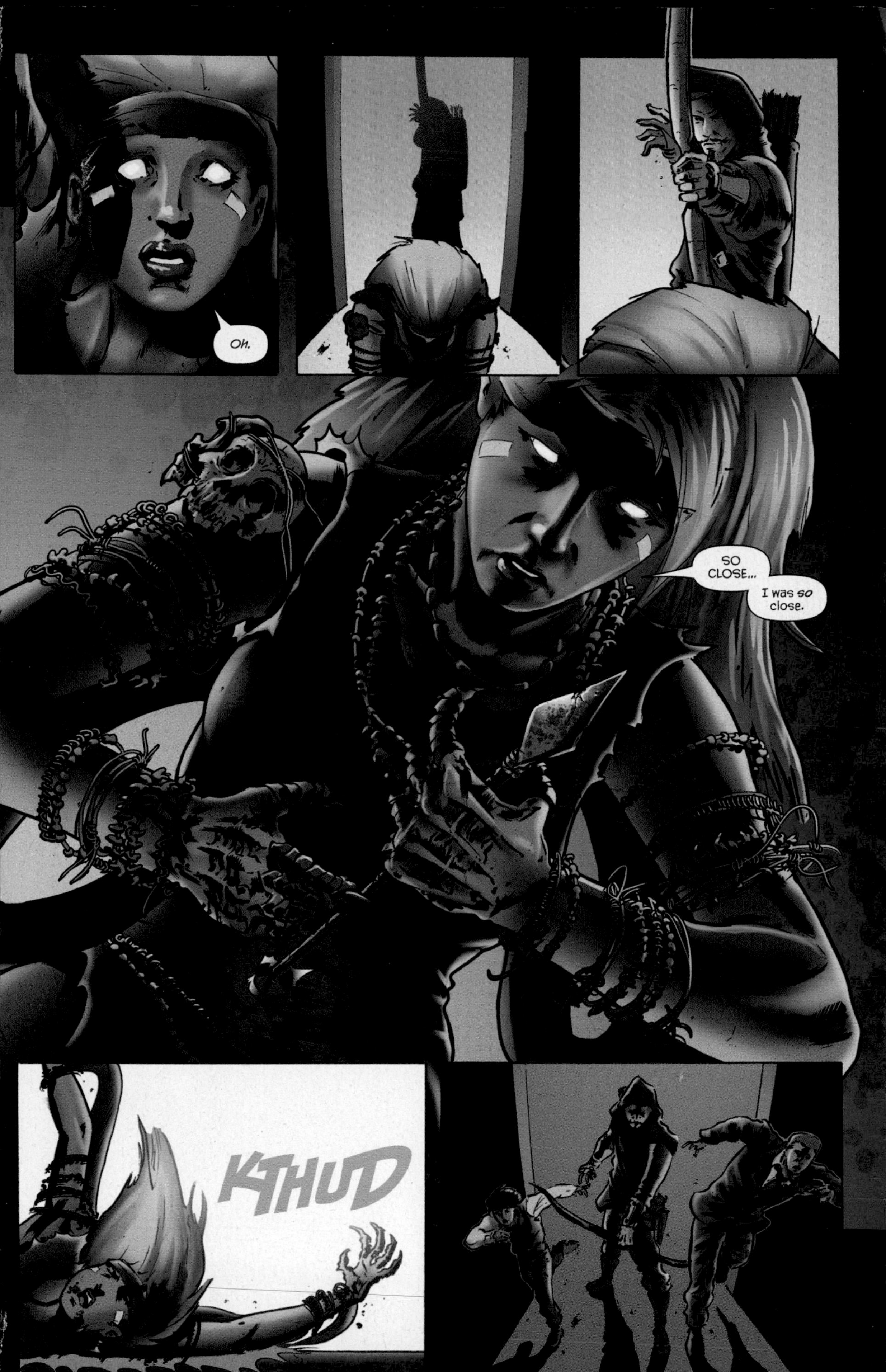
Oh.
SO CLOSE...
I was *so* close.
KTHUD

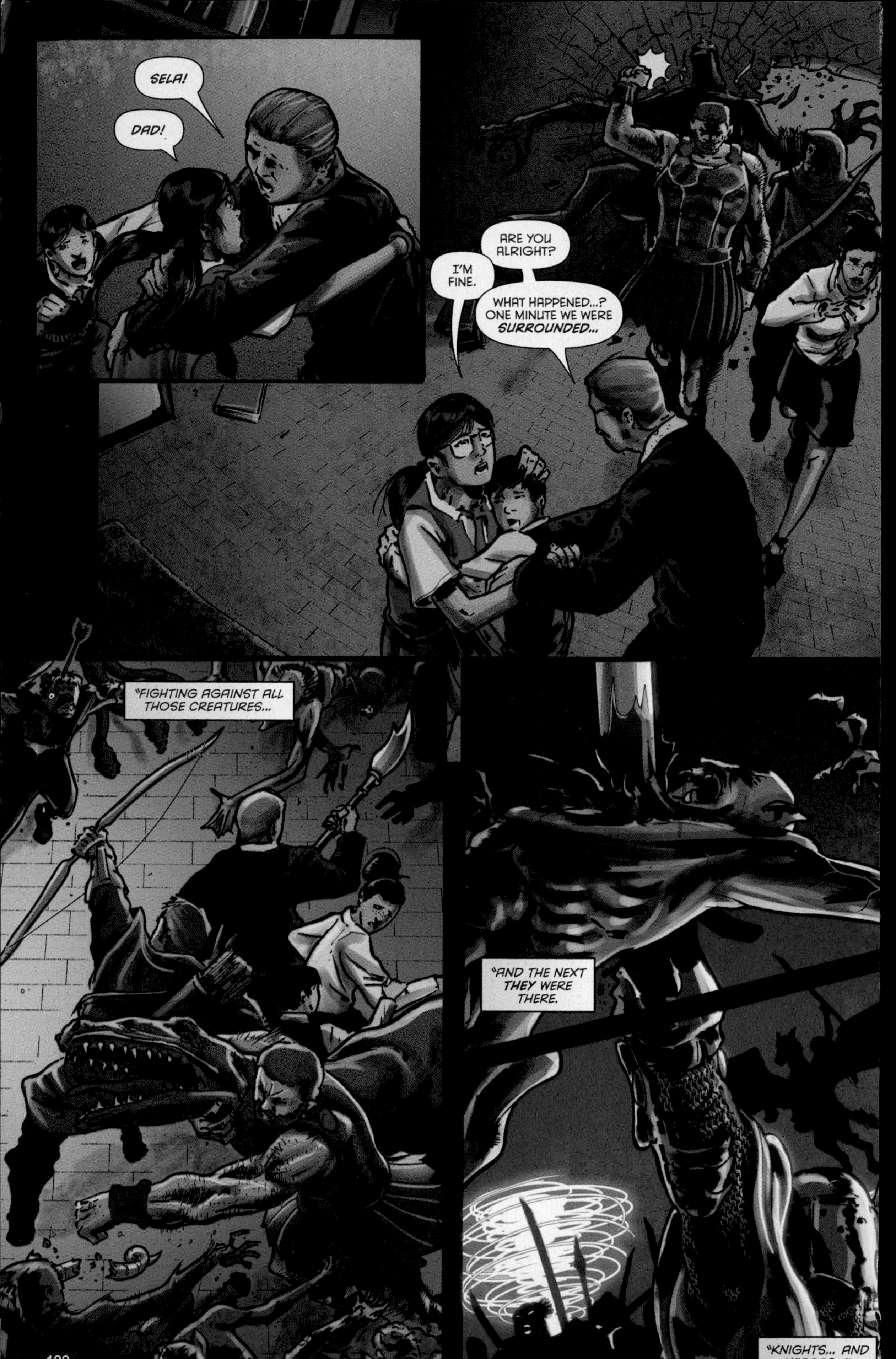
SELA!
DAD!
ARE YOU ALRIGHT?
I'M FINE.
WHAT HAPPENED...? ONE MINUTE WE WERE SURROUNDED...
"FIGHTING AGAINST ALL THOSE CREATURES...
"AND THE NEXT THEY WERE THERE.
"KNIGHTS... AND HEROES..."

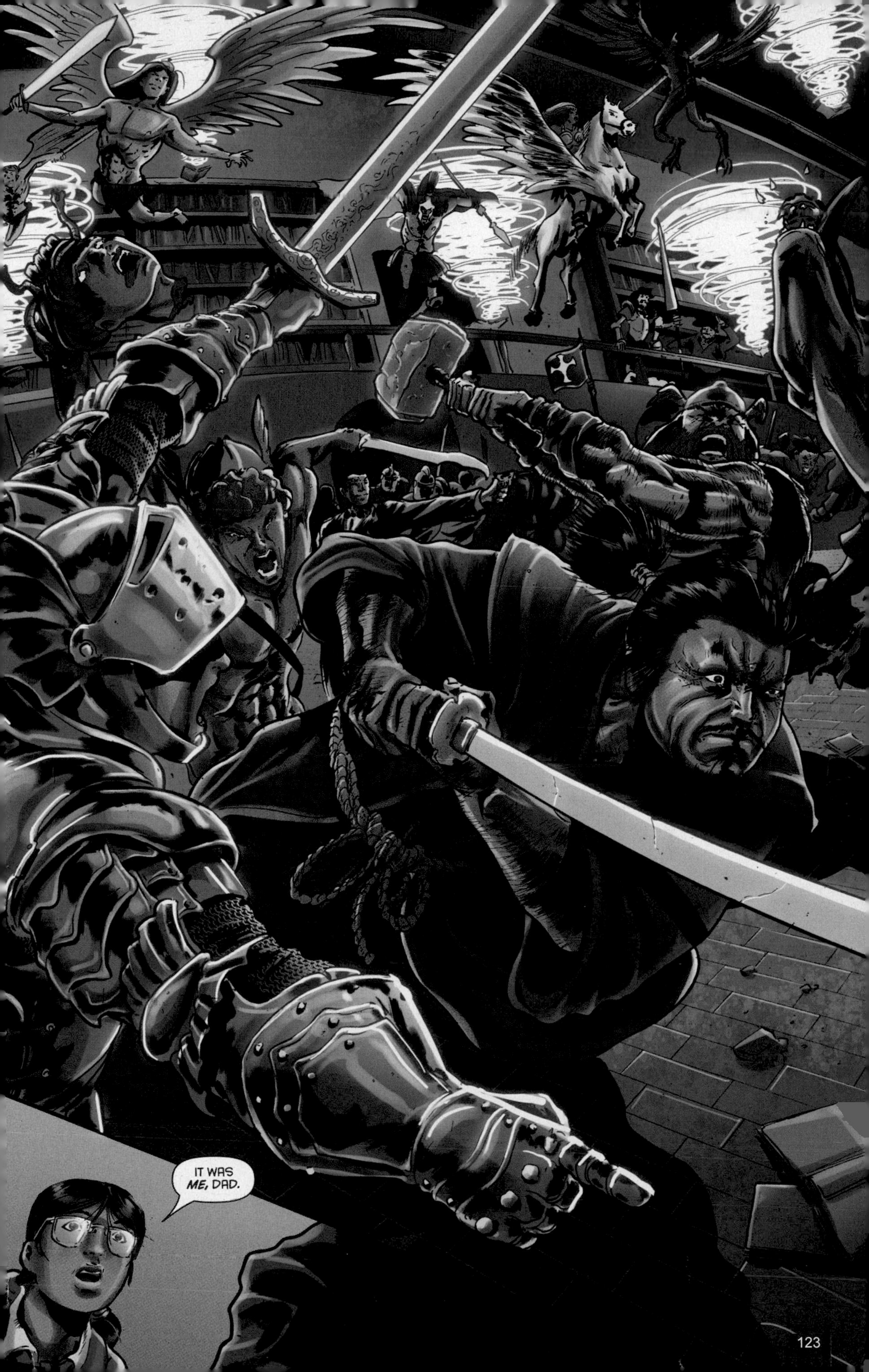
IT WAS *ME*, DAD.

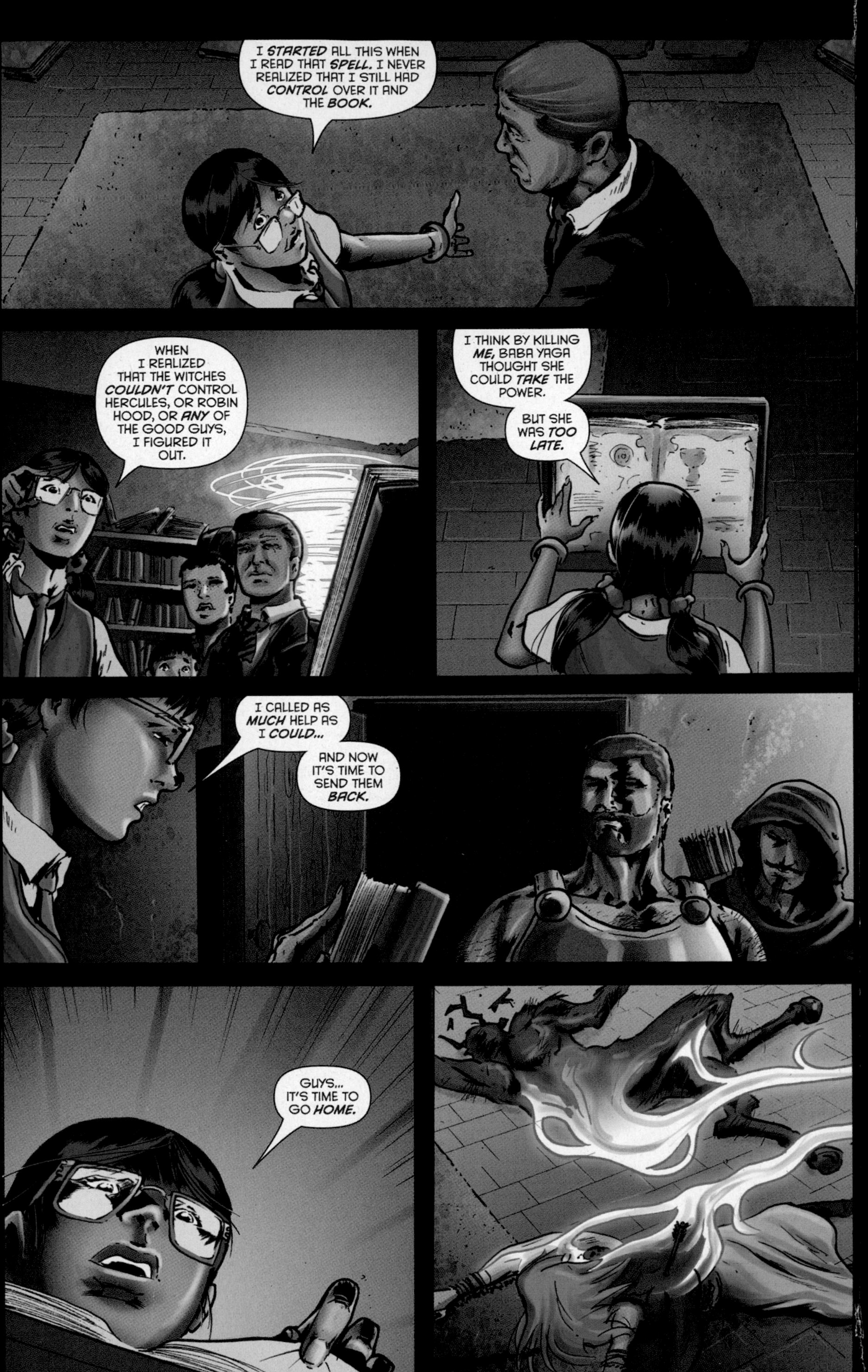
I STARTED ALL THIS WHEN I READ THAT SPELL. I NEVER REALIZED THAT I STILL HAD CONTROL OVER IT AND THE BOOK.
WHEN I REALIZED THAT THE WITCHES COULDN'T CONTROL HERCULES, OR ROBIN HOOD, OR ANY OF THE GOOD GUYS, I FIGURED IT OUT.
I THINK BY KILLING ME, BABA YAGA THOUGHT SHE COULD TAKE THE POWER.
BUT SHE WAS TOO LATE.
I CALLED AS MUCH HELP AS I COULD...
AND NOW IT'S TIME TO SEND THEM BACK.
GUYS... IT'S TIME TO GO HOME.

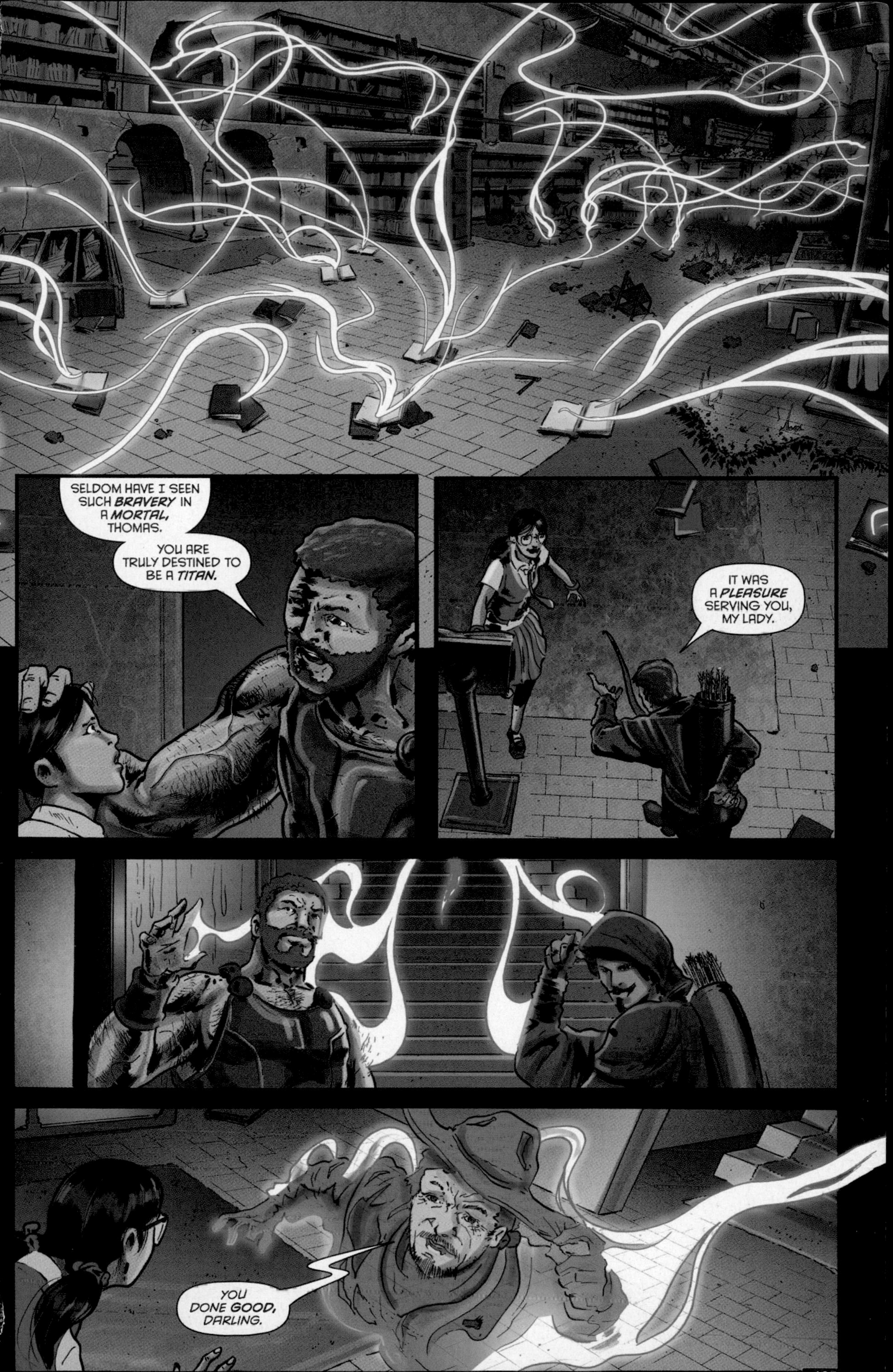
SELDOM HAVE I SEEN SUCH BRAVERY IN A MORTAL, THOMAS.
YOU ARE TRULY DESTINED TO BE A TITAN.
IT WAS A PLEASURE SERVING YOU, MY LADY.
YOU DONE GOOD, DARLING.

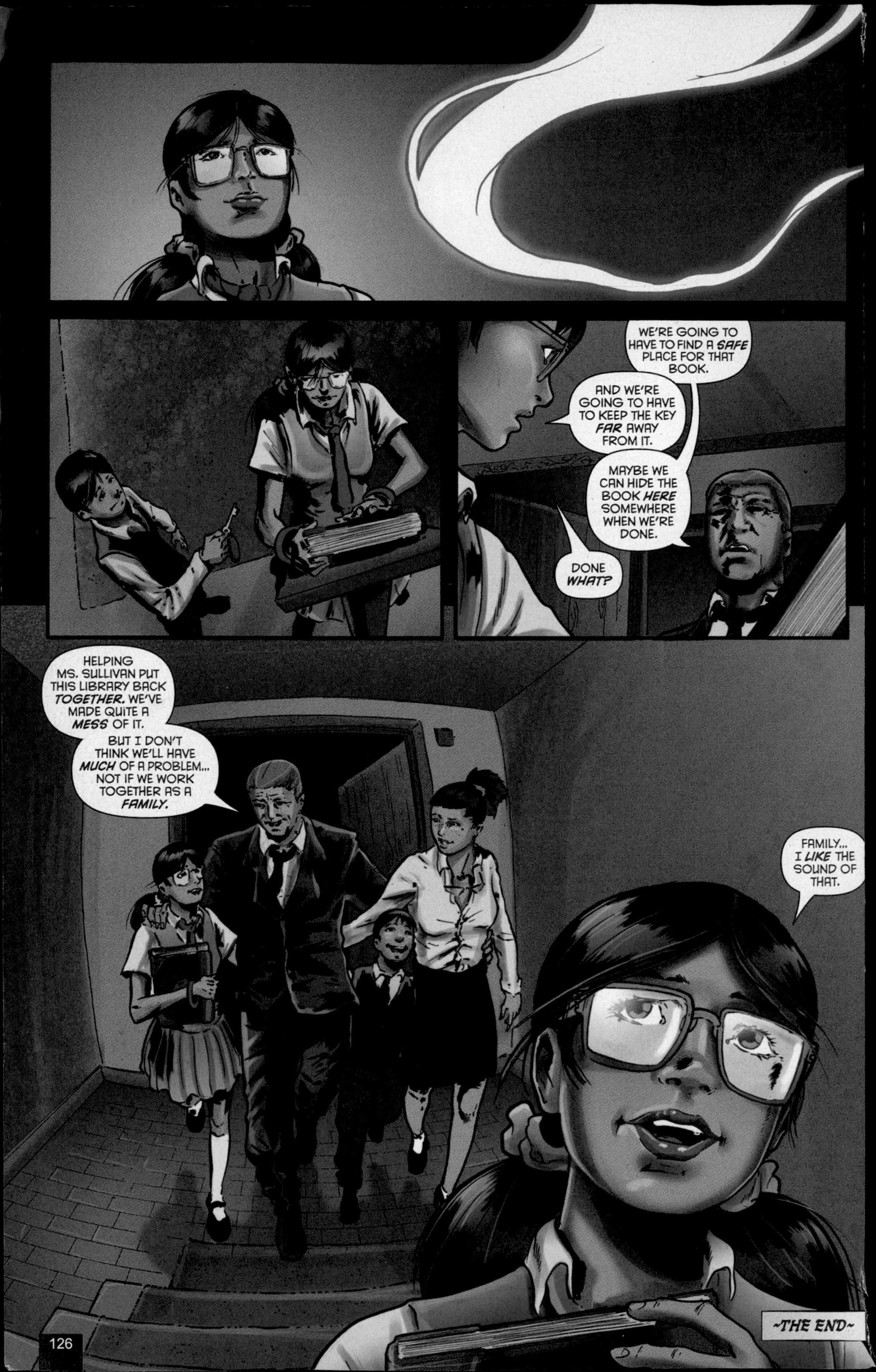

WE'RE GOING TO HAVE TO FIND A SAFE PLACE FOR THAT BOOK.
AND WE'RE GOING TO HAVE TO KEEP THE KEY FAR AWAY FROM IT.
MAYBE WE CAN HIDE THE BOOK HERE SOMEWHERE WHEN WE'RE DONE.
DONE WHAT?
HELPING MS. SULLIVAN PUT THIS LIBRARY BACK TOGETHER. WE'VE MADE QUITE A MESS OF IT.
BUT I DON'T THINK WE'LL HAVE MUCH OF A PROBLEM... NOT IF WE WORK TOGETHER AS A FAMILY.
FAMILY... I LIKE THE SOUND OF THAT.
~THE END~

Grimm Fairy Tales Presents the Library

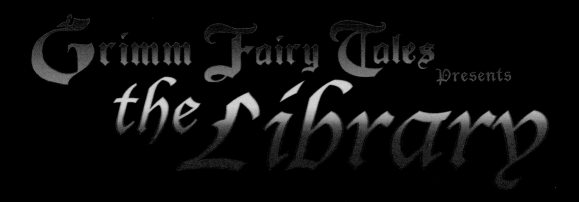

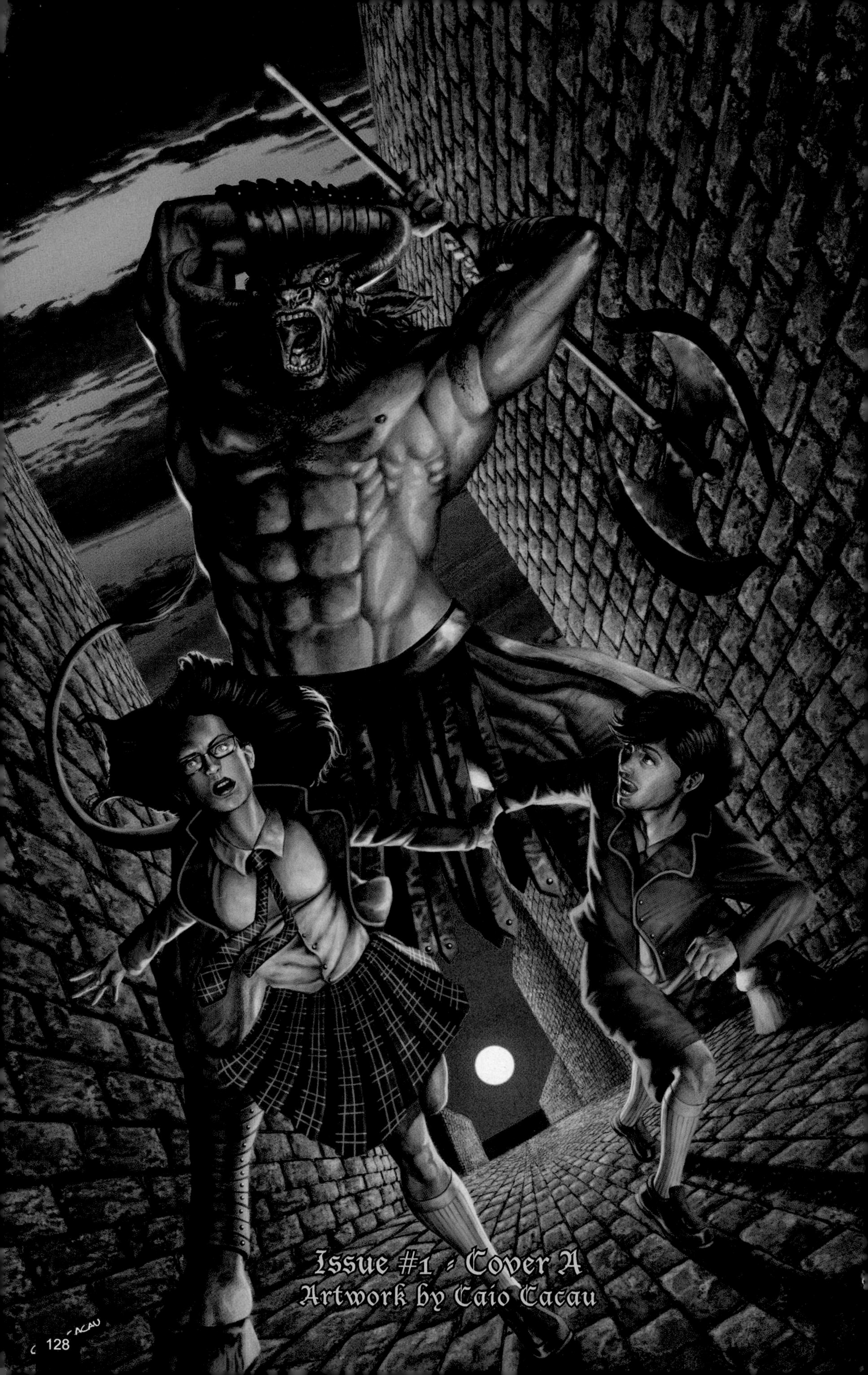

Issue #1 - Cover A
Artwork by Caio Cacau

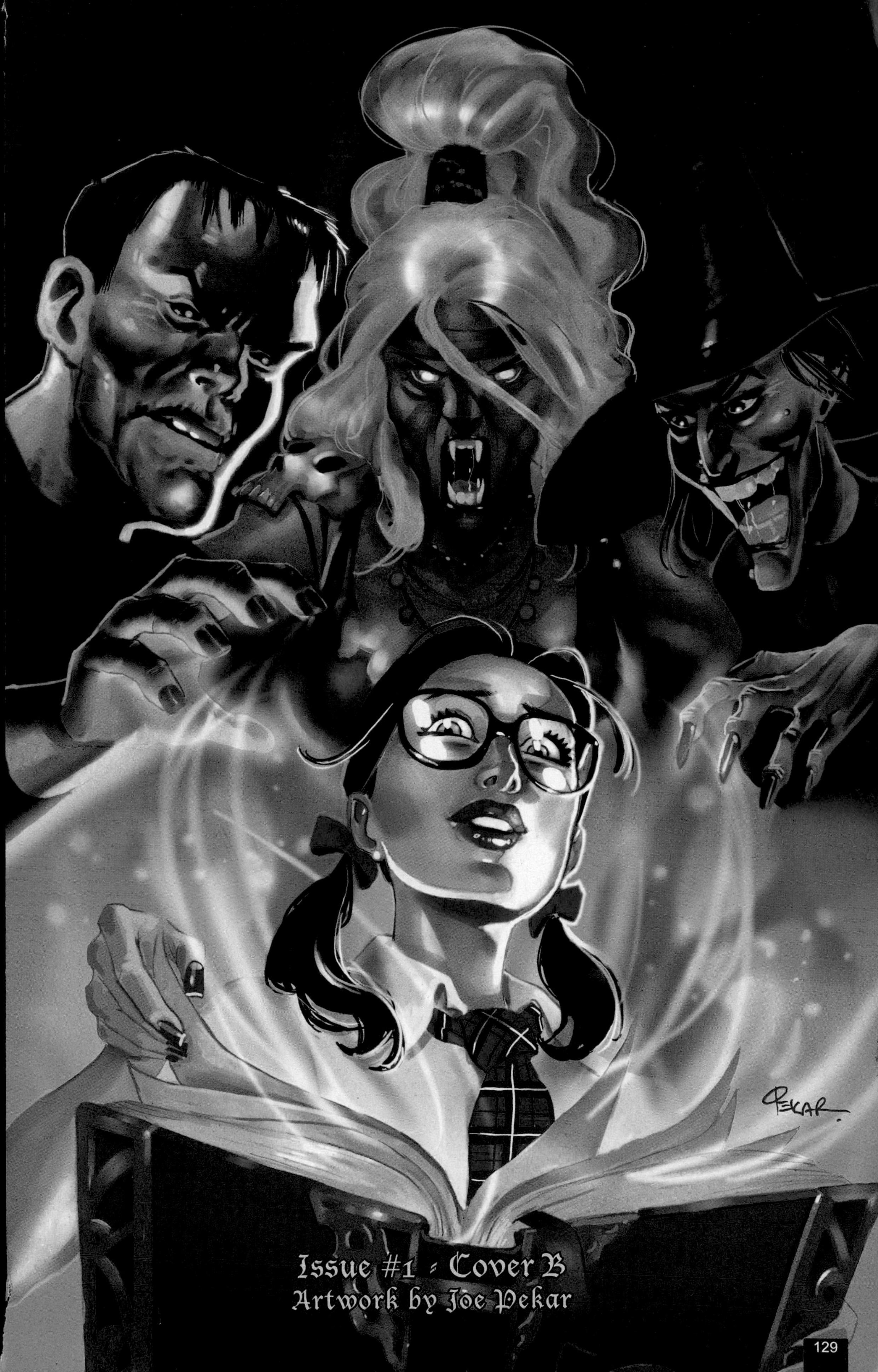
PEKAR

Issue #1 - Cover B
Artwork by Joe Pekar

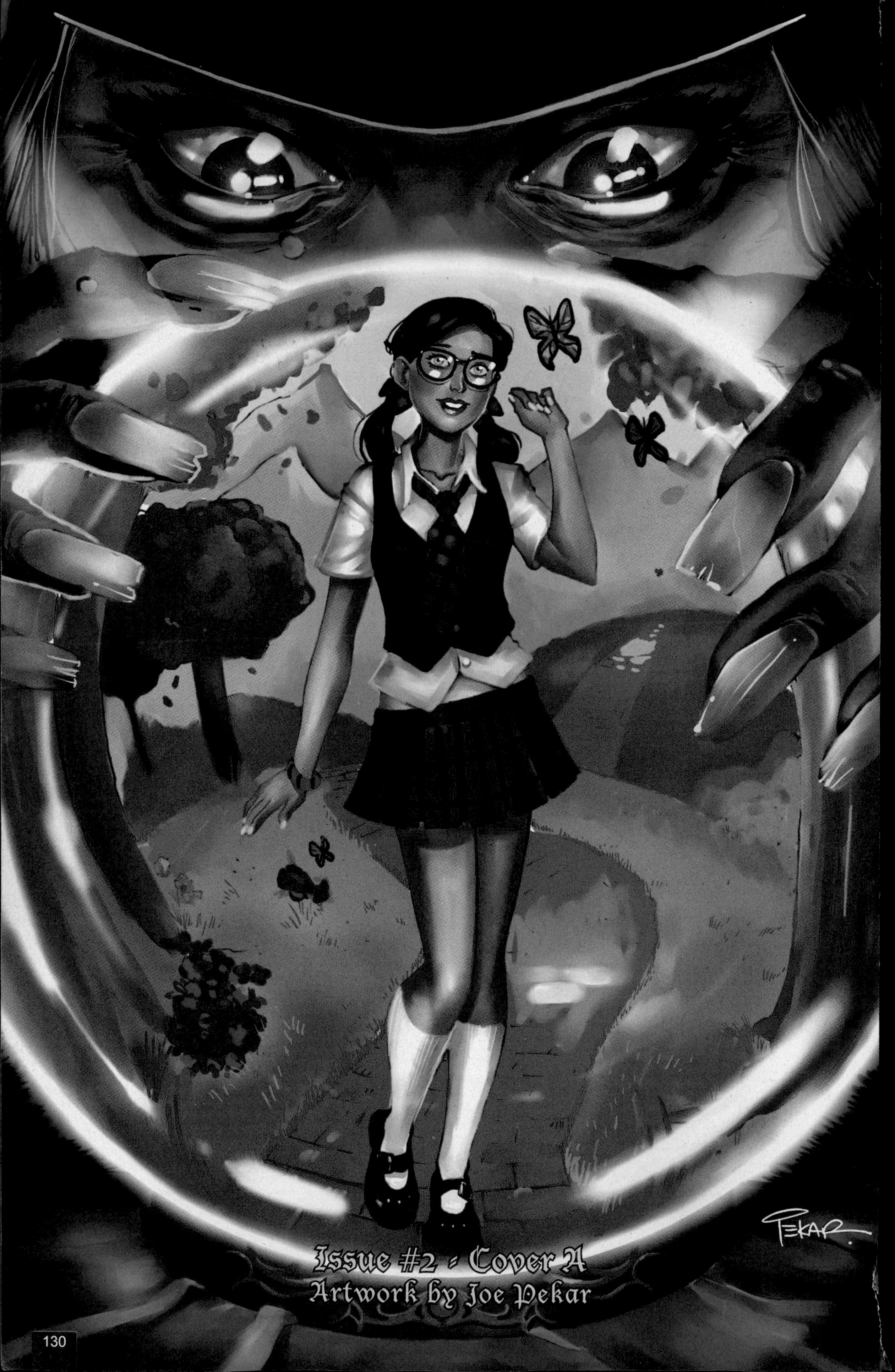
PEKAR

Issue #2 - Cover A
Artwork by Joe Pekar

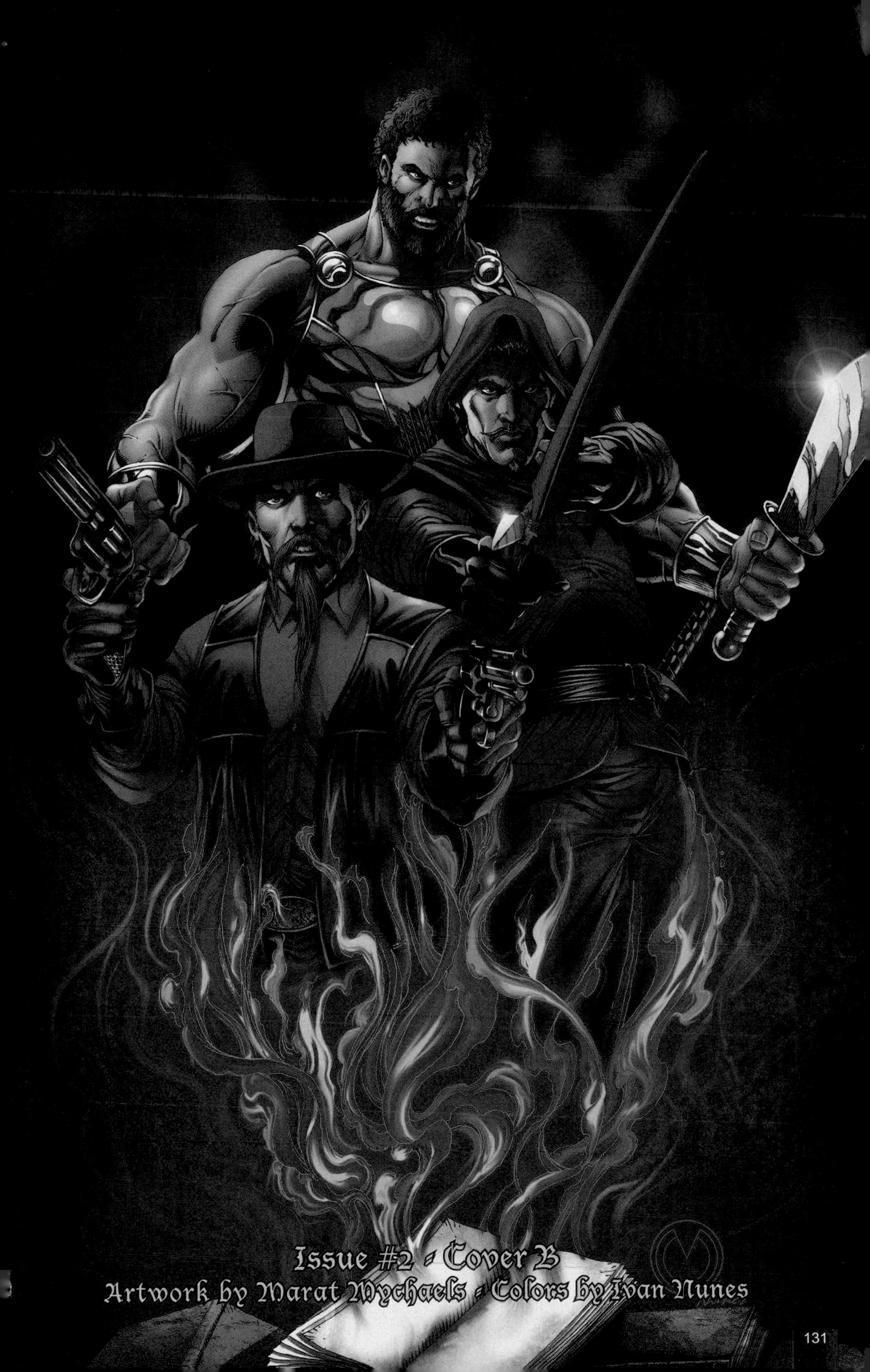

Issue #2 - Cover B
Artwork by Marat Mychaels - Colors by Ivan Nunes

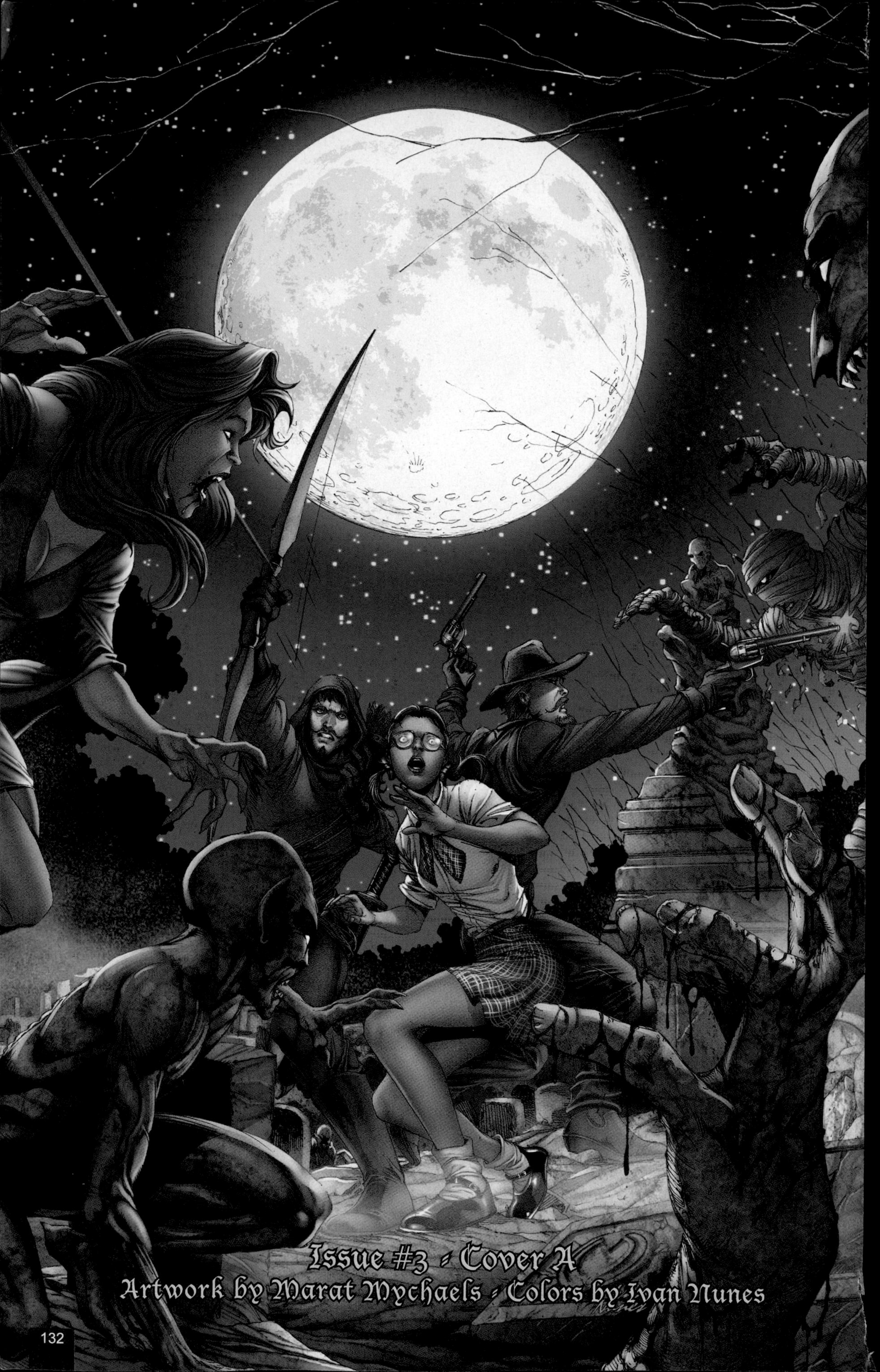

Issue #3 - Cover A
Artwork by Marat Mychaels - Colors by Ivan Nunes

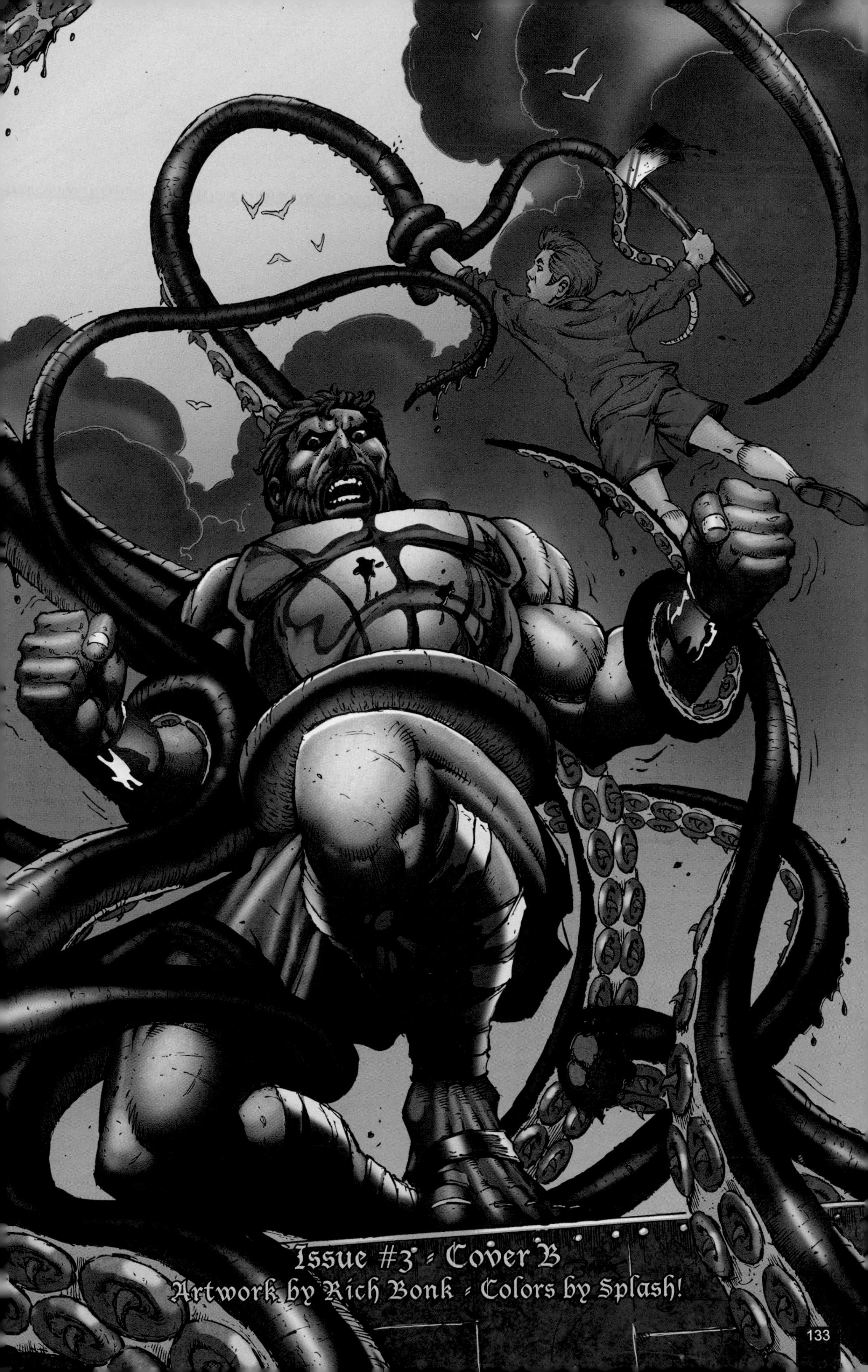

Issue #3 • Cover B
Artwork by Rich Bonk • Colors by Splash!

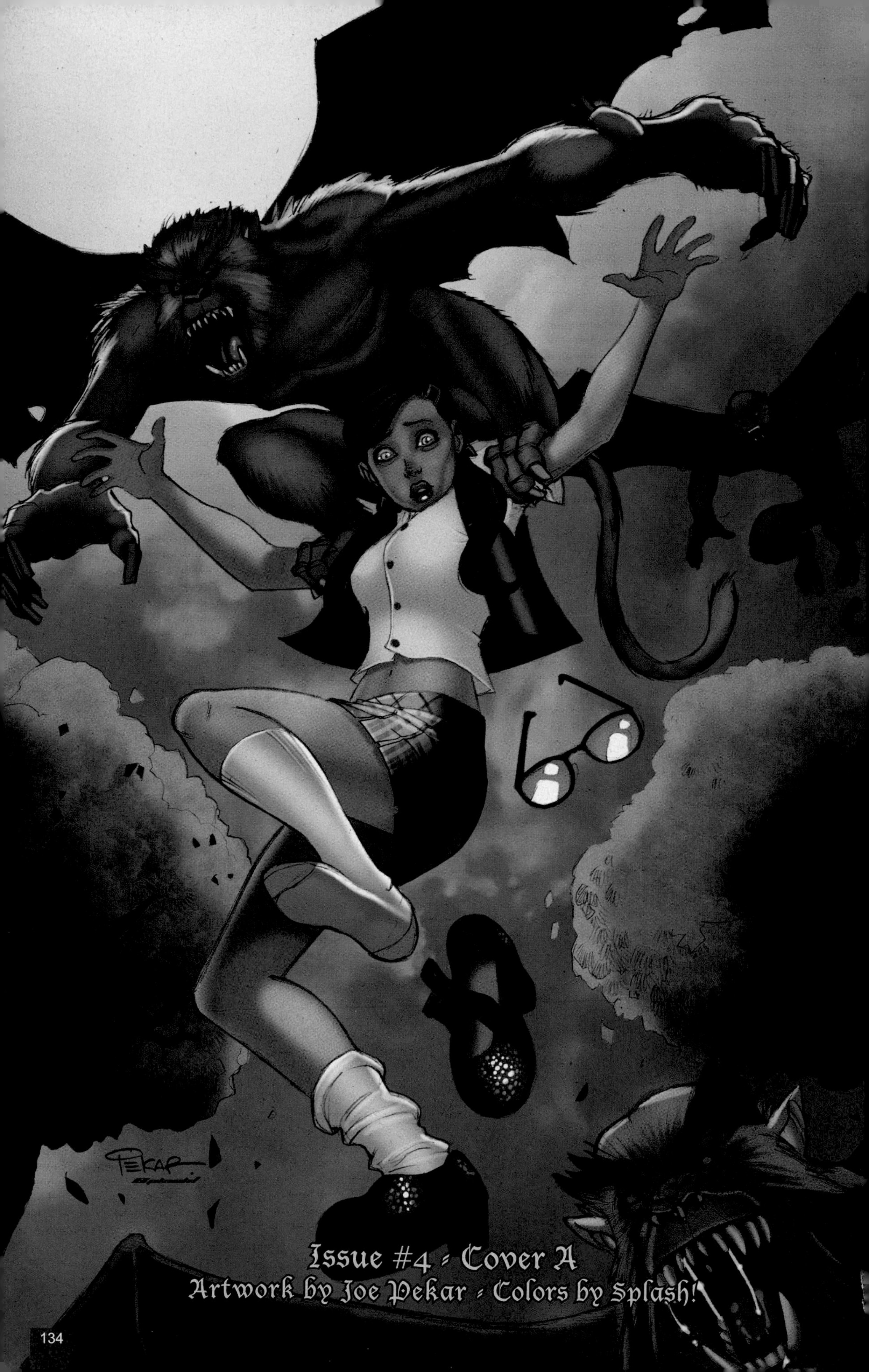
PEKAR

Issue #4 - Cover A
Artwork by Joe Pekar - Colors by Splash!

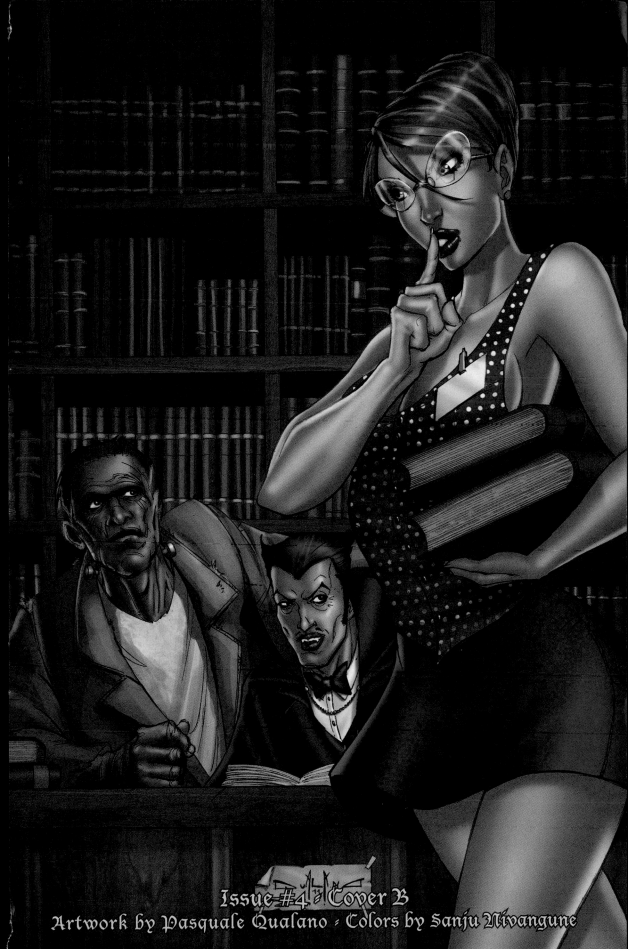

Issue #4 Cover B
Artwork by Pasquale Qualano - Colors by Sanju Nivangune

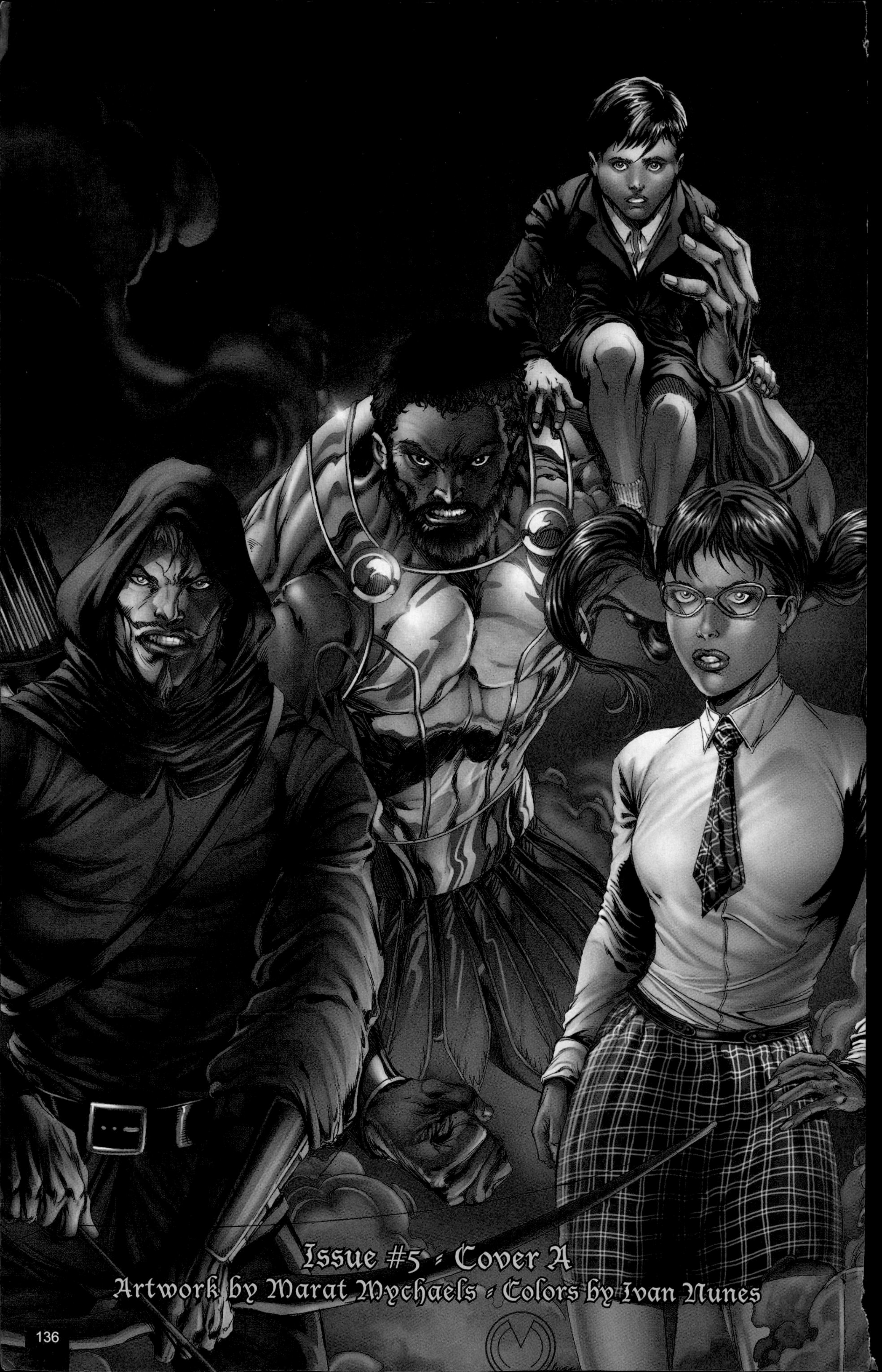

Issue #5 - Cover A
Artwork by Marat Mychaels - Colors by Ivan Nunes

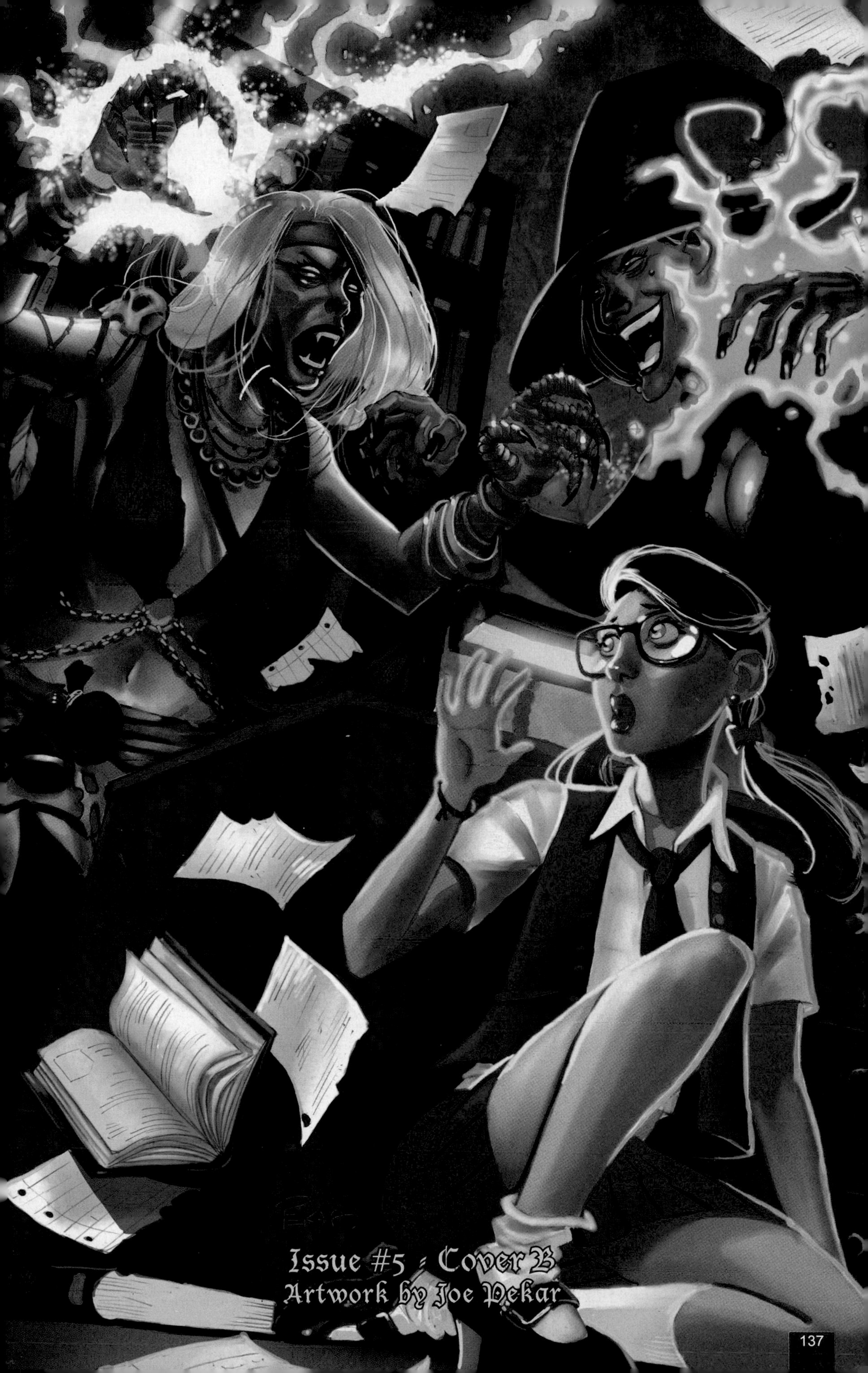

Issue #5 - Cover B
Artwork by Joe Pekar

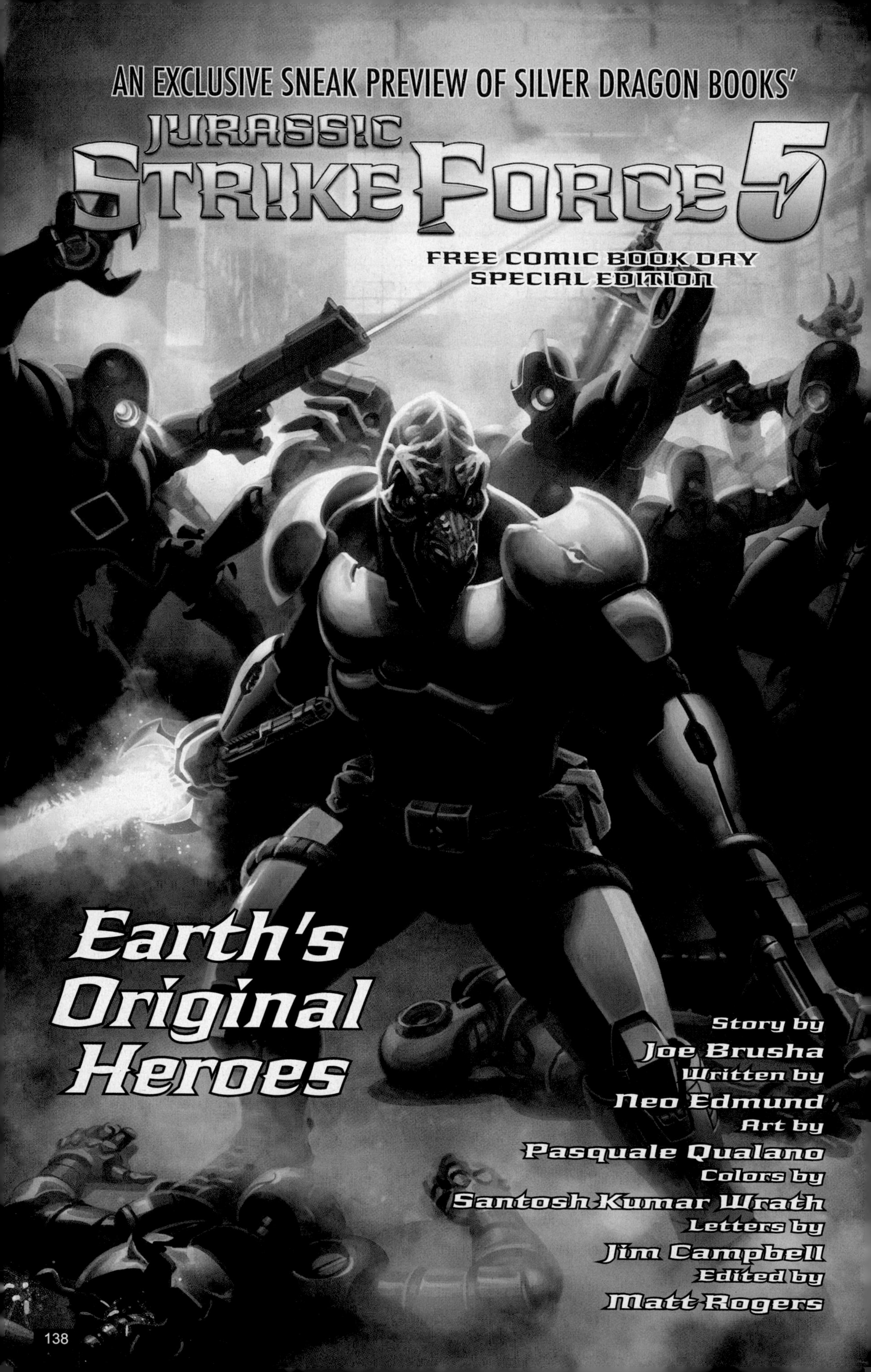
AN EXCLUSIVE SNEAK PREVIEW OF SILVER DRAGON BOOKS'
JURASSIC STRIKE FORCE 5
FREE COMIC BOOK DAY SPECIAL EDITION
Earth's Original Heroes
Story by
Joe Brusha
Written by
Neo Edmund
Art by
Pasquale Qualano
Colors by
Santosh Kumar Wrath
Letters by
Jim Campbell
Edited by
Matt Rogers

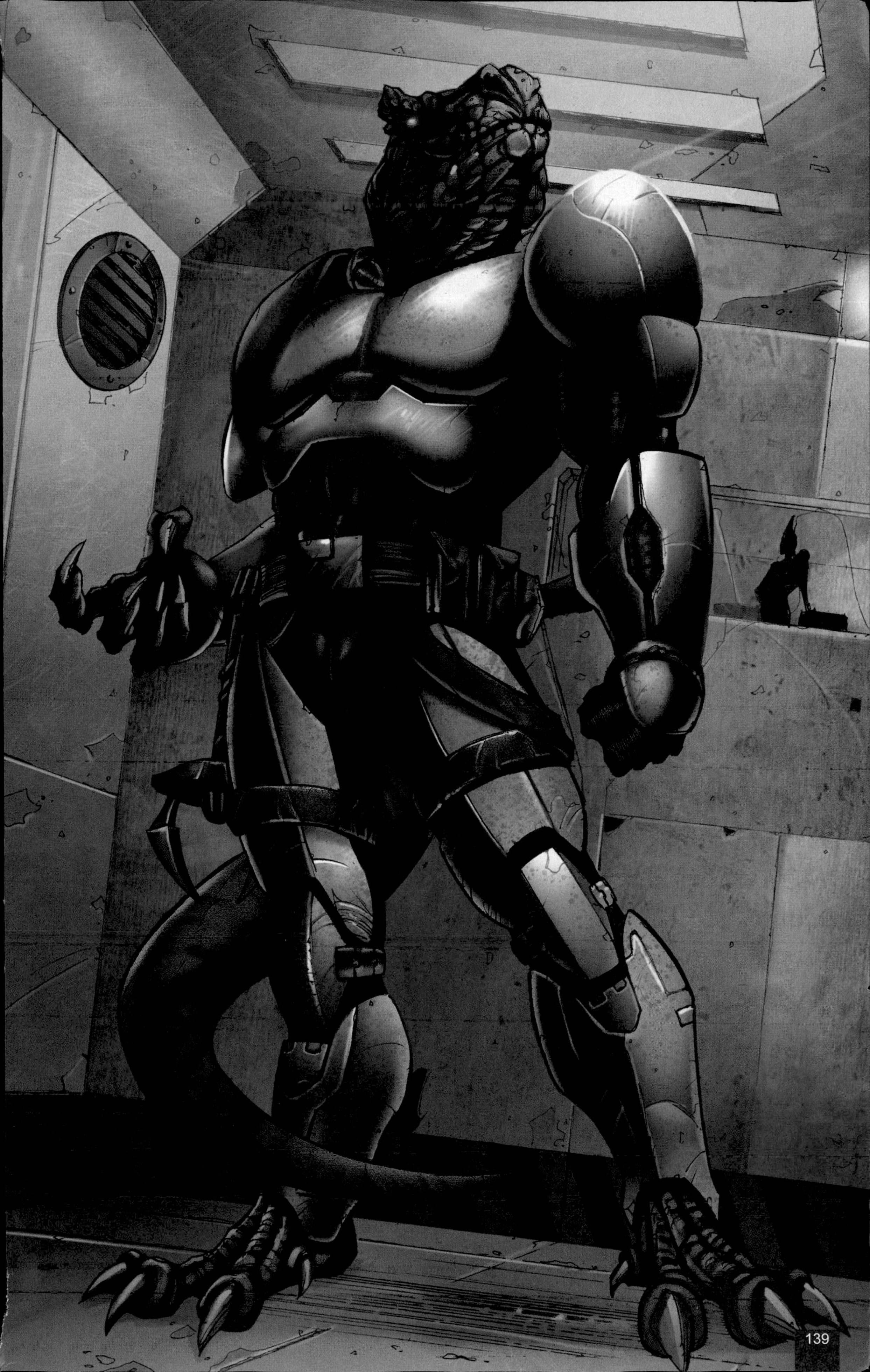

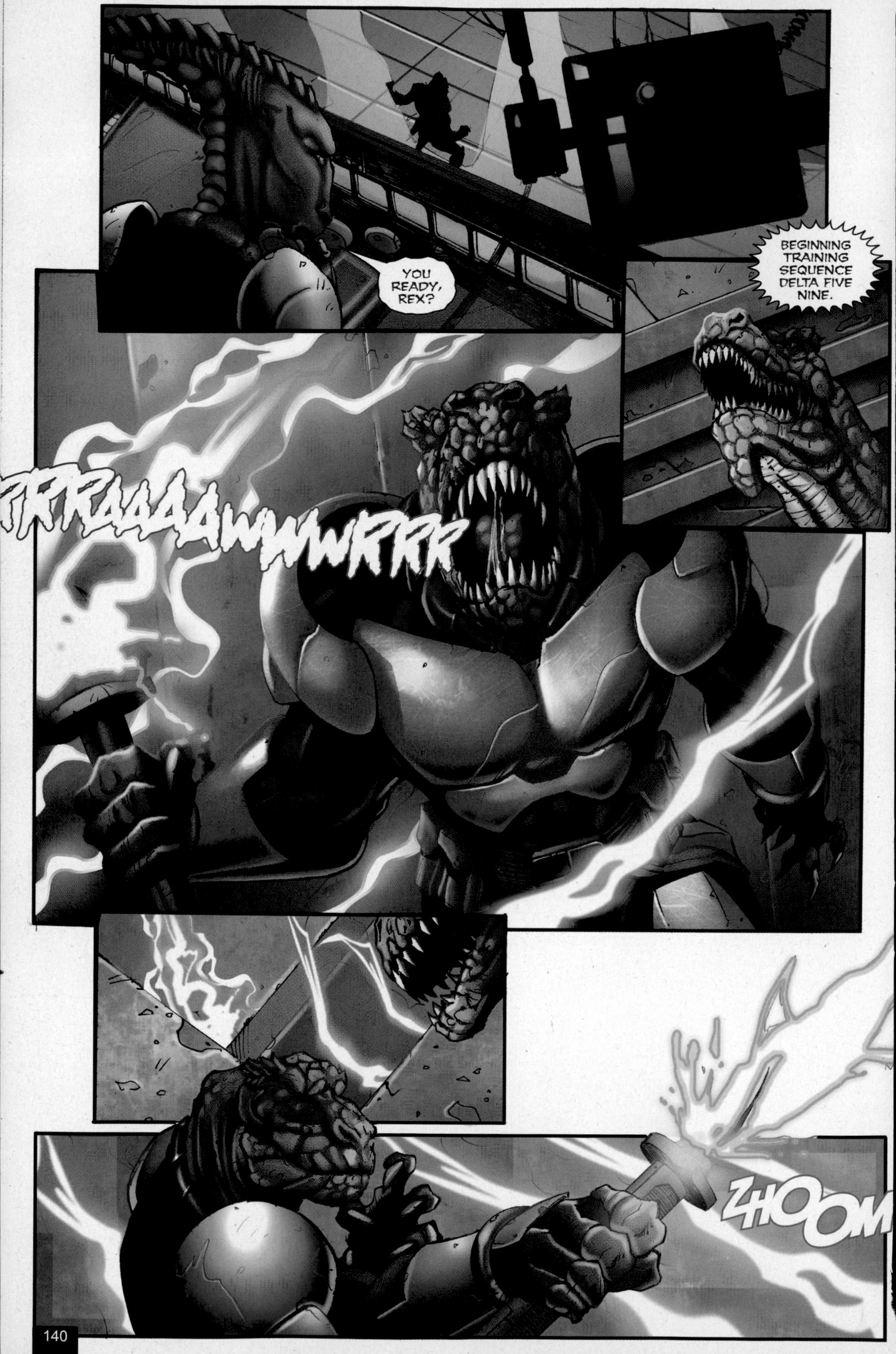

YOU READY, REX?
BEGINNING TRAINING SEQUENCE DELTA FIVE NINE.
RRRAAAAAWWWRRR
ZHOOM

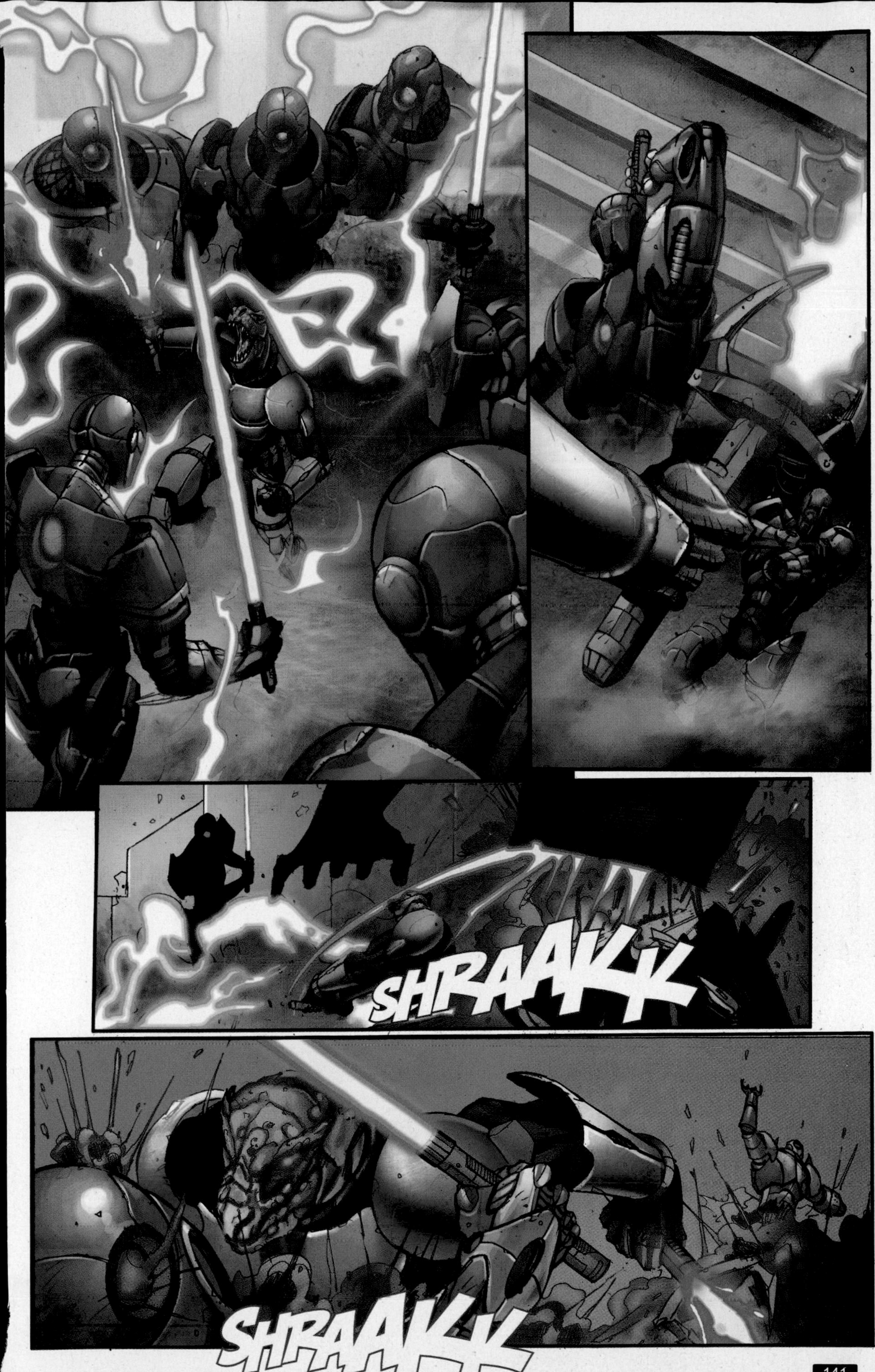
SHRAAKK
SHRAAKK

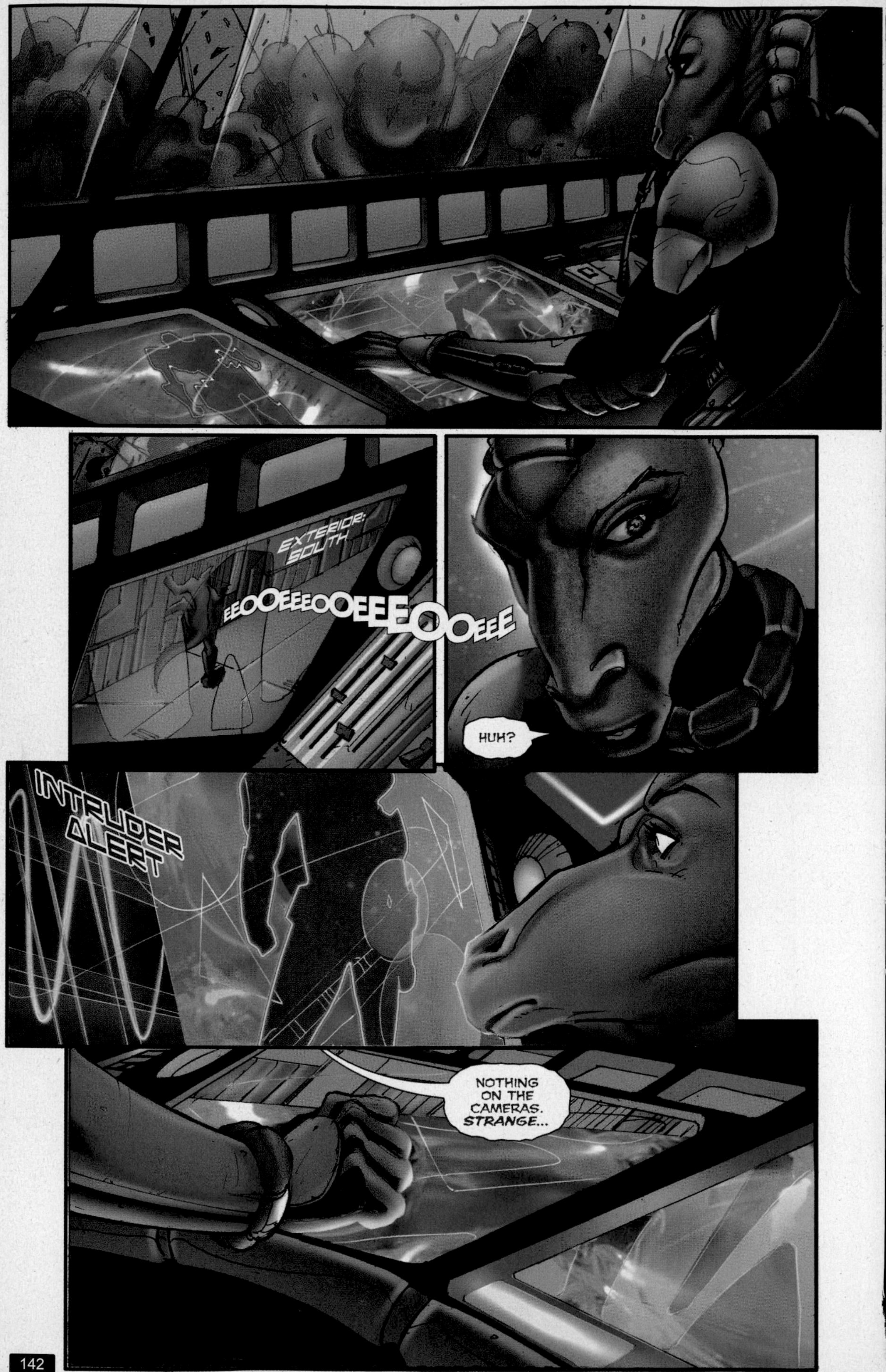
EXTERIOR: SOUTH
EEOOEEEOOEEEOOEEE
HUH?
INTRUDER ALERT
NOTHING ON THE CAMERAS. STRANGE...

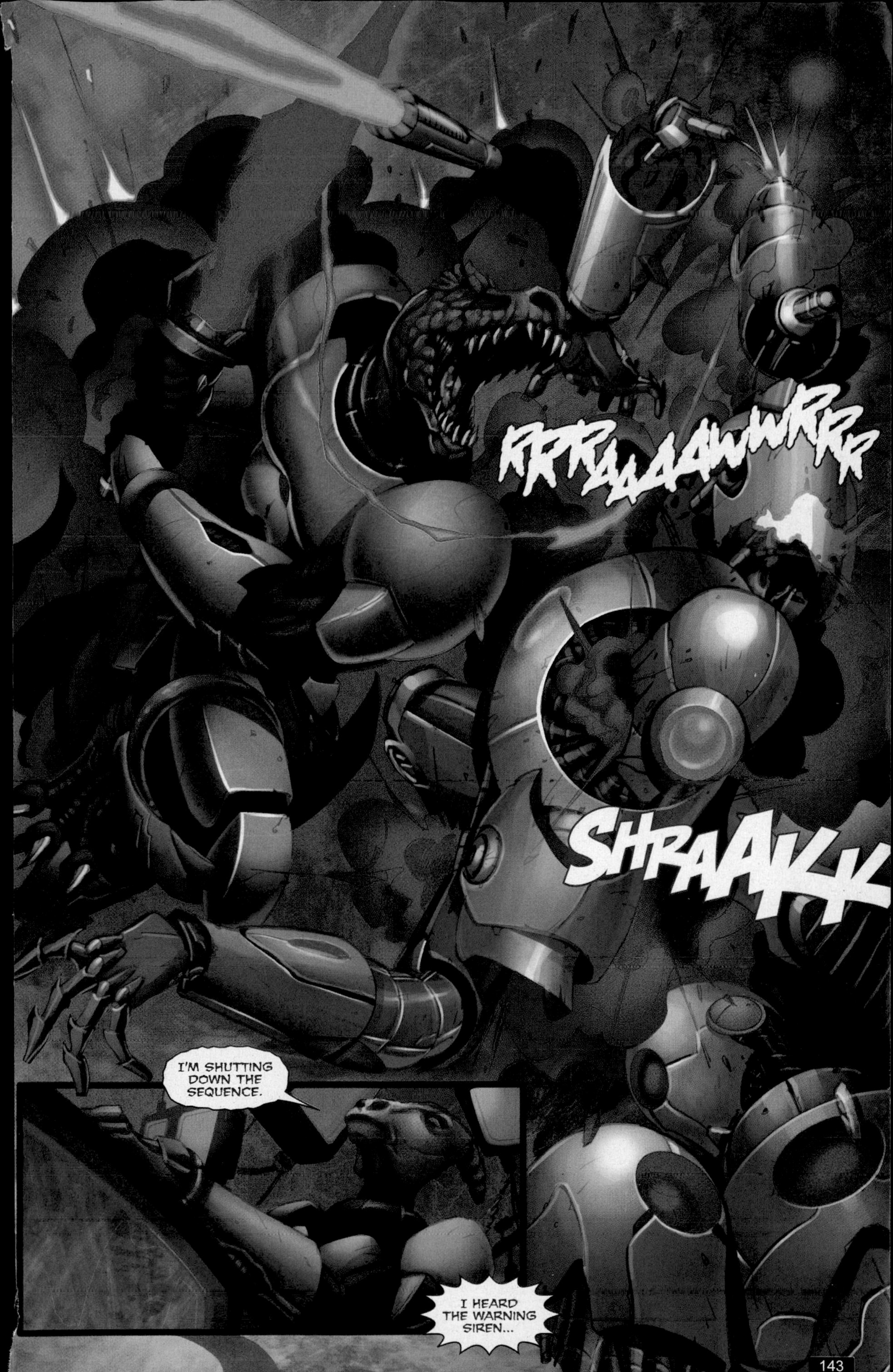
KRRRAAAAWWRRR
SHRAAKK
I'M SHUTTING DOWN THE SEQUENCE.
I HEARD THE WARNING SIREN...

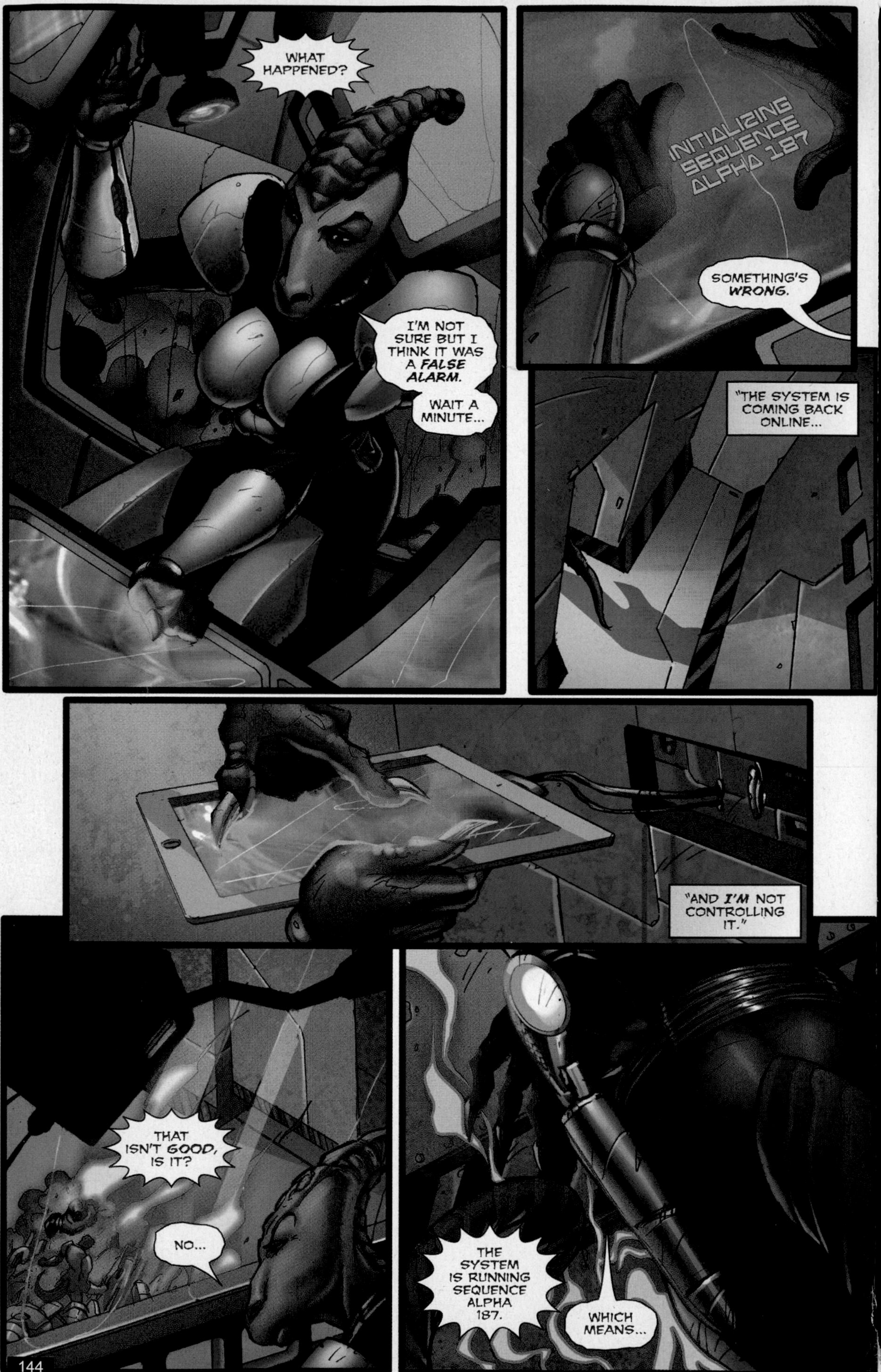
WHAT HAPPENED?
I'M NOT SURE BUT I THINK IT WAS A *FALSE ALARM*.
WAIT A MINUTE...
INITIALIZING SEQUENCE ALPHA 187
SOMETHING'S *WRONG*.
"THE SYSTEM IS COMING BACK ONLINE...
"AND *I'M* NOT CONTROLLING IT."
THAT ISN'T *GOOD*, IS IT?
NO...
THE SYSTEM IS RUNNING SEQUENCE ALPHA 187.
WHICH MEANS...

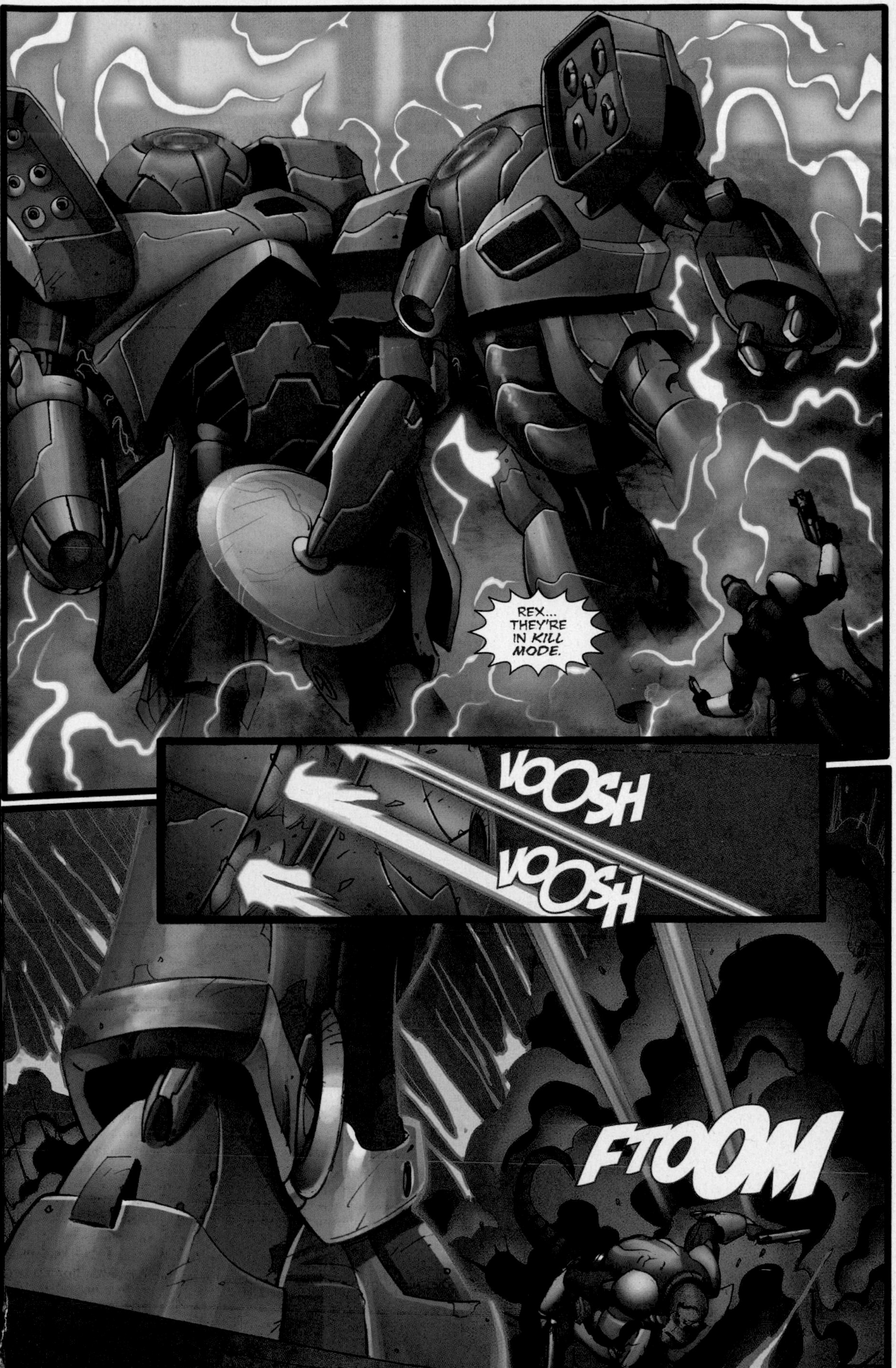
REX... THEY'RE IN KILL MODE.
VOOSH
VOOSH
FTOOM

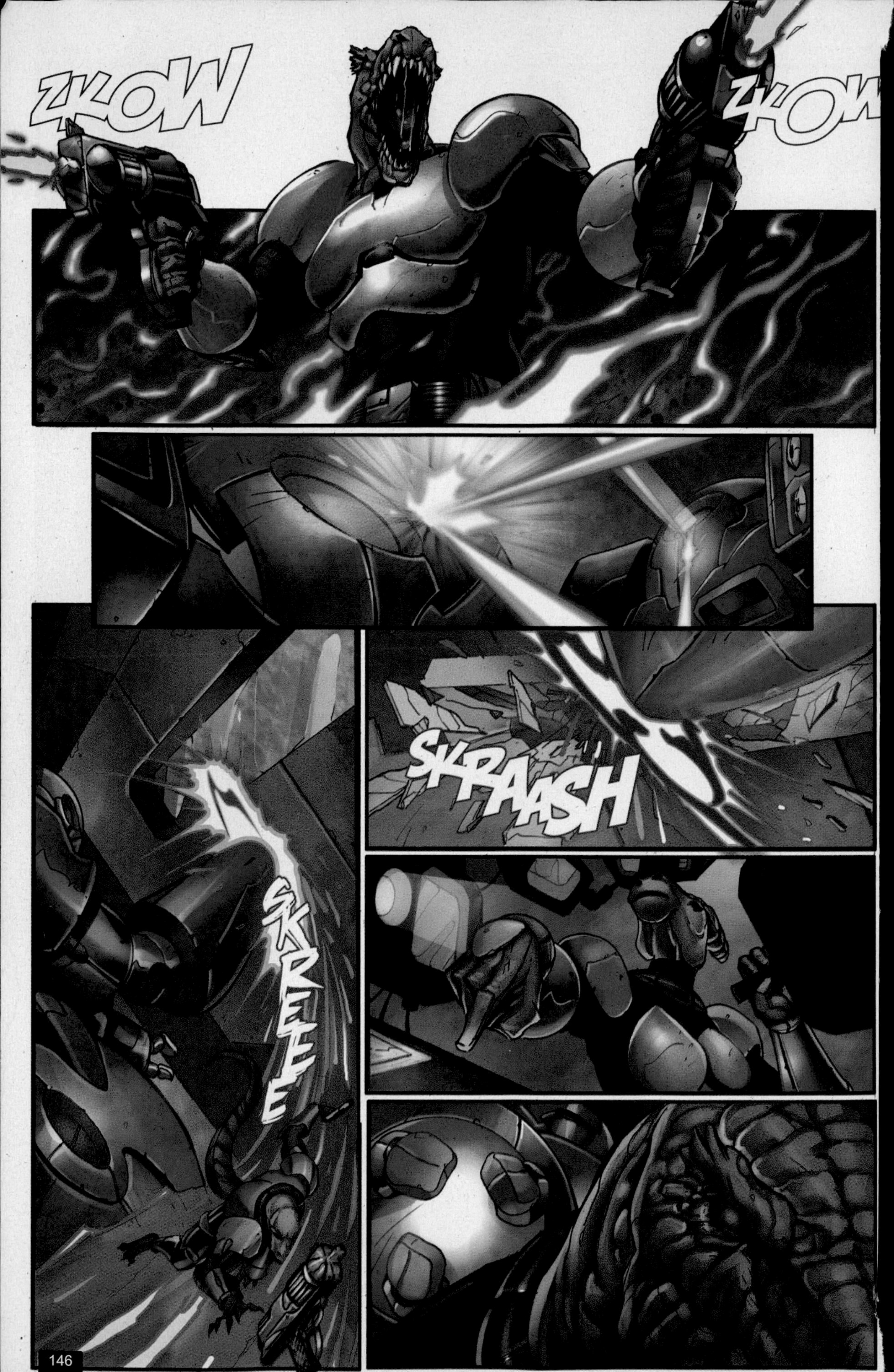
ZKLOW
ZKLOW
SKRAASH
SKREEEE

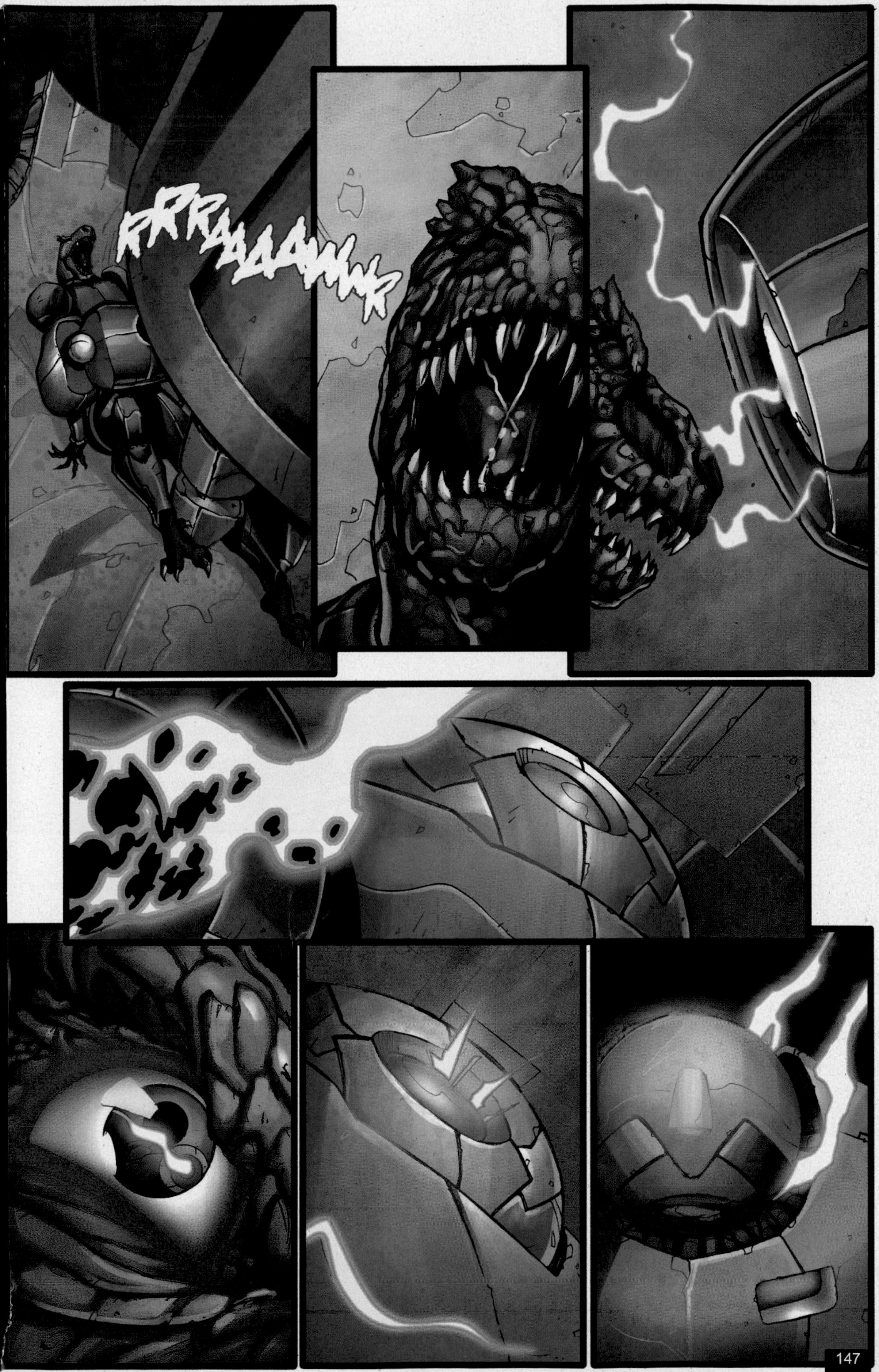
RRRAAAAAWWR

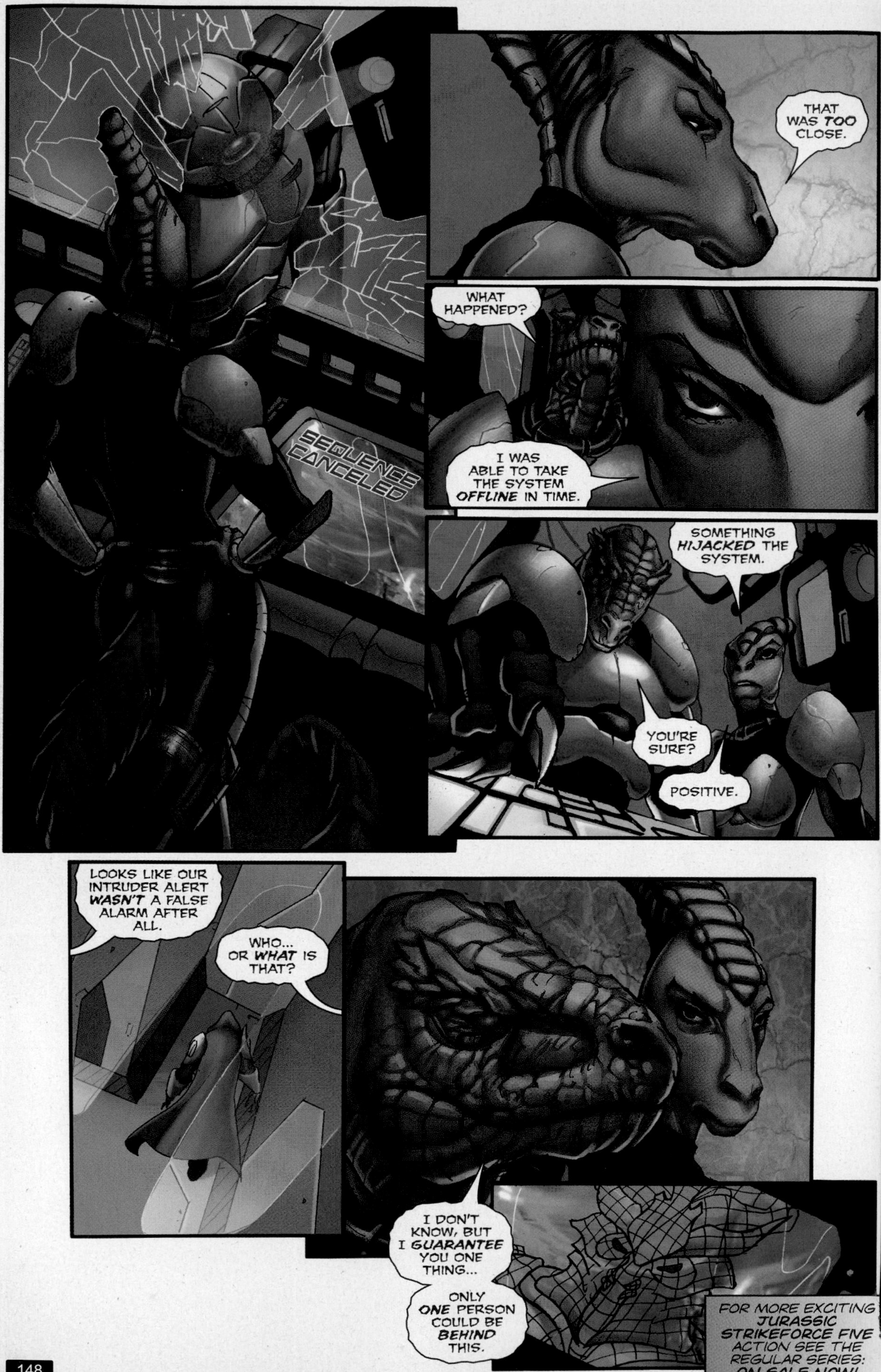
SEQUENCE CANCELED
THAT WAS TOO CLOSE.
WHAT HAPPENED?
I WAS ABLE TO TAKE THE SYSTEM OFFLINE IN TIME.
SOMETHING HIJACKED THE SYSTEM.
YOU'RE SURE?
POSITIVE.
LOOKS LIKE OUR INTRUDER ALERT WASN'T A FALSE ALARM AFTER ALL.
WHO... OR WHAT IS THAT?
I DON'T KNOW, BUT I GUARANTEE YOU ONE THING...
ONLY ONE PERSON COULD BE BEHIND THIS.
FOR MORE EXCITING JURASSIC STRIKEFORCE FIVE ACTION SEE THE REGULAR SERIES: ON SALE NOW!

Grimm Fairy Tales Presents the Library

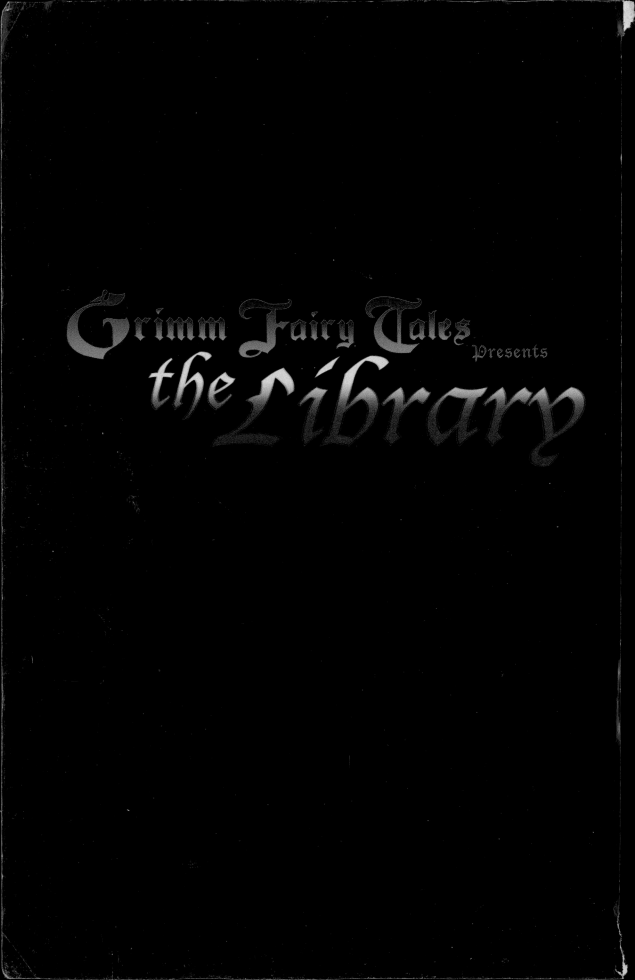